Notably NASHVILLE

a medley of tastes and traditions

Junior League of Nashville

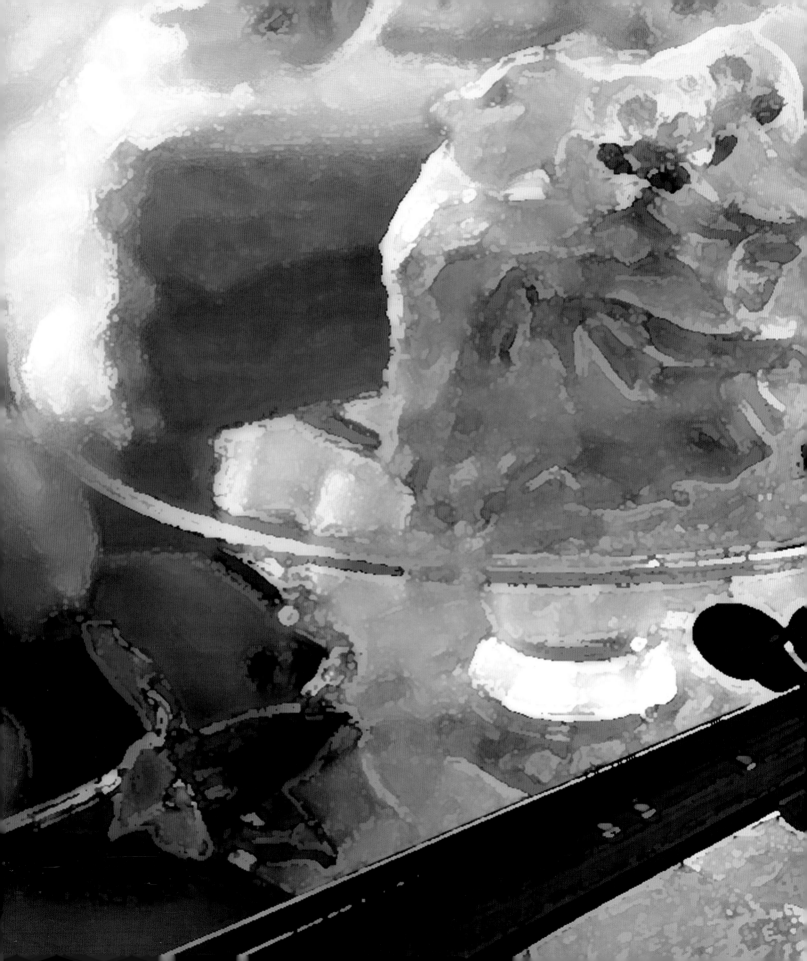

Notably NASHVILLE

a medley of tastes and traditions

Copyright © 2003
Junior League of Nashville
2405 Crestmoor Road
Nashville, Tennessee 37215
615.269.9393
www.jlnashville.org

Library of Congress Number:
   2002104720
ISBN: 0-9718381-0-0

Edited, Designed, and Manufactured
by Favorite Recipes® Press
An imprint of

FRP

PO Box 305142
Nashville, Tennessee 37230
1-800-358-0560

Art Director: Steve Newman
Project Editor: Jane Hinshaw
Project Manager: Susan Larson
Copy Editing: Junior League of Nashville
   Cookbook Committee
Photography: © 2003 by
   Mike Rutherford

Manufactured in China

First Printing 2003—20,000 copies
Second Printing 2005—15,000 copies

JUNIOR LEAGUE OF
NASHVILLE
Women building a better community

Our Mission: The Junior League of Nashville is an organiztion of women committed to promoting voluntarism, developing the potential of women and improving the community through the effective action and leadership of trained voluntccrs. Its purpose is exclusively educational and charitable. The Junior League of Nashville reaches out to women of all races, religions and national origins who demonstrate an interest in and a commitment to voluntarism.

Our Vision: The Junior League of Nashville is a premier women's volunteer organization that offers our members the opportunity to build meaningful relationships with others who are unified by a desire to give back to our community. Through the talents of a diverse membership, we will support and enrich the lives of women, children and families in our community. Together we have greater impact than we do individually.

Milestones: The Junior League of Nashville was founded in 1922. The Junior League Home was founded in 1923 and continues to provide volunteer services and financial assistance to Vanderbilt Children's Hospital, where the Junior League Home has resided since 1970. The Junior League of Nashville has founded 21 community projects since 1923. Some of the latest collaborations include: The Junior League of Nashville Child Care Center at the Red Shield Family Initiative and the Junior League of Nashville Children's Services at the downtown branch of the Nashville Public Library.

Publications: The Junior League of Nashville is very proud of *Notably Nashville,* our most recent community cookbook which continues the legacy of our predecessor publications. The Junior League of Nashville has been publishing cookbooks since 1964 when *Nashville Seasons* was introduced. *Nashville Seasons* was reprinted 11 times in 17 years. Having enjoyed success in the cookbook field and having become absorbed in the history of Nashville through our volunteer endeavors, a combination of the two seemed inevitable. The Junior League of Nashville released *Nashville Seasons Encore* in 1977 as a travel guide to our city. The second edition of *Nashville Seasons Encore* included additional recipes from country music celebrities, and the cookbook was reprinted in 1982 and 1985 under the name *Encore! Nashville.*

The proceeds from the sale of the cookbook support the vital mission of the Junior League of Nashville and continue to improve our community through the effective action and leadership of our trained volunteers.

Acknowledgments

We would like to thank the following for their generous financial contributions for the second printing of *Notably Nashville: a medley of tastes and traditions.*

Music Row Contributors

THE **TENNESSEAN**
Every day matters.   www.tennessean.com

PUBLIX SUPER MARKETS
CHARITIES

Parthenon Contributors

HECHT'S

MONROE CARELL JR.
Children's Hospital
at Vanderbilt

Natchez Trace Supporters

Publix Super Markets

Phillip P. Shipp IV, DDS

Iroquois Steeplechase Supporters

Crystal's

Kandle Kitchen

Contents

PUBLIX SUPER MARKETS
CHARITIES

Foreword

Notably Nashville is the sort of cookbook that must be read and savored, preferably with a cup of tea at your elbow, while a cat sleeps at your feet. The pages almost beg to be folded down, or else fingerprinted with chocolate icing. It's the sort of book that doesn't mind if you draw a star next to "Asparagus Soup," and it especially doesn't mind if you carry it around, reading recipes at odd moments—during lulls in traffic or pauses in your child's soccer game. Chances are, you might draw a crowd. Someone is bound to say, "Have you tried that recipe? Is it good? May I see it, please?"

Generations of southerners have honed their culinary skills with the assistance of various Junior League cookbooks, and I am no exception. When I was a small girl, my grandmother gave me a copy of *River Road Recipes*. To soothe my ruffled spirit—I was only eight years old—she took me aside and said, "Michael Lee, I know you were hoping for a doll, but honey, it's *never* too early to dabble with food. Always remember, the best recipes come from the Junior League."

This belief held true for my mother, who owned hundreds of league cookbooks, all of them spiral-bound and deliciously thick. I spent many afternoons leafing through them. My personal favorite was *The Memphis Cookbook*. I loved the more alluring recipes, such as "Red Devil Sauce," offered by Mrs. Joseph C. Loughheed, or the simple, comforting ones, like "Marmalade Muffins," by Mrs. R. Carl Dickerson, Jr. I especially loved the foreword, which included detailed instructions for "How To Cook A Husband."

Now, from some of Tennessee's most creative kitchens, comes a spectacular book for your shelf: *Notably Nashville*. The recipes are not only mouthwatering, they capture the city's essence—and it is a challenge to define the cuisine of Tennessee. In fact, many people have wondered if such a thing existed. Certainly, Nashville can't be likened to the cuisine of Louisiana, with its mysterious gumbos and étouffées that simmer all the way through *River Road Recipes*, or the holy trinity (celery, onions, peppers). When it comes to the dishes of Tennessee, most people scratch their heads a moment, then they list traditional foods: white beans and green onions, country ham sizzling in an iron skillet, cornbread pulled from the oven. While this fare is heartwarming and tasty, it does not give an accurate picture of the city's culinary IQ. True, Nashville is surrounded by rolling hills, and it has its share of guitar pickers; but at the same time, the city is filled with athletes, intellectuals, bookworms, and art collectors. It's a mix of the discriminating and the dashing, the audacious and the aristocrat. Its diversity has molded the city into a place where anything goes: Some Nashvillians listen to Garth, others prefer Pavarotti; some residents prefer cowboy boots, while others prefer Manolo Blahniks.

The same might be said for corn bread—some folks want it buttered, others mush it into a tall glass of milk, but who would think of tossing it into a salad? You can find this recipe in *Notably Nashville*. It's the sort of dish that defines the cuisine of the city, which has always been a tasteful blend of the classic and the chic. Of course, if you prefer plain fried chicken and buttered corn bread, you will find those dishes, too; but I myself can't wait to prepare the corn bread salad. I can already taste the crunchy red onions, the tang of the sour cream and mayonnaise, juxtaposed with black beans and corn.

But first, I raise my glass, toasting the women behind these recipes—they are not only sharing the best from their kitchens, but from themselves.

Michael Lee West

Michael Lee West is the author of *She Flew the Coop, American Pie, Consuming Passions,* and the upcoming *Mad Girls in Love.* She lives with her family in a renovated funeral home outside Nashville, Tennessee.

History

*I*n 1922, the Junior League of Nashville began assisting the community when Cornelia Keeble Ewing chartered the JLN with 45 members. These dedicated women established an unprecedented commitment to the crippled children of Middle Tennessee when, in 1923, the Junior League Home for Crippled Children opened its doors. Its mission was "to provide free and skilled attention to crippled children whose parents or guardians are unable to pay for service, and whose disabilities can be sufficiently improved to enable them to be self-supporting in later life." Most of the children suffered from polio, and, at that time, there were no rehabilitation services available to the crippled children of Tennessee. Junior League members contributed countless hours and dollars to help the Home get started.

The twenties were a time of prohibition, flappers, and modern conveniences and a time when women began to work outside the home as secretaries, bookkeepers, and telephone operators. They were also a time of reaction against the reform movement of the previous decade. However, the women of the Junior League of Nashville were determined to make the Home a success. To raise money, JLN members began the Paper Sale, later known as the Palm Sunday Paper Sale. In the first year of the event, 1924, the sale raised $5,500. The JLN recognized and fulfilled a need for convalescent care of crippled children. Many of the patients in the Home were from rural areas of Middle Tennessee.

In 1970, the Junior League Home for Crippled Children moved from Ninth and Monroe, its location for more than five decades, to Vanderbilt Children's Hospital, where it remains today. The Junior League Home for Crippled Children continues to serve the needs of the crippled child. Today's League has adopted a broader definition of "crippled" to include mental health problems as well as other disabling conditions. In 1998, a $2,000,000 capital campaign donation was approved from the JLN Trust for a new children's hospital. This special donation was the largest gift ever given by the Junior League of Nashville and the first gift given to the capital campaign. In the Fall of 2003, the Monroe Carell, Jr., Children's Hospital at Vanderbilt opened and the Home's presence there is greater than ever. The Junior League Home is again expanding its scope in order to continue to provide quality care for the children of our community.

Introduction

Distinctly southern at its roots, Nashville today is a growing city resonating with a medley of varied sights, sounds, and flavors. Long considered the "Athens of the South," Nashville seamlessly blends music, history, family, art, education, sports, and government into a city that sings. Indeed, Nashville has been able to embrace the best of both worlds—big city life and small town values. These are the things that make Nashville Notable.

A capital city with a life of its own, Nashville has more to offer visitors than just country music. In *Notably Nashville,* you will find a guide to some of the finest locales and special events Nashville has to offer—tour Andrew Jackson's Hermitage, run with the horses at the Iroquois Steeplechase, fire up the grill in the shadow of the Titans' home coliseum, float down the Cumberland on a riverboat, and, of course, listen to some of the world's best music, not just country, mind you. Nashville's burgeoning music scene encompasses blues, jazz, gospel, bluegrass, opera, and, yes, the best of country. Walk into the "Mother Church of Country Music" and hear the songs of old resonating off her wooden pews. Climb the stairs of Athena's temple and sit at the feet of the goddess of wisdom. Sit in on a lecture by one of the world-renowned professors at one of Nashville's many colleges and universities and feel your own wisdom expand. After feeding your mind, comfort your soul with food at one of many restaurants favored by Nashville families for years. A city of hidden talents, Nashville will surprise and delight both young and old and enliven and enrich the lives of those who come here. Come with us and sample firsthand what Nashville has to offer.

MONROE CARELL JR.
children's Hospital
at Vanderbilt

Appetizers and Beverages

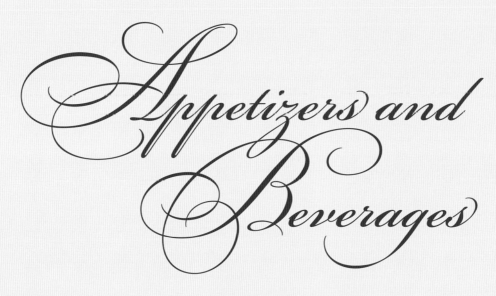

Appetizers and Beverages

Tally Ho!
Nashville's Iroquois Steeplechase has become
one of the city's premier outdoor sporting events.
The internationally renowned race, held annually since
1941 at the Percy Warner Park course, is one of the nation's
major venues for "weight for age" steeplechase racing.

The Steeplechase, held every year on the second Saturday in May, has evolved into a charity fund-raiser for Vanderbilt Children's Hospital. It's also a grand opportunity to don your best hat, grab a hot hors d'oeuvre, and sip a Belle Meade Mint Julep. The race is named for Iroquois, the first and one of only two American-bred horses to win the English Derby. You can pay homage to Iroquois at Belle Meade Plantation, located in the heart of the city of Belle Meade.

The original Federal-style house located on Belle Meade Plantation was built by the Harding family in 1820, and suffered devastating fire damage in 1851. The current house, featuring six 22-foot solid limestone columns, a cantilever staircase, and a beautiful front porch, was rebuilt in 1853 and is twice the size of the original. Belle Meade Plantation survived a major Civil War battle that raged all about the plantation. The limestone columns bear the battle scars, and the bullet holes remain visible today for visitors to see. After surviving the Civil War, Belle Meade Plantation built a reputation as a premier thoroughbred nursery and stud farm. The Plantation's carriage house is home to one of the largest collections of antique carriages in existence. The grounds of Belle Meade Plantation host a yearly calendar of seasonal events, including summer's weekly Jazz & Blues on the Lawn. Visitors can dine and enjoy local jazz and blues artists under the summer evening sky. The Mansion is preserved at its Victorian finest, open to the public, and situated in one of Nashville's oldest and most beautiful neighborhoods not far from the Steeplechase course. So, when the weather warms and the roses bloom, grab a picnic hamper, blanket, and cooler, and settle in for the race. When the horses come pounding over Heartbreak Hill and cross the finish line, you'll be in for the thrill of a lifetime!

Walnut and Bleu Cheese Tart with Cranberries

Great as a side dish served with salads.

Walnut Pastry
1 cup White Lily flour
2/3 cup ground walnuts
1 tablespoon sugar
1/2 teaspoon dry mustard
1/4 teaspoon salt
1/8 teaspoon cayenne pepper
*6 tablespoons (3/4 stick) unsalted
    butter*
1 to 2 teaspoons milk

Filling
2 tablespoons olive oil
1 large onion, finely chopped
1/2 teaspoon salt
1 cup fresh cranberries
1 tablespoon sugar
1 1/3 cups chopped walnuts
2 teaspoons minced fresh thyme
3 ounces bleu cheese, crumbled
2 eggs
1 cup heavy cream

To prepare the pastry, combine the flour, walnuts, sugar, dry mustard, salt, cayenne pepper and butter in a food processor and pulse until the mixture resembles fine crumbs. Add the milk and pulse until the mixture forms a dough. Shape into a ball and press over the bottom and side of a 9-inch tart pan.

Prick the pastry with a fork. Place in the freezer for 30 minutes. Bake at 375 degrees for 15 to 20 minutes or until light brown. Reduce the oven temperature to 350 degrees.

To prepare the filling, heat the olive oil in a heavy saucepan over medium heat. Add the onion and sprinkle with the salt. Sauté for 10 to 15 minutes or until the onion is tender and golden brown, stirring frequently. Add the cranberries and sugar. Cook until the cranberries begin to pop. Stir in the walnuts and thyme and remove from the heat.

Spread the cranberry mixture in the tart shell. Sprinkle the bleu cheese over the top. Combine the eggs and cream in a mixing bowl and whisk until smooth. Pour over the filling.

Bake the tart at 350 degrees for 15 to 20 minutes or until the filling is set and golden brown. Let stand for 15 minutes before serving.

Serves 8

Basil Torte

An all-time favorite for entertaining.

1 cup loosely packed fresh spinach leaves
3/4 cup fresh Italian parsley
1/4 cup fresh basil leaves
1 teaspoon minced garlic
1/4 cup vegetable oil
1/4 cup finely chopped walnuts
1 cup freshly grated Parmesan cheese
8 ounces cream cheese, softened
4 ounces Roquefort cheese, softened
1/4 cup slivered sun-dried tomatoes, patted dry

Line a 3×5-inch loaf pan with a piece of plastic wrap large enough to hang over the sides.

Combine the spinach, parsley, basil and garlic in a food processor and process until chopped. Add the vegetable oil gradually, processing constantly until smooth. Combine with the walnuts and Parmesan cheese in a bowl and mix well.

Blend the cream cheese and Roquefort cheese in a mixing bowl until smooth. Spread 1/3 of the mixture evenly in the prepared pan. Spread half the spinach mixture over the cheese and arrange half the sun-dried tomatoes over the spinach. Spread half the remaining cream cheese mixture over the tomatoes.

Layer with the remaining spinach and sun-dried tomatoes and spread the remaining cream cheese mixture over the top. Fold the plastic wrap over the layers and chill for 24 hours.

Let stand until room temperature before serving. Invert onto a serving plate and remove the plastic wrap. Serve with crackers.

Serves 6 to 8

Baked Brie in Puff Pastry with Honey Walnut Sauce

Great for a Valentine's Day dinner for two.

Brie
1 frozen puff pastry sheet, thawed
2 (4-ounce) wedges Brie cheese,
    about 1½×6½ inches each
1 egg, beaten

Honey Walnut Sauce
¼ cup (½ stick) butter
3 tablespoons honey
1½ teaspoons minced garlic
2 tablespoons chopped walnuts
1 tablespoon chopped fresh parsley

To prepare the Brie, roll the pastry sheet to a 12×12-inch square on a lightly floured surface. Cut into halves diagonally to form 2 triangles. Place 1 Brie wedge on each triangle with the wide edge of the cheese toward the long side of the pastry.

Fold the pastry to enclose the cheese and press the edges of the pastry gently with a fork to seal completely. Place seam side up on a baking sheet and brush with the beaten egg. Bake at 400 degrees for 18 minutes or until golden brown.

To prepare the sauce, combine the butter, honey and garlic in a small saucepan over low heat. Cook until the butter melts, stirring constantly. Spoon the sauce onto 2 serving plates and sprinkle with the walnuts and parsley. Place the pastry-wrapped Brie in the center of the plates.

The Brie may be prepared up to 6 hours in advance, covered and stored in the refrigerator until time to bake and serve.

Serves 2

Honey Mustard Almond Brie

1 (13-ounce) round Brie cheese
1 (8-ounce) jar honey mustard
2 to 4 ounces toasted almonds

Place the Brie in a microwave-safe serving dish. Spread the mustard over the cheese. Microwave for 3 to 5 minutes or until the cheese is soft. Sprinkle with the almonds and serve warm.

Serves 8

Asparagus Cheese Puffs

8 ounces fresh asparagus
3/4 cup White Lily flour
1/4 teaspoon curry powder
1/2 teaspoon salt
cayenne pepper to taste
3/4 cup milk
5 tablespoons unsalted butter, chopped
3 large eggs
4 ounces (1 cup) coarsely shredded Manchego cheese
1/2 cup finely grated Parmigiano-Reggiano cheese
salt and black pepper to taste

Trim the asparagus and cut into 1/4-inch pieces. Blanch briefly in boiling water in a saucepan; drain and rinse with cold water.

Mix the flour, curry powder, 1/2 teaspoon salt and cayenne pepper in a small bowl. Combine the milk and butter in a medium saucepan and bring to a boil over medium-high heat. Remove from the heat. Add the dry ingredients all at once and mix with a wooden spoon until the mixture pulls away from the side of the pan and forms a ball.

Return to the heat and cook for 20 to 30 seconds or until the mixture appears slightly dry. Remove to a large bowl and let stand until slightly cool. Beat in the eggs 1 at a time. Add the asparagus and cheeses and mix well. Season with salt and black pepper to taste.

Spoon by rounded tablespoonfuls onto baking sheets lined with baking parchment. Bake at 400 degrees on the center oven rack for 15 to 20 minutes or until golden brown. Serve immediately.

Serves 4

Fresh Asparagus and Puff Pastry Pinwheels

16 to 20 asparagus spears
1/2 cup sweet-hot mustard
4 ounces cream cheese, softened

1 sheet frozen puff pastry, thawed
1 egg, beaten
poppy seeds to taste

Trim the asparagus and steam or simmer in boiling water in a saucepan for 3 minutes or until tender-crisp. Immerse in cold water, drain and chill in the refrigerator.

Combine the mustard and cream cheese in a small bowl and mix until smooth. Roll the puff pastry 1/8 inch thick on a lightly floured surface. Cut into halves lengthwise. Spread each pastry half with the cream cheese mixture. Arrange 8 to 10 asparagus spears along the narrow edge of each pastry and roll the pastry tightly to enclose the asparagus.

Brush the rolls with egg and sprinkle with the poppy seeds. Wrap in plastic wrap and freeze until firm enough to slice. Cut into 1/2-inch slices.

Arrange the slices on a baking sheet and bake at 400 degrees for 15 minutes or until golden brown.

You may place the slices in an airtight container and store in the freezer until time to bake and serve.

Makes 4 dozen

Mexican Roll-Ups

If you are not serving a crowd, reduce the recipe by two-thirds.

24 ounces cream cheese, softened
1 envelope ranch salad dressing mix
chopped green onions to taste
1 red bell pepper, chopped

2 or 3 jalapeño peppers, finely chopped
4 ounces (1 cup) finely shredded
    Cheddar cheese
6 (9-inch) flour tortillas

Combine the cream cheese, salad dressing mix, green onions, bell pepper, jalapeño peppers and Cheddar cheese in a bowl and mix well.

Spread the cream cheese mixture over the tortillas and roll to enclose the filling. Wrap in plastic wrap and store in the refrigerator for up to several days. Cut into 1/2-inch slices with a sharp knife and arrange on a serving plate. Serve with salsa or taco sauce.

Makes 9 dozen

Picnic Café's Cheese Wafers

From the Picnic Café in Belle Meade.

2¹/2 cups White Lily flour
¹/3 teaspoon salt
¹/3 teaspoon cayenne pepper
1¹/2 pounds (6 cups) sharp Cheddar cheese, finely shredded
1¹/2 cups (3 sticks) butter

Mix the flour, salt and cayenne pepper in a bowl. Add the cheese and mix well. Place the butter in a microwave-safe bowl and microwave until melted and bubbling. Add to the cheese mixture and mix well. Shape into small balls with a melon scoop and place on an ungreased baking sheet. Cover with waxed paper and press into circles or desired shape. Bake at 350 degrees for 30 minutes or until crisp and golden brown.

Makes 5 dozen

Cocktail Cheese Biscuits

¹/2 cup (1 stick) butter, softened
4 ounces (1 cup) shredded sharp Cheddar cheese
1 cup White Lily flour
1 teaspoon salt
¹/2 teaspoon (or more) cayenne pepper
pecan halves

Beat the butter in a large mixing bowl until creamy. Add the cheese, flour, salt and cayenne pepper and mix well. Shape into small balls and place on an ungreased baking sheet. Place 1 pecan half on each ball and press to flatten. Bake at 350 degrees for 15 minutes.

Makes 3 dozen

For Olive-Stuffed Cheese Biscuits, shape tablespoons of the dough around pimento-stuffed olives and bake as above.

Occasions

Belle Meade Plantation hosts a variety of exciting events for families and friends, among which is the annual Fall Fest. This two-day harvest festival features artisans and craftsmen from around the country, musicians, a fine antiques show, great food, and lots of children's rides and activities. Enjoy the fabulous fall weather and foliage on the grounds of the antebellum home.

Cayenne Toasts

Very spicy! Great with soups, salads, and cream cheese spreads.

1 cup olive oil
1½ teaspoons sugar
1½ teaspoons garlic powder
1½ teaspoons onion powder
1 teaspoon paprika

1½ teaspoons salt
1 to 2 teaspoons cayenne pepper
½ teaspoon finely ground black
    pepper
3 loaves French bread

Combine the olive oil, sugar, garlic powder, onion powder, paprika, salt, cayenne pepper and black pepper in a small bowl and mix well. Cut the French bread into ¼-inch slices and arrange in single layers on ungreased baking sheets. Brush with the olive oil mixture. Bake at 200 degrees for 1 hour or until very crisp. Cool on wire racks.

Serves 12 to 18

Marinated Cheese

½ cup olive oil
½ cup white wine vinegar
1 (2-ounce) jar pimento, drained
3 tablespoons chopped parsley
3 tablespoons chopped green onions
3 garlic cloves, minced
1 teaspoon sugar
¾ teaspoon dried basil leaves,
    crushed

½ teaspoon salt
½ teaspoon freshly ground pepper
1 (8-ounce) rectangle sharp Cheddar
    cheese, chilled
1 (8-ounce) rectangle cream cheese,
    chilled

Garnish
fresh parsley

Combine the olive oil, vinegar, pimento, parsley, green onions, garlic, sugar, basil, salt and pepper in a jar and shake to mix well.

Cut the Cheddar cheese into halves lengthwise. Cut the halves crosswise into ¼-inch slices. Repeat the process with the cream cheese. Alternate the Cheddar cheese slices and cream cheese slices in a shallow dish, standing the slices on edge to make a log.

Pour the olive oil mixture over the log. Marinate, covered, for 8 hours or longer. Remove the log to a serving plate and drizzle with the marinade. Garnish with parsley. Serve with wheat crackers.

Serves 12

Jack's Sweet and Hot Party Pecans

1/4 cup (1/2 stick) butter
3 tablespoons sugar
1/4 cup Jack Daniel's Tennessee Whiskey
2 tablespoons Tabasco sauce, or to taste
1/2 teaspoon garlic powder
1 1/2 teaspoons salt
4 cups (about 1 pound) pecan halves

Combine the butter, sugar, whiskey, Tabasco sauce, garlic powder and salt in a large saucepan. Bring to a boil over medium heat, stirring to mix well. Boil for 3 minutes. Add the pecans and mix to coat well.

Spread the pecans in a single layer in a shallow baking pan. Bake at 300 degrees for 30 minutes or until crisp, stirring occasionally. Cool and store in an airtight container. Do not substitute margarine for butter in this recipe.

Makes 4 cups

Sugar and Spice Pecans

Makes a great holiday gift.

1/2 cup sugar
2 tablespoons cinnamon
1/2 teaspoon salt
1 egg white
3 cups pecan halves

Mix the sugar, cinnamon and salt in a small bowl. Beat the egg white in a bowl until foamy. Add the pecans and mix to coat evenly. Add the sugar mixture and mix well. Spread in a single layer in a shallow baking pan. Bake at 300 degrees for 30 minutes, stirring every 7 to 10 minutes. Cool and store in an airtight container.

Makes 3 cups

Mushroom and Spinach Pinwheels

Cream Cheese Pastry

8 ounces reduced-fat cream cheese, softened
2/3 cup butter, softened
1 cup all-purpose White Lily flour
1 cup self-rising White Lily flour

Pinwheels

1 (10-ounce) package frozen chopped spinach
2 1/2 cups chopped fresh mushrooms
1 large onion, chopped (1 cup)
2 tablespoons butter
1 tablespoon all-purpose White Lily flour
1/2 teaspoon lemon juice
Tabasco sauce to taste
1/8 teaspoon garlic powder
1/2 teaspoon dried oregano leaves, crushed
1/2 teaspoon salt
1/4 cup grated Parmesan cheese
1 egg white
1 tablespoon water

To prepare the pastry, beat the cream cheese with the butter in a large bowl until light and fluffy. Add the all-purpose flour and self-rising flour and mix well. Divide into 2 equal portions. Shape each portion into a ball and wrap in plastic wrap. Chill for 30 to 60 minutes or until firm enough to handle easily.

To prepare the pinwheels, cook the spinach using the package directions. Drain and press to remove excess liquid. Sauté the mushrooms and onion in the butter in a large skillet over medium heat for 3 minutes or until the onion is tender. Add the spinach, flour, lemon juice, Tabasco sauce, garlic powder, oregano and salt. Cook until thickened, stirring constantly. Stir in the cheese; cool.

Roll the pastry into 7×12-inch rectangles on a floured surface. Spread the spinach mixture over the pastry, leaving a 1/2-inch border on the sides. Roll the dough from the narrow edge to enclose the filling. Moisten the edges with a small amount of water and press to seal. Wrap in plastic wrap and chill for 1 hour. Cut the rolls into 1/2-inch slices and arrange the slices on ungreased baking sheets. Brush with a mixture of the egg white and 1 tablespoon water. Bake at 400 degrees for 20 minutes or until golden brown. Remove to wire racks to cool.

Makes 28

New Year's Cakes

1 small onion, finely chopped
1 tablespoon olive oil
2 (16-ounce) cans black-eyed peas, drained
8 ounces cream cheese, softened
1 tablespoon chopped fresh chives
1 large egg
1 teaspoon (or more) hot sauce
1 teaspoon dried onion flakes
1/2 teaspoon salt
1 (8-ounce) package hush puppy mix
olive oil

Garnish
sour cream
pepper jelly

Sauté the onion in 1 tablespoon olive oil in a small skillet until tender. Combine with 1 can of peas, cream cheese, chives, egg, hot sauce, onion flakes and salt in a food processor and process until smooth. Combine with the hush puppy mix and remaining can of peas in a bowl and mix well.

Shape by 2 tablespoonfuls into small patties and place on a baking sheet covered with waxed paper. Chill, covered, for 1 hour.

Add just enough olive oil to a nonstick skillet to cover the bottom and heat over medium heat. Add the patties and sauté for 4 minutes on each side or until crisp. Drain on paper towels. Garnish with sour cream and/or pepper jelly or serve with Pico de Gallo (page 184).

Serves 12

Tomato Basil Bruschetta

1 pound Roma or vine-ripened tomatoes, chopped
6 fresh basil leaves, finely slivered
1¹/₂ teaspoons minced garlic
2 tablespoons olive oil
2 tablespoons white balsamic vinegar
1 teaspoon kosher salt
1¹/₂ teaspoons finely ground pepper
2 tablespoons olive oil
1 teaspoon granulated garlic
1 French baguette

Combine the tomatoes, basil, minced garlic, 2 tablespoons olive oil, vinegar, kosher salt and pepper in a bowl and mix well. Let stand at room temperature for 1 hour or longer.

Mix 2 tablespoons olive oil with the granulated garlic in a small bowl. Slice the baguette diagonally ¹/₂ inch thick. Brush with the olive oil mixture. Grill or broil until lightly toasted. Top with the tomato mixture to serve.

Makes 20

Roasted Garlic

2 large whole garlic bulbs
¹/₄ cup white wine
¹/₄ cup chicken stock
1 tablespoon butter, melted
¹/₄ teaspoon chopped fresh basil
¹/₄ teaspoon salt

Slice off the tops of the whole garlic bulbs and place the bulbs in a foil-lined baking pan. Combine the wine, chicken stock, butter, basil and salt in a small bowl and mix well. Pour over the garlic and cover with foil. Bake at 300 degrees for 3 hours. Cool to room temperature.

Separate into cloves and squeeze from the skins into a bowl. Mash until smooth. Serve with Melba toast or sliced baguette.

You may also wrap the bulbs in foil, place in a baking pan and grill for 2 hours.

Serves 8

Tenderloin with Horseradish Cream Sauce

Great served on rolls with either the Horseradish Cream Sauce or with honey mustard for an elegant buffet.

Horseradish Cream Sauce

1 cup whipping cream
1/2 cup drained horseradish
2 tablespoons Dijon mustard
1/2 cup mayonnaise
salt and pepper to taste

Tenderloin

1 1/2 teaspoons dried rosemary
1/4 teaspoon each dry mustard and ginger
1/8 teaspoon garlic powder
1 teaspoon each seasoned salt and kosher salt
1/2 teaspoon onion salt
1 teaspoon freshly ground pepper
1 (3- to 4-pound) beef tenderloin
2 tablespoons each butter and olive oil

To prepare the sauce, beat the whipping cream in a mixing bowl just until soft peaks form. Whisk the horseradish, Dijon mustard and mayonnaise in a medium bowl. Whisk 1/2 cup of the whipped cream gently into the horseradish mixture. Fold the remaining horseradish mixture into the whipped cream. Season with salt and pepper to taste. Chill until serving time.

To prepare the tenderloin, mix the rosemary, dry mustard, ginger, garlic powder, seasoned salt, kosher salt, onion salt and pepper in a small bowl. Rub evenly over the tenderloin.

Heat the butter and olive oil in a large roasting pan over medium heat. Add the tenderloin and brown on all sides for 15 minutes. Roast at 425 degrees for 22 minutes for medium-rare. Remove from the oven and let stand for 20 minutes before serving. Slice and serve with the horseradish sauce.

Serves 16

A short drive from Nashville to Shelbyville, Tennessee, will get you to the home of another notable Tennessee equestrian event, the Tennessee Walking Horse National Celebration. Each summer these remarkable horses, known for their gentle ride and smooth gait, compete for titles, ribbons, trophies, and $650,000 in prize money. The premier event for Tennessee Walking Horses, the Celebration crowns the breed's World Grand Champion and some twenty World Champions. It is billed as the "World's Greatest Horse Show," with 4,000 equine entrants. Annual attendance exceeds 220,000, so be sure to make your reservations in advance.

Tomato Chutney and Ham Pinwheels

2 (8×12-inch) whole wheat flatbread wraps, or 4 (10-inch) flour tortillas
8 ounces cream cheese, softened
³/4 cup roasted tomato chutney
¹/3 cup chopped cilantro
6 to 8 thin slices Virginia ham

Place the wraps on a work surface and spread with the cream cheese. Spread the chutney lengthwise down the centers of the wraps. Sprinkle with the cilantro and arrange the ham slices evenly over the wraps.

Roll the wraps from the long sides to enclose the filling. Wrap in plastic wrap and chill for 1 hour or longer. Cut the rolls into ³/4-inch slices to serve.

Makes 32

Not Your Mother's Ham Biscuits

1 (20- to 24-roll) package dinner rolls in a foil pan
¹/2 cup (1 stick) margarine, softened
1¹/2 tablespoons poppy seeds
1¹/2 tablespoons Dijon mustard
1¹/2 tablespoons grated onion
1 teaspoon Worcestershire sauce
8 ounces thinly sliced smoked ham
8 ounces thinly sliced Swiss cheese

Split the entire pan of rolls into halves horizontally with a serrated knife, leaving both halves intact. Combine the margarine, poppy seeds, Dijon mustard, onion and Worcestershire sauce in a bowl and mix well. Spread over the cut sides of the rolls. Layer the ham and cheese alternately on the bottom roll section and replace the top section.

Wrap the pan in foil and bake at 400 degrees for 20 minutes or until the cheese melts. Cut into rolls with a sharp knife to serve.

You may use the rolls while they are still frozen and/or freeze the filled rolls before baking.

Makes 20 to 24

Bacon-Stuffed Cherry Tomatoes

2 pounds large cherry tomatoes
salt to taste
1 pound sliced bacon
4 scallions, finely chopped
1/2 cup mayonnaise

Place the tomatoes on their stem ends and cut off about 1/4 of the blossom ends. Scoop out the seeds and pulp with a small spoon. Salt the cavities lightly and invert to drain.

Fry the bacon in a large skillet over medium heat until crisp and brown. Remove to paper towels to drain and chop fine. Combine with the scallions and mayonnaise in a bowl and mix well. Spoon the mixture into the tomatoes with a small spoon, mounding the filling slightly. Place on a serving plate and chill, covered, until serving time.

Makes 36 to 48

Phyllo Sausage Cups

An elegant alternative to sausage balls.

1 pound hot sausage
16 ounces cream cheese, softened
1 bunch green onions, finely chopped
2 packages miniature phyllo cups

Brown the sausage in a skillet, stirring until crumbly; drain well. Combine with the cream cheese and green onions in a bowl and mix well. Spoon into the phyllo cups and arrange on a baking sheet. Bake at 350 degrees for 10 to 15 minutes or until heated through. Serve warm.

You may prepare the cups in advance and store in the refrigerator until time to heat and serve.

Makes 30

Thai Curried Chicken Salad

8 ounces chicken breasts

1 tablespoon vegetable oil

1/2 teaspoon cardamom

1/2 teaspoon each ginger, cumin,
   coriander, turmeric and
   cayenne pepper

1/4 cup plain yogurt

1/4 cup mayonnaise

salt and black pepper to taste

14 sturdy crackers

1/2 cup sliced grapes

chopped cilantro

Cook the chicken in enough boiling water to cover in a covered saucepan for 7 minutes or until cooked through. Cool in the cooking liquid and drain. Cut into 1/2-inch pieces. Heat the vegetable oil in a small skillet over low heat. Add the cardamom, ginger, cumin, coriander, turmeric and cayenne pepper and cook for 3 minutes or until the spices are aromatic. Combine with the yogurt and mayonnaise in a bowl. Stir in the chicken, salt and black pepper. Arrange the crackers on a platter and top with the chicken mixture and 1 or 2 grape slices. Sprinkle with chopped cilantro.

Makes 14

The Tailgate Sandwich

For a heartier sandwich, just add more ham or turkey.

1 large red bell pepper

1 thin and crusty French baguette

1 tablespoon extra-virgin olive oil

1 tablespoon red wine vinegar

2 or 3 slices mozzarella cheese

4 to 6 large arugula leaves or
   radicchio leaves

4 thin slices tomato

freshly ground pepper to taste

4 thin slices smoked ham or turkey

Cut the bell pepper into halves lengthwise, discarding the seeds and membranes. Place cut side down on a baking sheet and flatten slightly. Broil until evenly charred. Place in a plastic bag, seal and let stand for 10 minutes. Remove and discard the skin.

Trim the ends of the baguette to form an 8-inch loaf. Split horizontally and scoop out most of the centers, leaving shells. Brush the cut sides with a mixture of the olive oil and vinegar.

Layer the mozzarella cheese, arugula, and tomatoes on the bottom bread half; season with pepper. Cut the roasted bell pepper halves into halves again lengthwise. Arrange on the layers and top with the ham and remaining bread. Wrap with plastic wrap, pressing down lightly. Let stand at room temperature for 1 hour. Cut crosswise to serve.

Serves 8 as an appetizer or 2 as a main course

Crab Meat Crisps

Also tasty made with chicken instead of crab meat.

1/2 cup (1 stick) butter, softened
1 (5-ounce) jar Old English cheese spread
1 1/2 teaspoons mayonnaise
1/2 teaspoon each garlic salt and seasoned salt
6 ounces crab meat, drained
6 English muffins, split

Mix the butter, cheese, mayonnaise, garlic salt and seasoned salt in a bowl. Stir in the crab meat. Spread on the cut sides of the muffins and arrange on a baking sheet. Bake at 400 degrees for 15 minutes or until bubbly. Cut into quarters to serve.

Makes 48

Curry Cream Cheese Spread

8 ounces cream cheese, softened
4 ounces (1 cup) shredded sharp Cheddar cheese
1 tablespoon Worcestershire sauce
1 tablespoon curry powder
1/4 teaspoon salt
4 ounces chutney
1/4 cup shredded coconut
1/4 cup chopped green onions
1/4 cup chopped peanuts or cashews

Combine the cream cheese, Cheddar cheese, Worcestershire sauce, curry powder and salt in a bowl and mix well. Shape into a flat disk on a piece of plastic wrap. Cover with the plastic wrap and chill for several hours or until firm.

Place the disk on a serving plate and spoon the chutney over the top. Sprinkle with the coconut, green onions and peanuts. Serve with crackers.

Serves 8

Black-Eyed Pea Dip

1 (16-ounce) can black-eyed peas
1 (16-ounce) can field peas
1 (16-ounce) can Shoe Peg corn
1 cup chopped onion
2 garlic cloves, minced
1/2 cup olive oil
1/4 cup red wine vinegar
1 teaspoon Tabasco sauce
1/2 teaspoon dry mustard
1/2 teaspoon pepper
1 cup chopped parsley
2 tablespoons chopped fresh basil

Drain and rinse the black-eyed peas, field peas and corn. Combine with the onion and garlic in a bowl. Add the olive oil, vinegar, Tabasco sauce, dry mustard and pepper and mix well. Chill, covered, for 8 hours or longer.

Add the parsley and basil at serving time. Serve with corn chip scoops.

Serves 16

Goat Cheese Garlic Dip

8 ounces cream cheese, softened
8 ounces fresh goat cheese, softened
8 ounces sour cream
2 teaspoons minced garlic
1 tablespoon chopped fresh chives
1 teaspoon chopped fresh thyme
1/2 teaspoon salt
1/2 teaspoon cracked black pepper
cayenne pepper to taste

Combine the cream cheese and goat cheese in a food processor and pulse to mix well. Add the sour cream, garlic, chives, thyme, salt, cracked pepper and cayenne pepper and mix until smooth. Spoon into a serving bowl and chill, covered, until serving time. Serve with crackers or pita chips.

Serves 12

Kahlúa Dip

8 ounces cream cheese, softened
1 cup whipping cream, whipped
3/4 cup packed brown sugar
1 cup sour cream
1/3 cup Kahlúa
1/3 cup salted nuts (optional)

Blend the cream cheese and whipped cream in a bowl. Add the brown sugar, sour cream, Kahlúa and nuts and mix well. Spoon into a serving dish and chill, covered, for up to 2 days. Serve with sliced Granny Smith apples or other seasonal fruit.

Serves 24

Layered Guacamole

A popular recipe from Encore.

2 large ripe avocados, mashed
2 tablespoons mayonnaise
1 tablespoon lemon juice
1/8 teaspoon each garlic powder and garlic salt
1 cup sour cream
1 or 2 (8-ounce) jars picante sauce, or to taste, drained
3/4 cup chopped black olives
3 medium tomatoes, peeled and chopped
6 ounces (1 1/2 cups) shredded Cheddar cheese
bacon, crisp-fried and crumbled
1 (16-ounce) can refried beans

Combine the first 5 ingredients and mix well. Spread in an 8×12-inch dish. Spread the sour cream and then the picante sauce over the top. Layer with the olives, tomatoes, cheese and bacon. Pipe the refried beans around the edge with a pastry tube. Chill, covered, until serving time. Serve with corn chips or tortilla chips.

Serves 16

Roasted Corn Guacamole

1 cup fresh or frozen corn kernels
1 tablespoon vegetable oil
2 large avocados, chopped
1 large tomato, chopped
1/4 cup chopped cilantro
2 tablespoons finely chopped red onion
1 teaspoon minced jalapeño pepper

1 teaspoon minced garlic
2 tablespoons fresh lime juice
2 tablespoons vegetable oil
1 teaspoon white wine vinegar
1/4 teaspoon cumin
1 1/2 teaspoons sea salt

Toss the corn kernels with 1 tablespoon vegetable oil in a bowl. Spread on a baking sheet and roast at 450 degrees for 7 to 8 minutes or until golden brown, stirring frequently. Cool to room temperature.

Combine the corn with the avocados, tomato, cilantro, onion, jalapeño pepper and garlic in a bowl and mix well. Stir in the lime juice, 2 tablespoons vegetable oil, vinegar, cumin and sea salt. Chill, covered, for up to 6 hours. Serve with tortilla chips.

Serves 12

Pimento Cheese with a Twist

Makes a delicious and easy spread for sandwiches, too.

4 ounces cream cheese, softened
1/4 cup mayonnaise
1 garlic clove, minced
1 teaspoon drained sweet pickle relish
8 ounces (2 cups) shredded sharp
   Cheddar cheese

1 (4-ounce) jar chopped pimentos,
   drained
1 (4-ounce) can chopped green chiles,
   drained
salt to taste

Combine the cream cheese, mayonnaise, garlic and pickle relish in a food processor and process until smooth. Add the Cheddar cheese, pimentos, green chiles and salt and process to mix well. Spoon into a serving dish and cover. Chill for up to 8 hours. Serve with crackers.

You may use reduced-fat cream cheese, mayonnaise and/or Cheddar cheese for a lighter version.

Serves 8

Spicy Olive Tapenade

A great alternative to salsa. For variety, use an assortment of imported black and green olives.

1 (4-ounce) can chopped green chiles
1 (4-ounce) can chopped black olives
1 (6-ounce) jar pimento-stuffed green olives, chopped
4 green onions with tops, finely chopped
2 to 3 tomatoes, finely chopped
2 to 3 tablespoons seeded and chopped jalapeño pepper
1/2 cup olive oil
2 tablespoons cider vinegar
garlic powder to taste

Drain the green chiles, black olives and green olives. Combine with the green onions, tomatoes and jalapeño pepper in a bowl. Combine the olive oil, vinegar and garlic powder in a small bowl and mix to blend well. Add to the olive mixture and mix well. Chill, covered, for 8 to 10 hours. Serve with corn scoops or tortilla chips.

Serves 12

Creamy Salmon Dip

8 ounces Neufchâtel cheese, softened
1/3 cup chopped red onion
4 ounces smoked salmon
1/4 teaspoon lemon juice
1/4 teaspoon dillweed
1 tablespoon drained capers

Combine the Neufchâtel cheese and onion in a food processor and pulse to mix well. Add the salmon, lemon juice, dillweed and capers. Pulse to mix well. Serve immediately with crackers or store, covered, in the refrigerator for up to 24 hours.

Serves 8

Christmas Cheese Spread

A popular recipe from Encore.

6 ounces Roquefort cheese
1 (10-ounce) jar Cheddar cheese spread
12 ounces cream cheese
2 tablespoons minced onion
1/2 cup minced parsley
1 teaspoon Worcestershire sauce
1 cup finely chopped pecans
1/2 teaspoon cayenne pepper (optional)

Let the Roquefort cheese, Cheddar cheese and cream cheese stand at room temperature for 8 hours or longer to soften. Combine the cheeses with the onion, parsley, Worcestershire sauce, pecans and cayenne pepper in a bowl and mix well. Serve with baguette rounds.

Serves 12 to 15

Toasted Almond Spread

1/3 cup sliced almonds
8 ounces cream cheese, softened
6 ounces (1 1/2 cups) shredded Swiss cheese
1/3 cup mayonnaise
2 tablespoons chopped green onions
1/8 teaspoon nutmeg
1/8 teaspoon pepper

Spread the almonds on a baking sheet. Broil until lightly toasted. Reserve 1 tablespoon for the topping.

Combine the cream cheese, Swiss cheese, mayonnaise, green onions, nutmeg, pepper and the remaining almonds in a mixing bowl and mix well. Spread in a shallow quiche pan or pie plate.

Bake at 350 degrees for 10 minutes. Sprinkle with the reserved almonds and bake for 5 minutes longer. Serve warm with assorted crackers.

Serves 6

Sun-Dried Tomato Serendipity

4 ounces cream cheese, softened
4 ounces Neufchâtel cheese, softened
3 tablespoons sour cream
1/2 cup chopped oil-pack sun-dried tomatoes
3 green onions, chopped
1/4 cup (or more) chopped pecans
hot sauce to taste

Blend the cream cheese, Neufchâtel cheese and sour cream in a bowl. Add the sun-dried tomatoes, green onions and pecans and mix well. Season with hot sauce.

Serves 12 to 15

Belle Meade Mint Julep

In the fashion of Belle Meade Country Club.

1 cup sugar
1 cup water
fresh mint
crushed ice
water
bourbon

Bring the sugar and 1 cup water to a boil in a saucepan. Boil for 5 minutes without stirring. Pour over 1 bunch mint leaves in a heatproof bowl and crush the mint gently with the back of a spoon. Pour into an airtight container and chill for 8 to 10 hours. Strain into a pitcher for juleps or store in the refrigerator for up to several weeks.

Muddle a few fresh mint leaves in the bottom of an 8-ounce glass for each serving. Fill with crushed ice and add 1 tablespoon of the sugar syrup and 1 tablespoon water. Stir in 2 ounces bourbon; mix gently. Garnish each glass with a fresh mint sprig.

Serves 16

Notable

Everything's coming up roses for horses whose bloodlines can be traced to Belle Meade Plantation. General William Harding knew what he was doing when he purchased nineteen-year-old Bonnie Scotland as a breeding horse. Even though the horse was lame in one leg at the time of purchase, his blood still runs true. With the exception of only five, every winner of the Kentucky Derby since 1972 has come from bloodstock of Belle Meade's Bonnie Scotland—Seattle Slew, Charismatic, Sunday Silence, and Secretariat to name a few. So before you place your bet at the Derby, you might want to check for the Belle Meade connection. If you see Bonnie Scotland, odds are you'll pick a winner!

Champagne and Banana Punch

3 bananas
juice of 2 lemons
6 cups water
4 cups sugar
sections of 2 oranges, chopped
1 (12-ounce) can frozen orange juice concentrate
1 (48-ounce) can unsweetened pineapple juice
1/2 bottle Champagne

Mash the bananas with the lemon juice in a heatproof bowl. Bring the water to a boil in a saucepan and add the sugar, stirring until completely dissolved. Add to the bananas and stir in the oranges, orange juice concentrate and pineapple juice. Let stand until cool.

Spoon into an airtight container and freeze until firm. Let stand at room temperature for 45 minutes. Combine with the Champagne in a punch bowl and mix gently.

Serves 20 to 24

Holiday Cranberry Drink

Keep warm on the stove for holiday fragrance.

2 cups cranberry juice cocktail
2 1/2 cups unsweetened pineapple juice
1/2 cup water
1/3 cup packed brown sugar
1/2 teaspoon each ground cloves and ground allspice
3 cinnamon sticks

Garnish
cinnamon sticks

Combine the cranberry juice cocktail, pineapple juice, water and brown sugar in a saucepan and mix well. Stir in the cloves and allspice and add the cinnamon sticks. Bring to a boil over medium heat. Reduce the heat to low and simmer for 10 minutes. Pour into mugs, discarding the used cinnamon sticks. Garnish with fresh cinnamon sticks.

Serves 10

Chocolate Coffee Dream

Great après ski.

1¹/₂ cups brewed coffee
2¹/₂ cups milk
1¹/₂ cups water
3 (1-ounce) squares semisweet chocolate, chopped
1 teaspoon ground cinnamon
¹/₂ cup Kahlúa
vanilla ice cream

Garnish
chocolate curls or sprinkles

Combine the coffee, milk, water, chocolate and cinnamon in a 2¹/₂-quart microwave-safe bowl. Microwave on High for 7 to 8 minutes, whisking after 4 minutes to blend in the chocolate. Cover with plastic wrap and microwave on High for 4 to 5 minutes. Stir in the Kahlúa. Ladle into serving mugs. Add a small scoop of ice cream and garnish with chocolate curls.

Serves 6 to 8

Coffee Punch

A punch from Encore *that is milder than Irish coffee.*

6 tablespoons sugar
6 cups brewed strong coffee
2 cups whipping cream, whipped
1 cup Jamaican rum
5 quarts vanilla ice cream

Dissolve the sugar in the coffee in a bowl. Fold in the whipped cream and rum. Scoop the ice cream into a punch bowl and pour the coffee mixture over the top; mix gently.

Serves 15 to 20

Historical

In 1892, Joel Cheek, cousin and business partner of Leslie Owen Cheek, developed a specialized blend of coffee for the Maxwell House Hotel. Due to popular demand, it became the only blend served by the hotel and began Nashville's prominence in the coffee industry in the early 1900s. Teddy Roosevelt was served the Maxwell House coffee on a visit to Nashville in 1907 and noted that it was "good to the last drop."

Killer Margaritas

2 cups tequila
1/2 cup fresh lime juice
1 cup water
1/4 cup Grand Marnier
1 1/2 cups sweet-and-sour mix
1 1/2 cups margarita mix
8 to 10 lime wedges

Garnish
8 to 10 lime wedges or slices

Combine the tequila, lime juice, water, Grand Marnier, sweet-and-sour mix and margarita mix in a pitcher and mix well. Pour over ice in glasses. Squeeze the juice of 1 lime wedge into each glass and garnish with additional lime.

Serves 8 to 10

Jack Daniel's Celebration Citrus Cider

1 1/2 cups Jack Daniel's Tennessee Whiskey
1 cup apple cider
1/2 cup orange juice
1/2 cup lemon juice
1 (1-liter) bottle ginger ale
orange, lemon and apple slices

Garnish
lemon slices

Combine the whiskey, apple cider, orange juice, lemon juice and ginger ale in a punch bowl or large pitcher and mix gently. Add the fruit slices. Ladle over ice in punch cups and garnish with additional lemon slices.

Serves 8 to 10

Whiskey Slush

2 cups water
5 tea bags
1 cup sugar
1 (6-ounce) can frozen orange juice concentrate
1 (12-ounce) can frozen lemonade concentrate
1¹/2 cups bourbon
7 cups water

Bring 2 cups water to a boil in a saucepan and add the tea bags. Remove from the heat and let steep for several minutes; discard the tea bags. Add the sugar and stir to dissolve completely. Combine with the remaining ingredients in a freezer container and mix well. Freeze until slushy.

Serves 10 to 15

Potting Shed Sangria

A recipe from a flower shop with a Happy Hour every Friday afternoon from 4:00 to 6:00. Customers could buy one plant and get one free in a social atmosphere made more festive by Potting Shed Sangria.

6 tablespoons sugar
3 jiggers apricot brandy
1 gallon burgundy
cinnamon to taste
3 cups lemon-lime soda
orange and lemon slices

Combine the sugar with the brandy in a large container and stir to dissolve the sugar completely. Add the wine and cinnamon and mix gently. Chill, covered, until serving time. Combine with the lemon-lime soda and fruit slices in a punch bowl or large pitchers at serving time and mix gently.

Makes 20 cups

Lemonade Syrup

Use this delicious syrup to create a variety of refreshing drinks.

1¹/2 cups water
1¹/2 cups sugar
1 tablespoon finely grated lemon zest
1¹/2 cups fresh lemon juice, about 6 to 8 lemons

Bring the water to a simmer in a saucepan and remove from the heat. Add the sugar and lemon zest. Stir until the sugar dissolves. Stir in the lemon juice. Chill, covered, in the refrigerator.

For Lemonade, combine equal parts of the syrup and water or club soda in a pitcher and mix well.
For Lemonade Cooler, combine equal parts of the syrup and white, rosé or zinfandel wine in a pitcher and mix gently.
For Lemonade Cocktail, combine equal parts of the syrup and club soda with half as much vodka or whiskey in a pitcher and mix gently.

Makes 3 cups syrup

Mint Tea

1¹/2 cups water
2 family-size tea bags
leaves of 6 mint sprigs
1¹/2 cups water
³/4 cup sugar
¹/2 cup fresh lemon juice (optional)
4 cups cold water

Bring 1¹/2 cups water to a boil in a saucepan and add the tea bags and mint. Remove from the heat and let steep for 15 minutes. Bring 1¹/2 cups water to a boil in a saucepan and add the sugar, stirring until the sugar dissolves. Stir in the lemon juice. Strain the tea into a 2-quart container. Add the sugar syrup and the cold water and mix well. Store in the refrigerator for up to several days.

You may easily double the recipe to serve a crowd. For a sugar-free version, substitute 22 packets of artificial sweetener for the sugar.

Makes 2 quarts

Show House Tea Punch

Gallons of Show House Tea Punch, a recipe from Nashville Seasons, *disappear daily at the Junior League Show House Tea Room.*

4 cups water
8 tea bags
2 cups sugar
2 cups water
2 cups orange juice
3/4 cup lemon juice
2 quarts water

Bring 4 cups water to a boil in a saucepan and add the tea bags. Remove from the heat and steep for several minutes; discard the tea bags. Combine the sugar with 2 cups water in a saucepan and boil for 5 minutes or until the sugar is completely dissolved. Combine the tea and the sugar water in a clean plastic 1-gallon container. Add the orange juice and lemon juice and mix well. Add 2 quarts water and shake to mix well. Store in the refrigerator.

Makes 1 gallon

Culinary

For festive ice cubes, fill the cups of an ice tray 1/3 full with water, tea or lemonade. Place decorative items such as mint leaves, raspberries, pansies or citrus zest in each cup. Freeze until firm. Fill the cups with additional water and freeze again. These make an unexpected and festive touch for any occasion.

Breads and Brunches

Breads and Brunches

Sterling silver. Fine porcelain. Crystal goblets.
These elegant serving pieces might have been found on a
sideboard laden with food served to guests at The
Hermitage, home of Andrew Jackson, seventh President of
the United States of America, and Rachel Donelson Jackson,
his beloved wife. Old Hickory, Hero of the Common
Man, and Self-Made Man are just a few of the titles
bestowed on Andrew Jackson and are befitting of the man
who came to influence and dominate the early 1800s to
such an extent that it is known as the "Age of Jackson."

His home, The Hermitage, is a testament to his transformation from a penniless orphan to President of the United States. Purchased in 1804, The Hermitage was originally a few log buildings on approximately 425 acres. A much larger Federal-style brick home was built beginning in 1819, with wings added in 1831 for Jackson's library and the dining room.

Damaged by fire in 1834, the home required renovations that resulted in the beautiful Greek-revival mansion that greets visitors today. Next to the house sits a carefully planned formal garden envisioned by Rachel Jackson and inspired by her love of flowers. Nearly all the objects on display at The Hermitage are original and include the Jacksons' furniture, books, eyeglasses, a sword, and their Bible. Since 1889, The Hermitage has been preserved by the dedicated members of The Ladies' Hermitage Association. Secure in its place in history, The Hermitage is but one stop on the multi-home tour of the Antebellum Trail in Middle Tennessee.

From Columbia to Nashville, these fine southern homes transport visitors to another time—when Scarletts and Rhetts were more than just memories—and showcase southern hospitality at its best. Carnton Plantation in Franklin is another home on the trail and, like The Hermitage, is a fine example of Greek Revival architecture. It was built in 1825 by Randal McGavock, a former mayor of Nashville. A profitable, self-supporting plantation prior to the Civil War, Randal's son, John, and his wife, Carrie, turned the mansion into a field hospital for injured soldiers seeking aid during the Battle of Franklin in November of 1864. Carnton was owned by the McGavocks until 1911. In 1978 the Carnton Association, Incorporated, saved the home from decades of neglect, and today's property, in addition to the home, features a restored 1840s garden and a Civil War cemetery.

Saved in 1954 by the National Society of Colonial Dames of America in Tennessee from scheduled demolition, Travellers Rest also takes its place on the Antebellum Trail. Begun in 1799, wealthy lawyer John Overton's original four-room home underwent three expansions between 1808 and 1828. The last addition included a veranda on the east side of the first story, which altered the home's original southern orientation. It was named Travellers Rest in deference to the visitors who had traveled far to discuss legal, political, and business matters with Judge Overton and were very weary from their journey. Currently, it houses one of the largest collections of early 1800s Tennessee-made furniture in the state. The home was restored by the Society to its 1830s style and is now open for public tours, school and scouting groups, and summer camp programs. These three homes along with Belle Meade Plantation, Belmont Mansion, Carter House, President Polk Home, and Rattle & Snap Plantation, give visitors a well-preserved snapshot of life in the Nashville area and the South during the 1800s.

No-Knead Bread

1 envelope dry yeast
1 1/4 cups lukewarm water
2 tablespoons shortening
2 tablespoons sugar

2 teaspoons salt
1 1/2 cups White Lily all-purpose flour
1 1/2 cups White Lily bread flour
butter

Dissolve the yeast in the lukewarm water in a large mixing bowl. Add the shortening, sugar, salt and all-purpose flour and beat for 2 minutes. Add the bread flour and mix with a wooden spoon until smooth. Let rise, covered, for 30 to 35 minutes or until doubled in bulk.

Beat the dough down with 25 strokes and place in a greased loaf pan, spreading evenly. Let rise, covered, for 40 minutes or until the dough reaches the top of the pan.

Bake at 375 degrees for 40 to 50 minutes or until the top is crisp and golden brown. Rub the top with butter and remove to a wire rack to cool.

Serves 12

Orange Date Nut Bread

A delicious bread from Nashville Seasons.

1 orange
1 cup chopped dates
sugar
3/4 cup broken pecans or walnuts
2 tablespoons melted shortening
1 egg, beaten

2 cups White Lily flour
1 cup sugar
1 teaspoon baking powder
1 teaspoon baking soda
1/2 teaspoon salt
1 teaspoon vanilla extract

Cut the orange into halves and squeeze the juice into a 1-cup measure. Add enough water to the juice to measure 1 cup. Roll the dates in enough sugar to prevent sticking together.

Grind the orange halves with the dates and pecans and combine in a large bowl. Add the orange juice mixture and shortening and mix well. Mix in the egg.

Sift the flour, 1 cup sugar, baking powder, baking soda and salt together. Add to the orange mixture and mix well. Stir in the vanilla.

Spoon into a greased loaf pan. Bake at 350 degrees for 1 hour. Cool on a wire rack.

You may double or triple the recipe if desired. Wrap loaves in foil to store in the freezer.

Serves 12

Cranberry Bread

Wonderful buttered and toasted for breakfast.

2 cups White Lily flour
1 cup sugar
1/2 teaspoon each baking powder and baking soda
1 egg, beaten
1/2 cup orange juice
2 tablespoons vegetable oil
1 tablespoon water
1 cup whole fresh cranberries
1/2 cup chopped pecans

Mix the flour, sugar, baking powder and baking soda in a large bowl. Combine the egg, orange juice, vegetable oil and water in a medium bowl and mix well. Add to the dry ingredients and mix until smooth. Stir in the cranberries and pecans. Spoon into a greased loaf pan. Bake at 325 degrees for 1 hour and 10 minutes or until golden brown. Remove to a wire rack to cool.

Serves 15

Beer Batter Bread

1/2 cup (1 stick) butter, melted
3 cups White Lily self-rising flour
2 tablespoons sugar
1 (12-ounce) can beer

Pour enough of the butter into a 5×9-inch loaf pan to coat the bottom. Combine the flour, sugar and beer in a large mixing bowl and mix until smooth. Spoon into the prepared loaf pan. Drizzle the remaining butter over the top.

Bake at 350 degrees for 50 to 60 minutes or until light golden brown. Remove to a wire rack and let stand for 10 minutes before serving.

Serves 12

Historical

Named after the game of chance that led to William Polk's ownership of 5,600 acres, the Rattle & Snap Plantation house in Columbia, Tennessee, was built by his son George Washington Polk between 1842 and 1845. Listed as a National Historic Landmark, the fully restored and furnished grand Greek Revival house is on the Antebellum Trail and open for public tours.

Streusel Corn Bread with Honey Pecan Butter

As served in the Minnie Pearl Junior League Decorators' Show House Tea Room.

Streusel Topping
1/4 cup (1/2 stick) butter
1/2 cup packed brown sugar
1 tablespoon honey
1 cup White Lily flour

Corn Bread
2 (8-ounce) packages corn muffin mix
1/2 cup sugar
2 eggs
2/3 cup cold water
1 1/2 tablespoons dark corn syrup
2 to 3 ounces (1/2 to 3/4 cup) shredded
   Cheddar cheese
1/4 to 1/3 cup corn kernels

Honey Pecan Butter
1 cup (2 sticks) butter, softened
3 tablespoons plus 3/4 teaspoon light
   brown sugar
1 teaspoon vanilla extract
2 3/4 tablespoons honey
6 tablespoons chopped roasted pecans

To prepare the topping, cream the butter in a mixing bowl until light. Add the brown sugar and honey and beat for 1 minute. Add the flour gradually, mixing well after each addition.

To prepare the corn bread, combine the corn muffin mix and sugar in a mixing bowl. Add the eggs, water and corn syrup and mix well. Stir in the cheese and corn.

Spoon into a greased 9×13-inch baking pan and bake at 300 degrees for 20 minutes. Crumble the topping over the top and bake for 10 to 15 minutes longer or until golden brown.

To prepare the butter, beat the butter in a mixing bowl until light. Add the brown sugar, vanilla, honey and pecans 1 ingredient at a time, beating constantly until well mixed. Serve immediately with the corn bread or store in the refrigerator and let stand at room temperature for 1 hour before serving.

Serves 8

Poppy Seed Bread

Bread

3 cups White Lily flour
1 1/2 teaspoons baking powder
1 1/2 teaspoons salt
2 teaspoons poppy seeds
3 eggs
2 1/2 cups sugar
1 1/4 cups vegetable oil
1 1/2 cups milk
1 1/2 teaspoons vanilla extract
1 teaspoon almond extract

Orange Almond Glaze

1/4 cup orange juice
3/4 cup sugar
2 tablespoons margarine
1/2 teaspoon vanilla extract
1/2 teaspoon almond extract

To prepare the bread, mix the flour, baking powder, salt and poppy seeds together. Combine the eggs and sugar in a mixing bowl and beat until thickened and pale yellow. Add the vegetable oil, milk and flavorings and beat until smooth. Mix in the dry ingredients.

Spoon into 3 greased and floured loaf pans. Bake at 325 degrees for 1 hour. Cool in the pans for 5 minutes.

To prepare the glaze, combine the orange juice, sugar, margarine and flavorings in a saucepan. Bring to a boil over medium heat, stirring to mix well.

Pierce holes in the bread and pour the hot glaze over the top. Remove to a wire rack to cool completely.

The batter will also make 7 small loaves or 14 miniature loaves. Reduce the baking time to 45 minutes for the small loaves and to 35 minutes for the miniature loaves.

Serves 12

Culinary

To make Lemon Butter, beat 1/2 cup butter in a mixing bowl. Add 1 tablespoon confectioners' sugar, 1/2 teaspoon finely grated lemon zest and 1 teaspoon lemon juice and beat until smooth. Store in the refrigerator and let stand at room temperature until soft before serving.

For Orange Butter, substitute orange zest for the lemon zest and orange juice for the lemon juice.

For Savory Lime Butter, add 1 tablespoon chopped fresh savory or thyme and 1/2 teaspoon finely shredded lime zest to 1/2 cup beaten butter.

For Herb Butter, add 1 teaspoon crushed dried basil or 1/2 teaspoon crushed dried thyme and 1/2 teaspoon crushed dried marjoram to 1/2 cup beaten butter.

For Parmesan Garlic Butter, add 1/3 cup grated Parmesan cheese, 1/4 teaspoon garlic powder and 2 tablespoons chopped fresh parsley or 2 teaspoons crushed dried parsley to 1/2 cup beaten butter.

Pumpkin Chocolate Chip Muffins

1²/3 cups White Lily flour
3/4 cup sugar
1/4 teaspoon baking powder
1 teaspoon baking soda
1 tablespoon pumpkin pie spice

1/4 teaspoon salt
2 eggs, beaten
1/2 cup (1 stick) butter, melted
1 cup canned pumpkin
6 ounces (1 cup) chocolate chips

Mix the flour, sugar, baking powder, baking soda, pumpkin pie spice and salt in a large bowl. Combine the eggs with the butter and pumpkin in a bowl and beat until smooth. Stir in the chocolate chips. Fold into the dry ingredients.

Spoon into greased muffin cups and bake at 350 degrees for 20 to 25 minutes or until golden brown. Serve immediately or remove to a wire rack to cool.

To bake 24 miniature muffins, reduce the baking time to 12 to 15 minutes.

Makes 1 dozen

Oatmeal Muffins

A popular recipe from Nashville Seasons.

1 cup quick-cooking oats
1 cup buttermilk
1 egg, beaten
1/2 cup packed brown sugar
1 cup White Lily flour

1 teaspoon baking powder
1/2 teaspoon baking soda
1 teaspoon salt
1/3 cup melted shortening

Mix the oats with the buttermilk in a large bowl and let stand for 1 hour. Add the egg and brown sugar and mix well.

Sift the flour, baking powder, baking soda and salt together. Add to the oats mixture and mix well. Add the shortening and mix just until moistened.

Spoon into greased muffin cups, filling 2/3 full. Bake at 400 degrees for 20 minutes. Serve immediately or remove to a wire rack to cool.

Makes 16

Morning Glory Muffins

Great tucked in your backpack for hiking in the Warner Parks or biking the Natchez Trace.

4 cups White Lily flour
2¹/₂ cups sugar
4 teaspoons baking soda
4 teaspoons cinnamon
1 teaspoon salt
6 eggs
2 cups vegetable oil
4 teaspoons vanilla extract
4 cups grated carrots, about 8 carrots
1 cup raisins
1 cup shredded coconut
2 apples, peeled and shredded, or 1 (8-ounce) can crushed
    pineapple, drained
1 cup chopped pecans

Sift the flour, sugar, baking soda, cinnamon and salt together. Beat the eggs in a large mixing bowl just until smooth. Add the vegetable oil and vanilla and mix well. Add the dry ingredients and mix just until moistened. Stir in the carrots, raisins, coconut, apples and pecans.

Spoon into greased muffin cups. Bake at 350 degrees for 15 to 20 minutes or until light brown. Cool in the pans for 5 minutes and remove to a wire rack to cool completely.

Makes 3 to 3¹/₂ dozen

Entertainment

On your way back to Nashville from Carnton Plantation, plan to spend the day in downtown Franklin, designated a Great American Main Street by the National Trust for Historic Preservation. The entire 15-block downtown area, carefully revitalized by the Downtown Franklin Association, is on the National Register of Historic Places. Have a warm muffin at Merridee's Breadbasket, browse Franklin Booksellers for the latest best-seller, and follow the bubbles to Bathos to find handmade soaps for at home pampering. Then stroll leisurely through the unique antiques, clothing, and gift shops surrounding the town square. When lunch time rolls around, walk to one of the many restaurants in the downtown area or dash up Franklin Road to The Factory, a 1929 manufacturing facility painstakingly restored into 250,000 square feet of antiques, art, specialty shops, theater, and dining— Franklin's newest and most unusual shopping venue.

English Tea Muffins

Pecan Topping
1/2 cup packed light brown sugar
1 teaspoon cinnamon
1/4 cup chopped pecans

Muffins
2 cups White Lily flour
2 teaspoons baking powder
1/4 teaspoon cinnamon
1/2 teaspoon salt
1/2 cup (1 stick) butter, softened
3/4 cup sugar
1 large egg
1 cup milk
3/4 cup raisins or dried cranberries

To prepare the topping, mix the brown sugar, cinnamon and pecans in a bowl and set aside.

To prepare the muffins, mix the flour, baking powder, cinnamon and salt together. Cream the butter and sugar in a large mixing bowl until light and fluffy. Beat in the egg. Add the flour mixture to the egg mixture 1/3 at a time, alternating with the milk and mixing just until moistened after each addition. Fold in the raisins.

Spoon by 1/4 cupfuls into greased muffin cups and sprinkle with the topping. Bake at 350 degrees for 20 minutes or until the tops spring back when lightly touched. Serve immediately or remove to a wire rack to cool.

The batter may be prepared in advance and stored, covered, in the refrigerator for up to 1 week before baking.

Makes 1 dozen

Hot Water Hoecakes

3/4 cup cornmeal
2 tablespoons butter, chopped

1/2 teaspoon salt
1 cup boiling water

Combine the cornmeal, butter and salt in a mixing bowl. Add the boiling water and mix well. Drop by tablespoonfuls onto greased baking sheets. Bake at 425 degrees for 20 to 25 minutes or until browned.

Serves 4

Cranberry Orange Scones

1^{1}/2 cups White Lily flour
^{1}/4 cup sugar
2 teaspoons grated orange zest
1^{1}/2 teaspoons baking powder
^{1}/4 teaspoon baking soda
^{1}/2 teaspoon salt
^{1}/2 cup dried cranberries
^{1}/2 cup (1 stick) unsalted butter, softened
1 egg
^{1}/4 cup (or more) orange juice
1 teaspoon vanilla extract

Mix the flour, sugar, orange zest, baking powder, baking soda and salt in a bowl. Add the cranberries. Cut in the butter until the mixture resembles coarse crumbs.

Beat the egg in a 1-cup measure. Add enough orange juice to measure ^{1}/2 cup. Beat in the vanilla. Add to the crumb mixture and mix just until moistened. Knead gently 8 to 10 times on a lightly floured surface. Shape into a 10-inch circle and cut into 8 wedges. Place on a greased baking sheet.

Sprinkle with additional sugar. Bake at 450 degrees for 12 minutes. Reduce the oven temperature to 400 degrees and bake for 5 minutes longer or until golden brown.

Makes 8

ulinary

Fairy Butter is a recipe from Hermitage Hospitality, *a cookbook from the time of Andrew Jackson. To make it, nineteenth-century cooks were instructed to: "Take the yelks of two hard-eggs, and beat them in a marble mortar, with a large spoonful of orange-flower water, and two tea spoonfuls of fine sugar beat to powder; beat this all together, till it is a fine paste, then mix it up with about as much fresh butter out of the churn, and force it through a fine strainer full of little holes, into a plate. This is a very pretty thing to set off a table at supper."*

Hermitage Hospitality *is edited by Ginger Helton and Susan Van Riper and published by Aurora Publishers Inc., Nashville and London, 1970. Fairy Butter is reprinted with permission from the Ladies' Hermitage Association.*

Apple Fritters

This recipe has been handed down for four generations and originated in the farming country of North Carolina. It is a truly southern recipe, sometimes referred to as apple dumplings. It can also be made with firm peaches.

2 cups White Lily flour
2 tablespoons sugar
1 tablespoon baking powder
1 teaspoon salt
2 eggs
1 cup milk
2 tablespoons butter, melted
2 cups chopped peeled apples or peaches
vegetable oil for frying
1/4 cup sugar
1/2 teaspoon cinnamon

Mix the flour, 2 tablespoons sugar, baking powder and salt in a large bowl. Beat the eggs with the milk and butter in a medium bowl. Add to the dry ingredients and mix just until moistened. Stir in the apples; the batter will be thick.

Heat enough vegetable oil to float the fritters in a deep saucepan or deep fryer over medium heat. Drop by spoonfuls into the hot oil, frying about 5 fritters at a time for 4 minutes or until golden brown and turning frequently.

Mix 1/4 cup sugar and the cinnamon in a paper bag made of nonrecycled material. Remove the fritters to the bag and shake to coat well.

If the fritters become brown in less than 3 or 4 minutes, the oil is too hot and the centers of the fritters will not be cooked completely.

Makes 2 dozen

Hush Puppies

2 cups cornmeal
1 tablespoon White Lily flour
1 teaspoon each baking powder and salt
1/2 teaspoon baking soda
3 tablespoons chopped green onions
1 cup plus 3 tablespoons buttermilk
1 egg, beaten
corn oil, peanut oil or vegetable oil for deep-frying

Sift the dry ingredients into a mixing bowl. Add the green onions, buttermilk and egg and mix well. Heat the oil to 375 degrees in a medium saucepan, deep fryer or electric skillet. Drop the batter by rounded tablespoonfuls into the oil and fry until golden brown on all sides. Drain on paper towels and serve hot.

Serves 6

When Southern soldiers cooked their meals over open campfires during the Civil War, they would toss some of the fried cornmeal batter to their yapping dogs, commanding them to "Hush, puppies," so they wouldn't give away their location to the approaching Yankee soldiers.

Sausage Crescents

1 pound bulk sausage
8 ounces cream cheese
2 (8-count) packages refrigerator crescent roll dough
1 egg white
poppy seeds

Brown the sausage in a skillet, stirring until crumbly; drain. Combine with the cream cheese in a bowl and mix well.

Separate the roll dough into 2 rectangles on a lightly floured surface. Shape the sausage mixture into a log lengthwise down the center of each rectangle and fold the sides of the dough over to enclose the sausage.

Place seam side down on an ungreased baking sheet. Brush with the egg white and sprinkle with poppy seeds. Bake at 350 degrees for 20 minutes or until golden brown. Cool completely and cut into 1 1/2-inch slices.

Serves 10

Raspberry Cream Cheese Coffee Cake

2¹/2 cups White Lily flour
³/4 cup sugar
³/4 cup (1¹/2 sticks) butter, softened
¹/2 teaspoon baking powder
¹/2 teaspoon baking soda
³/4 cup sour cream
¹/4 teaspoon salt
1 teaspoon almond extract
8 ounces cream cheese, softened
¹/4 cup sugar
1 egg
¹/2 cup raspberry jam
¹/2 cup sliced almonds

Mix the flour and ³/4 cup sugar in a large bowl. Cut in the butter with a pastry blender until the mixture resembles coarse crumbs. Reserve 1 cup of the crumb mixture for the topping. Add the baking powder, baking soda, sour cream, salt and almond extract to the remaining crumb mixture and mix well. Spread evenly in a buttered and floured 9-inch springform pan.

Combine the cream cheese, ¹/4 cup sugar and egg in a small bowl and mix until smooth. Spread evenly over the bottom layer. Spoon the jam evenly over the cream cheese layer. Mix the reserved crumb mixture with the almonds in a small bowl. Sprinkle over the top.

Bake the coffee cake at 350 degrees for 55 to 60 minutes or until the filling is set and the crust is deep golden brown. Cool in the pan on a wire rack for 15 minutes. Place on a serving plate and remove the side of the pan. Serve warm or cold. Store, covered, in the refrigerator.

Serves 12 to 16

Kahlúa Caramel French Toast

1/2 cup (1 stick) unsalted butter
1 cup packed brown sugar
2 tablespoons corn syrup
1 tablespoon Kahlúa
2 to 3 bananas, sliced 1/4 inch thick
6 (1-inch) slices Italian bread or challah
5 large eggs
1 1/2 cups half-and-half
1 teaspoon Kahlúa
1 teaspoon vanilla extract
1/4 teaspoon salt
1/2 cup toasted sliced almonds

Combine the butter, brown sugar and corn syrup in a saucepan and cook over medium heat until the butter melts, stirring to blend well. Stir in 1 tablespoon Kahlúa. Spoon into a 9×13-inch baking dish. Arrange the banana slices in the dish.

Trim the bread slices if desired. Arrange in a single layer in the prepared dish. Combine the eggs, half-and-half, 1 teaspoon Kahlúa, vanilla and salt in a bowl and whisk until smooth. Pour evenly over the bread. Chill, covered, for 8 to 24 hours.

Let stand until room temperature. Sprinkle with the almonds. Bake at 350 degrees on the center oven rack for 35 to 40 minutes or until golden brown. Top with fresh strawberries or blueberries and whipped cream if desired. Serve immediately.

Serves 6

Historical

The Wildhorse Saloon, located in an 1800s riverfront warehouse on historic Second Avenue, was renovated with the past in mind. The exterior was carefully preserved during renovation. At the start of construction, the existing façade was removed brick by brick and stored. Upon completion of the interior reconstruction, the bricks were replaced in their original order to maintain the integrity of the historic area. Though cattle no longer stampede past the front doors as they did for the June 1994 opening, the Wildhorse Saloon does have amazing sculptures of horses hanging from the ceiling. Come and join the more than six million people who have stepped through the doors to taste the food, see the shows, and become a part of country music today.

Peach French Toast

3 ounces cream cheese, softened
1/4 cup chopped fresh peach
1/4 cup confectioners' sugar
1 teaspoon Amaretto
1/8 teaspoon almond extract (optional)
8 slices (1/2 to 3/4 inch) challah or loaf
    brioche

4 eggs
1/2 cup milk
1 tablespoon confectioners' sugar
1/2 teaspoon vanilla extract
1/8 teaspoon cinnamon
1 tablespoon butter
confectioners' sugar

Combine the cream cheese, peach, 1/4 cup confectioners' sugar, Amaretto and almond extract in a blender or food processor and process until puréed. Spread between the bread slices to make 4 sandwiches.

Combine the eggs with the milk, 1 tablespoon confectioners' sugar, vanilla and cinnamon in a mixing bowl and beat until smooth.

Heat the butter in a large nonstick skillet or griddle over medium heat. Dip the sandwiches into the egg mixture and fry in batches in the skillet until golden brown and crisp on both sides. Remove and sprinkle with additional confectioners' sugar. Serve with maple syrup or orange marmalade.

Serves 4

Oatmeal Pancakes

A healthy and delicious pancake.

1 cup quick-cooking oats
3/4 cup White Lily flour
1 tablespoon baking powder
1/2 teaspoon salt

1 cup milk
1 egg
2 tablespoons vegetable oil

Mix the oats, flour, baking powder and salt in a medium bowl. Add the milk, egg and vegetable oil and mix just until moistened.

Heat a griddle or large nonstick skillet to 400 degrees over medium-high heat. Pour the batter by 1/4 cupfuls onto the heated surface and cook until golden brown on both sides, turning once. Serve with butter and maple syrup, honey or preserves.

Makes 10 to 12 (4-inch) pancakes

Cheese Blintz Casserole

When transplanted from Brunswick, Georgia, to Chicago, this family blintz recipe won the blue ribbon in a Windy City baking contest and now wins rave reviews here. Just add tuna, bagels, and fresh fruit for a complete brunch.

1 cup White Lily flour
1/2 cup sugar
1 tablespoon baking powder
salt to taste
1/2 cup (1 stick) butter, melted
2 eggs, beaten
1 cup milk
1 teaspoon vanilla extract
16 ounces cottage cheese
16 ounces cream cheese, softened
2 eggs, beaten
1/4 cup sugar
juice of 1 lemon

Garnish
sour cream
cherry pie filling, heated

Mix the flour, 1/2 cup sugar, baking powder and salt in a large bowl. Add the butter, 2 eggs, milk and vanilla and mix until smooth. Spread half the mixture in a greased 9×13-inch baking dish.

Combine the cottage cheese, cream cheese, 2 eggs, 1/4 cup sugar, lemon juice and salt in a bowl and mix well. Spread evenly in the prepared dish and top with the remaining batter.

Bake at 300 degrees for 1 hour or until golden brown. Cut into squares and serve warm. Garnish with sour cream or cherry pie filling.

Serves 12

Belmont Mansion was built in the mid-1850s as a second home for Joseph and Adelicia Acklen. Fashioned after an Italian villa, the mansion was among the most richly crafted homes in the South and boasted more than 30 rooms and 10,000 square feet of living space. The estate, which included a 200-foot greenhouse, an exotic animal zoo, and a bowling alley, was opened to city residents since there was no public park in the area. Adelicia also hosted grand late-night parties to save her guests from the heat of the day. The mansion, located on what is now the campus of Belmont University, is one of the gems open to the public on the Antebellum Trail.

Almond Torte

Torte Crust

2²/3 cups White Lily flour
1¹/3 cups sugar
1¹/3 cups unsalted butter, softened
1 egg
¹/2 teaspoon salt

Filling

1 cup ground almonds
¹/2 cup sugar
1 egg, lightly beaten
1 teaspoon grated lemon zest
4 whole almonds

To prepare the crust, combine the flour, sugar, butter, egg and salt in a mixing bowl and mix at low speed to form a dough. Chill if needed for ease of handling. Divide the dough into 2 equal portions. Press 1 portion over the bottom of a greased 10-inch springform pan, placing a sheet of greased waxed paper over the top to help spread evenly to the side; discard the waxed paper. Press the remaining portion of dough into a 10-inch circle between 2 sheets of waxed paper and reserve.

To prepare the filling, combine the ground almonds, sugar, egg and lemon zest in a mixing bowl and beat until well mixed. Spread over the crust, spreading to within ¹/2 inch of the side of the pan.

Remove the top sheet of waxed paper from the reserved dough circle and invert onto the torte; discard the remaining sheet of waxed paper. Arrange the whole almonds on the top.

Place on a sheet of foil in a 325-degree oven and bake for 55 to 65 minutes or until light golden brown. Cool in the pan for 15 minutes. Remove the side of the springform pan and transfer the torte to a serving plate to cool completely.

Serves 24

Beautiful Breakfast Strata

1 cup milk
1/2 cup dry white wine
1 loaf dried French bread
2 cups loosely packed chopped fresh cilantro
3 tablespoons olive oil
8 ounces smoked Gouda cheese, thinly sliced
3 ripe tomatoes, thinly sliced
1/2 cup basil pesto
4 eggs
salt and freshly ground pepper to taste
1/2 cup whipping cream

Blend the milk and wine in a shallow dish. Cut the bread into 1/2-inch slices. Dip 1 or 2 slices at a time in the milk mixture and press gently to remove excess liquid, taking care not to tear the bread. Arrange the bread in a lightly greased 12-inch baking dish or 10-inch pie plate. Sprinkle with the cilantro and drizzle with the olive oil. Layer the cheese, tomato slices and pesto 1/2 at a time in the dish.

Beat the eggs with the salt and pepper in a medium bowl. Pour evenly over the layers and pour the cream over the top. Cover with plastic wrap and chill for 8 hours or longer.

Let stand at room temperature for 1 1/2 hours. Place the baking dish on a baking sheet and bake at 350 degrees for 1 hour or until puffed and golden brown.

Serves 8

Historical

Andrew and Rachel Jackson were known for their fondness for entertaining. They seldom ate alone at The Hermitage and delighted in having company. Even when they were away, the overseer was told to serve guests that passed by their home. Since tomatoes were considered poisonous during his lifetime, Andrew Jackson's cook would not have prepared Beautiful Breakfast Strata. Luckily, that misconception was proved to be false, and today you can enjoy it for brunch.

Egg and Ham Strata

Serve the strata with iced tea, lemonade, wine, Champagne, or mimosas garnished with a fresh raspberry for a colorful presentation.

2 large slices country ham
1/2 large loaf dried French bread
3 tablespoons butter, melted
1/2 cup chopped green onions
4 ounces (1 cup) shredded Swiss cheese
4 ounces (1 cup) shredded Monterey Jack cheese
8 eggs
13/4 cups milk
1/4 cup white wine
2 teaspoons Dijon mustard
1/4 teaspoon black pepper
ground red pepper to taste
3/4 cup sour cream
1/2 cup grated Parmesan cheese

Cook the country ham in a large skillet just until the edges begin to brown. Remove to a cutting board and cut into bite-size pieces. Cut the bread into small cubes and sprinkle in a 9×13-inch baking dish; drizzle with the butter. Layer the ham pieces, green onions, Swiss cheese and Monterey Jack cheese over the bread.

Combine the eggs with the milk, wine, Dijon mustard, black pepper and red pepper in a bowl and whisk until smooth. Pour over the layers and dollop the sour cream over the top. Chill, covered with foil, for 8 hours or longer.

Bake, covered, at 325 degrees for 1 hour. Sprinkle with the Parmesan cheese and bake, uncovered, for 10 minutes longer.

Serves 8 to 12

Christmas Morning Eggs

Serve with fresh fruit, White Lily biscuits, and sweet rolls for a special holiday breakfast.

16 ounces (4 cups) shredded Monterey Jack cheese
3 ounces cream cheese, cut into cubes
8 ounces bacon, crisp-fried and crumbled
chopped bell peppers, onions and mushrooms to taste
6 eggs
1 cup cottage cheese
1/4 cup (1/2 stick) butter, melted
1 cup half-and-half
1/2 teaspoon baking powder
1 teaspoon salt

Sprinkle the Monterey Jack cheese in a greased 9×13-inch baking dish. Layer the cream cheese cubes, bacon and vegetables over the top.

Combine the eggs with the cottage cheese, butter, half-and-half, baking powder and salt in a mixing bowl and beat until smooth. Pour over the layers. Chill, covered, in the refrigerator for 8 hours or longer.

Bake at 375 degrees for 40 to 45 minutes or until set and golden brown. Serve immediately.

Serves 6

One of the best times to visit the homes on the Antebellum Trail is at Christmastime, when the mansions are beautifully decorated in their period holiday finery. Special Christmas tours and meals are offered at many of the homes, and no one leaves without a touch of the holiday spirit.

Yankee-Pleaser Casserole

A dish containing all the foods most Yankees want to sample when they come South.

1 pound bulk sausage with sage
4 ounces (1 cup) shredded sharp
   Cheddar cheese
1 (8-ounce) package corn muffin mix
1 cup hot cooked grits

$^1/_2$ cup (1 stick) butter, melted
4 eggs
$1^3/_4$ cups milk, heated
2 ounces ($^1/_2$ cup) shredded sharp
   Cheddar cheese

Brown the sausage in a skillet, stirring until crumbly; drain. Sprinkle into a greased 2-quart baking dish and top with 1 cup shredded cheese.

Combine the corn muffin mix, grits, butter, eggs and milk in a bowl and mix well. Pour into the prepared dish. Top with $^1/_2$ cup cheese. Bake at 325 degrees for 45 minutes.

You may prepare the dish in advance and store in the refrigerator or freezer until needed. Allow a frozen casserole to thaw before baking and increase the baking time to 55 minutes for a refrigerated casserole.

Serves 8 Southerners or 6 Yankees

Huevos Chiles Rellenos

10 eggs, beaten
$^1/_2$ cup (1 stick) butter, melted
$^1/_2$ cup White Lily flour
1 teaspoon baking powder
1 (8-ounce) can chopped green chiles

2 cups cottage cheese
16 ounces (4 cups) shredded Monterey
   Jack cheese
salsa (optional)

Beat the eggs with the butter in a mixing bowl. Add the flour and baking powder and mix well. Stir in the green chiles, cottage cheese and Monterey Jack cheese. Spoon into a buttered 9×13-inch baking dish.

Bake at 400 degrees for 15 minutes. Reduce the oven temperature to 350 degrees and bake for 35 minutes longer. Serve with salsa.

Serves 10

Basic Quiche

A basic quiche recipe with variations from Nashville Seasons Encore. *There may be too much custard for some of the fillings, so just bake the leftover custard in a separate dish and eat it when no one is looking.*

1¹/2 cups heavy cream
4 eggs
1 teaspoon salt
¹/4 teaspoon pepper
4 ounces (1 cup) shredded Swiss cheese
1 unbaked (9-inch) deep-dish pie shell

Beat the cream, egg, salt and pepper in a mixing bowl until smooth. Stir in the cheese.

Bake the pie shell at 400 degrees for 15 minutes. Reduce the oven temperature to 375 degrees. Arrange any of the ingredients in the suggested variations below in the pie shell and pour the egg mixture over the top. Bake for 30 to 40 minutes or until the filling is set and golden brown. Cool for 10 minutes before serving.

Serves 6

For Spinach Quiche, sauté 1 thawed 10-ounce package frozen spinach in ¹/4 cup butter in a saucepan. Add 2 teaspoons lemon juice and 2 minced garlic cloves and proceed as above.

For Chicken and Broccoli Quiche, sauté ³/4 cup chopped cooked chicken and ³/4 cup cooked and drained chopped broccoli in ¹/4 cup butter or margarine in a saucepan. Stir in 2 teaspoons lemon juice and proceed as above.

For Crab Quiche, add one 6¹/2-ounce can drained crab meat and proceed as above.

For Cheesy Artichoke and Tomato Quiche, combine 1 drained and chopped 14-ounce can marinated artichoke hearts with ¹/2 cup cherry tomato halves and ¹/2 cup shredded Cheddar cheese and proceed as above.

For Mushroom Quiche, sauté ³/4 cup sliced fresh mushrooms in ¹/4 cup butter in a saucepan. Stir in 2 teaspoons lemon juice and proceed as above.

Grits with Tomato Concassée and Shrimp

Tomato Concassée

1 (28-ounce) can whole tomatoes
1 medium onion, coarsely chopped
3 garlic cloves, minced
1 tablespoon butter
1/4 cup dry white wine
cayenne pepper to taste
4 bay leaves
1/4 cup coarsely chopped and loosely
    packed herbs, such as parsley,
    oregano and/or thyme

Garnish

shaved Parmigiano-Reggiano cheese

Cheesy Grits

2 cups water
2 cups milk
1 tablespoon butter
2 teaspoons coarse salt
1 cup uncooked grits
1/4 cup heavy cream
2 tablespoons freshly grated
    Parmigiano-Reggiano cheese

Shrimp

1 tablespoon butter
16 large shrimp, peeled
coarse salt and freshly ground black
    pepper to taste

To prepare the tomato concassée, drain and chop the tomatoes, reserving the liquid but discarding the seeds. Sauté the onion and garlic in the butter in a large skillet for 2 to 3 minutes or until very tender. Add the wine and cook for 2 to 3 minutes or until the liquid evaporates. Add the tomatoes, reserved juice, cayenne pepper and bay leaves. Reduce the heat and simmer for 10 minutes or until slightly thickened. Remove from the heat and stir in the herbs, discarding the bay leaves. Cover and keep warm.

To prepare the grits, bring the water, milk, butter and salt to a low boil in a medium saucepan. Sprinkle in the grits and reduce the heat. Simmer for 15 to 20 minutes or until the mixture is smooth and thickened, stirring frequently with a wooden spoon. Stir in the cream and cheese. Cover tightly and keep warm.

To prepare the shrimp, heat the butter in a large skillet over medium-high heat until sizzling. Add the shrimp and season with salt and black pepper. Sauté for 2 minutes on each side or until seared and cooked through.

To serve, spoon the grits onto serving plates. Top with the concassée and arrange the shrimp around the edge. Garnish with the cheese.

Serves 4

Cheese Grits Olé

Cotija is a Mexican cheese with a salty and pungent taste. The softer versions are somewhat like feta cheese, but there is also a very firm variety.

4¹/2 cups water
1 teaspoon salt
1¹/2 cups uncooked grits
16 ounces (4 cups) crumbled cotija or
    shredded Monterey Jack cheese
¹/4 cup (¹/2 stick) butter or margarine
8 ounces jalapeño chicken sausage
8 ounces cilantro chicken sausage
¹/4 cup chopped pickled jalapeño peppers
2 tablespoons chopped pimento
1 garlic clove, minced
3 eggs, beaten

Bring the water and salt to a boil in a saucepan. Stir in the grits and reduce the heat. Simmer, covered, for 5 minutes, stirring occasionally. Stir in the cheese and butter.

Remove the casings from the sausages. Brown the sausages in a skillet, stirring until crumbly; drain. Combine with the jalapeño peppers, pimento, garlic and beaten eggs in a bowl and mix well.

Spoon into a greased 9×13-inch baking dish. Bake at 350 degrees for 30 minutes.

You may substitute 1 pound smoked breakfast sausage for the chicken sausages in this recipe.

Serves 8

Cultural

Need to brush up on your 1860s etiquette, clothing, or ability to ride sidesaddle? The 1861 Athenaeum Girls School at the Athenaeum Rectory in Columbia annually provides young ladies between the ages of fourteen and eighteen with a week's training in everything from archery to penmanship and many other mid-nineteenth century experiences, concluding with a formal ball complete with escorts from the Jackson Cadets. It's a must for young "Scarletts-in-Waiting."

Fresh Fruit Bake

3 cups sliced fresh pineapple
2 cups sliced fresh apricots
2 cups sliced fresh peaches
1 cup sliced fresh pears
1 cup sliced fresh apples
1/2 cup sugar
2 tablespoons cornstarch
1/2 cup (1 stick) butter, melted
1 cup dry sherry

Layer the pineapple, apricots, peaches, pears and apples in a 2-quart baking dish. Mix the sugar and cornstarch in a saucepan. Stir in the butter. Add the wine gradually, stirring constantly. Cook over low heat until thickened and smooth, stirring constantly. Pour over the fruit. Chill, covered, for 8 hours or longer.

Let stand at room temperature for 15 minutes. Bake, uncovered, at 350 degrees for 30 minutes or until bubbly.

Serves 10

Savory Tomato Tarts

16 unbaked tart shells
1 1/2 bunches fresh basil
2 large tomatoes, seeded, chopped and drained
3 green onions, thinly sliced
1 cup mayonnaise
1 cup sour cream
8 ounces (2 cups) shredded Cheddar cheese
1 cup grated Parmesan cheese

Arrange the tart shells on a baking sheet and bake at 375 degrees until partially done. Place 2 or 3 leaves of fresh basil in each shell and sprinkle with the tomatoes and green onions.

Combine the mayonnaise, sour cream and Cheddar cheese in a bowl and mix well. Spoon into the tart shells and sprinkle with the Parmesan cheese. Bake for 20 to 30 minutes or until puffed and golden brown.

Serves 16

Breakfast Granola

From a bed-and-breakfast in Taos, New Mexico.

3 cups rolled oats
1/2 cup raisins
1/2 cup coarsely chopped walnuts
1/2 cup coarsely chopped pecans
1/2 cup coarsely chopped almonds
1/3 cup sunflower seeds
2 tablespoons sesame seeds
1/3 cup flaked dried coconut
1/4 cup wheat germ
1/2 cup packed brown sugar
1/4 cup unsulfered molasses
1/4 cup honey
1/4 cup cold water
3 tablespoons vegetable oil
2 teaspoons cinnamon

Combine the oats, raisins, walnuts, pecans, almonds, sunflower seeds, sesame seeds, coconut and wheat germ in a large roasting pan and mix well.

Combine the brown sugar, molasses, honey, cold water, vegetable oil and cinnamon in a small heavy saucepan. Bring to a boil over low heat, stirring constantly. Drizzle over the mixture in the roasting pan and stir to mix well.

Bake at 325 degrees for 40 minutes or until toasted, stirring frequently. Cool completely and store in an airtight container.

Makes 6 1/2 cups

Historical

The James K. Polk home in Columbia was built by his father Samuel in 1816, when son James was twenty-one. James later began a successful legal and political career, which led to his election in 1845 as the nation's eleventh President. During his self-imposed single term as President, Polk, also known as "Young Hickory," accomplished all the tasks he had set for himself, including extending the United States' territory from the Atlantic Ocean to the Pacific Ocean. The Federal-style house is furnished with memorabilia from the Polk White House and is on the Antebellum Trail for public tours.

Soups and Salads

Soups and Salads

Southern city . . . River city . . . Nashville,
like most older southern cities, settled on a riverbank.
Christmas Day, 1779, James Robertson led our city's founders
to settle on the banks of the frozen Cumberland River.
Four months later, the original settlement of Fort Nashborough
was joined by Colonel John Donelson and about sixty families.
The name was changed in 1784 to Nashville. Visitors to
downtown Nashville can visit Fort Nashborough and get
a real feel for the city's early days on the bluffs.

Named in honor of Revolutionary War hero General Francis
Nash, the city serves as the capital of Tennessee, and has done so since
1843. Downtown Nashville houses many city and state buildings. The
most prominent of these is the golden domed Greek revival state capitol
building, which sits high atop Capitol Hill. The building was designed in
1845 by architect William Strickland, who also designed the magnificent

Egyptian Revival Downtown Presbyterian Church. At the base of the Hill sits the Bicentennial Mall State Park, built in 1996 to commemorate Tennessee's 200 years of statehood. This is a great place to learn, alfresco, about the Volunteer State via the walkway of history. There are also fountains that represent all of Tennessee's rivers and whose intermittent bursts delight weary visitors.

The Cumberland River winds through the city and today's riverfront is vibrant. The beautifully restored brick riverfront warehouses of Second Avenue now serve as home to a variety of shops, restaurants, and residences. Also visible from the banks of the Cumberland is the 67,000-seat coliseum, home to the NFL's Tennessee Titans.

Another notable Nashville attraction that graces the riverbank is the grand Gaylord Opryland Resort and Convention Center. This magnificent hotel boasts nine acres of lush indoor gardens, winding pathways, and sparkling waterfalls. The hotel's Delta wing features flatboats that cruise an indoor river made up of water from thousands of rivers from around the nation and the world. To cruise the Cumberland Old South style, book a dinner cruise aboard the *General Jackson*. This 976-foot riverboat, which sails regularly from its own dock at the hotel, provides passengers with a spectacular view of the city's skyline. Once vital for transportation and for survival, the river is an influence that is ever present in our fair city.

Iced Melon Soup

A popular recipe from Encore.

2 cups fresh orange juice
$1/3$ cup fresh lime juice
3 tablespoons honey
1 cup finely chopped honeydew melon
2 cups finely chopped cantaloupe
2 cups dry Champagne
1 cup whipping cream

Garnish
mint leaves
strawberries

Combine the orange juice, lime juice and honey with half the honeydew melon and cantaloupe in a blender or food processor and process until smooth. Combine with the Champagne in a bowl and mix well. Add the remaining cantaloupe and honeydew. Refrigerate until chilled thoroughly. Ladle into chilled bowls and top with a dollop of whipped cream. Garnish with mint and a strawberry.

You may also use Crenshaw melon in this soup.

Serves 6

Cucumber Gazpacho

A cool delight for a hot summer night.

3 medium cucumbers, peeled, seeded
   and cut into chunks
1 garlic clove
3 cups chicken broth
3 cups sour cream
3 tablespoons white vinegar
2 teaspoons salt

Garnish
2 tomatoes, peeled and finely chopped
$1/2$ cup chopped green onions
$3/4$ cup toasted almonds, cashews or
   croutons

Combine the cucumbers and garlic with a small amount of the chicken broth in a blender and process until smooth. Combine with the remaining chicken broth in a bowl and mix well. Whisk in the sour cream, vinegar and salt. Chill, covered, until serving time. Garnish with tomatoes, green onions and/or nuts or croutons.

Serves 8 to 10

Asparagus Soup

2 pounds asparagus, trimmed
2 cups chopped onions
2 garlic cloves, minced
1/4 cup (1/2 stick) unsalted butter
3 cups chicken broth
1/2 cup minced Italian parsley
5 fresh basil leaves, chopped
2 teaspoons minced fresh tarragon
3 or 4 drops of Tabasco sauce
salt and pepper to taste

Cut the asparagus into 1/2-inch pieces and reserve the tips. Sauté the onions and garlic in the butter in a large saucepan over medium heat until tender. Add the chicken broth, asparagus pieces, parsley, basil, tarragon and Tabasco sauce and mix well. Simmer for 1 hour, stirring occasionally.

Process the mixture in batches in a blender until smooth. Combine the batches in the saucepan.

Bring a small saucepan half full of water to a boil over high heat and add the reserved asparagus tips. Cook for 2 to 3 minutes or just until tender; drain. Add to the soup and heat to serving temperature over medium-low heat; do not boil. Season with salt and pepper.

Serves 4

Cold soups are a delightful addition to summer menus. Always taste cold soups before serving as cold foods tend to need more seasoning than hot ones. Serve the cold soup in bowls placed in larger bowls of crushed ice as an appetizer course or in tall wine glasses before your guests are seated.

Cheddar Cheese Soup

Great in the fall when you feel that first nip in the air.

1/2 cup each finely chopped celery,
    onion and carrot
1/4 cup (1/2 stick) butter
1/4 cup White Lily flour
4 cups beef broth
1 (12-ounce) bottle beer
16 ounces (4 cups) shredded white
    Cheddar cheese

16 ounces (4 cups) shredded Cheddar
    cheese
salt, cayenne pepper and black pepper
    to taste

Garnish

chopped fresh chives

Sauté the celery, onion and carrot in the butter in a heavy saucepan over low heat for 3 minutes. Stir in the flour and cook for 2 minutes, stirring constantly. Add the beef broth and beer and bring to a simmer, stirring constantly. Simmer for 15 to 20 minutes or until the vegetables are tender. Add the cheeses gradually and cook until the soup is smooth, whisking constantly. Season with salt, cayenne pepper and black pepper. Cook just until heated through. Garnish servings with chives.

Serves 8

Dilled Cream of Carrot Soup

3 cups chopped carrots
1 potato, peeled and chopped
4 cups chicken broth
1 medium onion, finely chopped
2 teaspoons dill
1/4 cup (1/2 stick) butter

1/4 cup White Lily flour
2 cups half-and-half
salt and white pepper to taste

Garnish

minced parsley

Combine the carrots and potato with the chicken broth in a saucepan and bring to a boil. Reduce the heat and simmer until the vegetables are tender. Process the mixture in batches in the food processor until smooth. Combine the batches in the saucepan.

Sauté the onion and dill in the butter in a medium saucepan until tender. Stir in the flour and cook for several minutes, stirring constantly. Add the half-and-half and cook until thickened, stirring constantly. Stir into the puréed vegetable mixture and season with salt and white pepper. Cook until heated through. Garnish servings with parsley.

Serves 6 to 8

Sherried Mushroom Bisque

16 ounces fresh mushrooms
1 large onion, chopped
4 cups chicken broth
6 tablespoons (3/4 stick) butter
6 tablespoons White Lily flour
1 cup milk
3 cups half-and-half
salt and pepper to taste
2 tablespoons sherry

Garnish
sliced mushrooms

Process the mushrooms and onion in a food processor until finely chopped. Combine with the chicken broth in a saucepan and simmer for 15 minutes.

Melt the butter in a medium saucepan and stir in the flour. Cook for 2 minutes, stirring constantly. Whisk in the milk gradually and cook for 2 minutes or until thickened, whisking constantly.

Stir in the half-and-half and add to the mushroom mixture. Season with salt and pepper. Add the sherry and cook just until heated through. Garnish servings with sliced mushrooms.

Serves 8

Culinary

Garnishes add to the flavor of soups and allow you to customize your own serving. Some delicious and interesting garnishes include crisp-fried and crumbled bacon; chopped or sliced avocado; lemon, lime, or orange slices or grated zest; crumbled French-fried onions; sour cream or yogurt flavored with herbs; flavored whipped cream; minced cashews, peanuts, almonds, or pistachios; minced herbs; poppy seeds or caraway seeds; and slivered pimento or olives.

Tortilla Soup

Add cooked chicken if you like a heartier soup, and, for an authentic Mexican soup, shred the chicken instead of chopping it.

2 garlic cloves
1 large yellow onion
1 tablespoon butter
2 tablespoons vegetable oil
2 corn tortillas, cut up
1 (4-ounce) can chopped mild green chiles
1 (14-ounce) can Italian plum tomatoes
1 cup tomato sauce
3¹/2 cups chicken stock
1 teaspoon chili powder
¹/4 teaspoon dried oregano leaves
1 teaspoon salt
¹/2 cup minced fresh cilantro
6 corn tortillas
vegetable oil for frying
12 ounces (3 cups) shredded Monterey Jack cheese

Chop the garlic in a food processor fitted with the metal blade. Replace the blade with the slicing disk. Cut the onion into pieces to fit the feeder tube and slice with the disk.

Heat the butter and 2 tablespoons vegetable oil in a 3-quart saucepan. Add the onion and garlic mixture with the cut-up tortillas and sauté lightly. Stir in the green chiles, tomatoes, tomato sauce, chicken stock, chili powder, oregano and salt. Bring to a boil, stirring to break up the tomatoes. Reduce the heat and simmer for 15 to 20 minutes or to the desired consistency. Stir in the cilantro.

Process the soup in batches in the food processor. Combine the batches in the saucepan and keep warm.

Cut the whole tortillas into ¹/2×2-inch strips. Heat 2 inches vegetable oil to 375 degrees in a deep fryer or saucepan. Add the tortilla strips in 5 or 6 batches and fry until crisp. Drain on paper towels.

Ladle the soup into bowls and top with the cheese and fried tortilla strips.

You may prepare the soup in advance and reheat to serve.

Serves 6

West African Sweet Potato Soup

Delicious and nutritious.

2 medium onions, chopped
1 tablespoon vegetable oil or olive oil
2 or 3 carrots, chopped
2 teaspoons grated gingerroot
1/8 to 1/4 teaspoon cayenne pepper
2 medium sweet potatoes, peeled and sliced 1/2 inch thick
3 to 4 cups water or stock
2 cups tomato juice or vegetable juice cocktail
1 tablespoon peanut butter
1 tablespoon sugar (optional)

Garnish
chopped green onions and/or peanuts

Sauté the onions in the oil in a large saucepan. Add the carrots, ginger and cayenne pepper. Sauté for 5 minutes. Add the sweet potatoes and water and cook for 20 minutes or until the sweet potatoes are tender. Stir in the tomato juice.

Process the soup in batches in a food processor or blender until smooth. Combine the batches in the saucepan and whisk in the peanut butter and sugar. Garnish the servings with green onions and/or peanuts.

Serves 6 to 8

White Bean Chili

1 pound dried Great Northern beans
2 pounds chicken breasts, skinned
1 onion, cut into quarters
1 cup coarsely chopped celery
2 medium onions, chopped
1 tablespoon olive oil
4 garlic cloves, minced
2 (4-ounce) cans chopped mild green chiles
2 teaspoons ground cumin
1 1/2 teaspoons oregano
1/4 teaspoon ground cloves
1/4 teaspoon cayenne pepper
12 ounces (3 cups) shredded Monterey Jack cheese

Garnish
sour cream
salsa
chopped fresh cilantro

Sort and rinse the beans and soak in enough water to cover in a bowl for 8 hours or longer; drain.

Combine the chicken with the onion quarters, celery and enough cold water to cover in an 8 quart saucepot. Bring to a boil and reduce the heat. Simmer for 20 to 30 minutes or until the chicken is tender, skimming the surface occasionally. Strain, reserving 6 cups liquid. Cool and shred the chicken, discarding the bones. Cover with foil to keep moist.

Sauté the chopped onions in the olive oil in a large stockpot. Add the garlic, green chiles, cumin, oregano, cloves and cayenne pepper. Sauté for 2 minutes longer.

Add the beans and reserved cooking liquid. Simmer for 45 to 60 minutes or until the beans are tender. Add the chicken and cook just until heated through. Sprinkle the servings with the cheese and garnish with sour cream, salsa and cilantro.

Serves 8 to 10

Brazilian Stew

1 pound smoked sausage
1 pound pork loin
1 large onion, finely chopped
2 green bell peppers, finely chopped
1 jalapeño pepper, minced
1 tablespoon minced garlic
vegetable oil
2 (15-ounce) cans black beans, rinsed
2 (15-ounce) cans chopped tomatoes, drained
4 (14-ounce) cans chicken stock
1/4 cup fresh lime juice
1 tablespoon chopped fresh parsley
1 teaspoon ground cumin
1 teaspoon kosher salt
1/4 teaspoon cayenne pepper, or to taste
1 tablespoon black pepper
hot steamed brown rice

Commercial stocks are usually saltier than the homemade variety. Dilute them with beer, wine, or tomato juice, whichever complements the recipe, but do not exceed the total amount of liquid in the recipe. You can also eliminate the processed taste of canned soups by adding a tablespoon or two of wine or wine vinegar.

Cut the sausage diagonally into 1/2-inch slices. Cut the pork into 1/2×2-inch strips. Sauté the sausage and pork with the onion, bell peppers, jalapeño pepper and garlic in a small amount of vegetable oil in a saucepan over medium heat until the onion is translucent and the pork is brown; drain.

Add the beans, tomatoes, chicken stock, lime juice, parsley, cumin, salt, cayenne pepper and black pepper. Bring to a boil and reduce the heat. Simmer for 1 hour or until the pork is tender. Serve over rice.

Serves 8

Green Chile Stew

Nice over rice in a soup bowl and served with corn bread.

2 pounds pork loin, trimmed
2 tablespoons olive oil
1 medium yellow onion, chopped
1 tablespoon minced garlic
2 fresh poblano peppers, seeded and chopped
2 (4-ounce) cans chopped green chiles
1 chipotle pepper in adobo sauce, minced
2 teaspoons ground cumin
1 teaspoon kosher salt
2 teaspoons black pepper
3 (14-ounce) cans chicken stock
hot cooked white rice

Garnish
chopped fresh cilantro

Cut the pork into $1/2$-inch cubes. Brown on all sides in the olive oil in a saucepan. Remove the pork and set aside. Add the onion, garlic and poblano peppers to the saucepan and sauté over low heat until the onion is translucent. Add the green chiles, chipotle pepper, cumin, salt and pepper and mix well. Sauté for 5 minutes.

Stir in the chicken stock and pork. Bring to a boil and reduce the heat. Simmer for 1 hour or until the pork is tender. Ladle over rice in soup bowls to serve. Garnish servings with cilantro.

Serves 6

Chicken and Sausage Gumbo

1 cup White Lily flour
1 cup vegetable oil
1¹/2 cups chopped onions
1 cup chopped celery
1 cup chopped green bell pepper
1 pound smoked andouille or kielbasa sausage, cut crosswise
    into ¹/2-inch slices
2 or 3 bay leaves
1¹/2 teaspoons salt
¹/4 to ¹/2 teaspoon cayenne pepper
6 cups water
1 pound skinless boneless chicken breasts
1 teaspoon Cajun seasoning
1 cup sliced fresh okra (optional)
2 tablespoons chopped parsley
¹/2 cup chopped green onions
1 tablespoon filé powder
hot cooked white rice

Blend the flour into the oil in a large heavy saucepan over medium heat. Cook for 20 to 25 minutes or until dark brown, stirring constantly. Add the onions, celery and bell pepper and sauté for 4 to 5 minutes or until tender.

Add the sausage, bay leaves, salt and cayenne pepper. Sauté for 3 to 4 minutes or until the sausage is brown. Stir in the water. Bring to a boil and reduce the heat. Cook for 1 hour, stirring occasionally.

Cut the chicken into 1-inch pieces and season with the Cajun seasoning. Add to the gumbo with the okra and simmer for 1¹/2 hours, skimming the surface occasionally. Discard the bay leaves. Stir in the chopped parsley, green onions and filé powder. Cook until heated through. Serve over hot white rice in deep bowls.

You may substitute commercial roux for the homemade roux in this recipe to save time.

Serves 4 to 6

Tuscan Chicken Stew

A low-fat heart-healthy recipe that tastes wonderful.

1 pound skinless boneless chicken
    breasts
1/2 teaspoon crushed dried rosemary
1/2 teaspoon salt
1/4 teaspoon pepper
2 teaspoons olive oil
2 teaspoons minced garlic

1 (14-ounce) can chicken broth
1 (16-ounce) can cannellini beans,
    rinsed and drained
1 (7-ounce) jar roasted red bell pepper,
    drained and chopped
3 1/2 cups torn spinach

Cut the chicken into 1-inch pieces. Combine with the rosemary, salt and pepper and toss to coat well. Brown in the heated olive oil in a large nonstick skillet over medium-high heat for 3 minutes. Add the garlic and sauté for 1 minute longer.

Add the chicken broth, beans and roasted bell pepper and bring to a boil. Reduce the heat and simmer for 10 minutes or until the chicken is cooked through. Stir in the spinach and simmer for 1 minute.

Serves 5 or 6

Balsamic Apple and Spinach Salad

Balsamic Dressing
1 cup vegetable oil or olive oil
1/2 cup sugar
1/2 cup balsamic vinegar
1 teaspoon paprika
1/2 teaspoon ground dry mustard
1/2 teaspoon salt

Salad
2 Granny Smith apples, chopped
1 (10-ounce) package each fresh
    spinach and Italian salad greens
1/4 cup chopped red onion
1 cup crumbled feta cheese
1 cup toasted pecans

To prepare the dressing, combine the oil, sugar, vinegar, paprika, dry mustard and salt in a bowl and mix until smooth.

To prepare the salad, add the apples to the dressing and let stand for several minutes. Combine the spinach and salad greens with the onion, cheese and pecans in a salad bowl and mix well. Add the apples and dressing and toss to coat well.

Serves 6 to 8

Fruit and Nut Salad

1 head romaine lettuce, sliced
1 head red leaf lettuce, torn
1 to 2 cups seedless grapes
1 cup drained mandarin oranges
Curried Salad Dressing (below)
1/4 to 1/2 cup toasted slivered almonds

Combine the romaine lettuce and red leaf lettuce in a salad bowl and mix well. Add the grapes and mandarin oranges and toss gently. Add the desired amount of Curried Salad Dressing and toss to coat well. Sprinkle with the almonds.

Serves 8

Curried Salad Dressing

1/3 cup red wine vinegar
1/2 cup olive oil
2 tablespoons brown sugar
1 teaspoon soy sauce
1 garlic clove, minced
2 tablespoons chopped chives
1 tablespoon curry powder

Combine the vinegar, olive oil, brown sugar, soy sauce, garlic, chives and curry powder in a bowl and whisk to mix.

Serves 8

Mandarin Orange Salad

Try pomegranate seeds instead of cranberries for an unusual variation.

Salad
1/2 head leaf lettuce, torn
1/2 head romaine lettuce, chopped
2 scallions, chopped
1 cup chopped celery
1/2 cup dried cranberries
1 (8-ounce) can mandarin oranges,
   drained
Red Wine Vinaigrette (below)

Sugared Almonds
3 tablespoons sugar
1/2 cup sliced almonds

To prepare the almonds, combine the sugar and almonds in a skillet over medium-low heat and cook until the sugar melts, stirring occasionally. Cook until the almonds are evenly coated, stirring constantly. Spread on waxed paper and separate with forks to cool.

To prepare the salad, combine the leaf lettuce, romaine lettuce, scallions, celery, cranberries and oranges in a salad bowl and mix gently. Add the Red Wine Vinaigrette and toss to coat well. Sprinkle with the almonds.

Serves 8

Red Wine Vinaigrette

1/4 cup vegetable oil
2 tablespoons red wine vinegar
3 drops of Tabasco sauce
1 tablespoon chopped parsley
2 tablespoons sugar
1/2 teaspoon salt
pepper to taste

Mix the vegetable oil, vinegar, Tabasco sauce, parsley, sugar, salt and pepper in a bowl.

Serves 8

Napa Salad

Taken on picnics to rave reviews for over two generations.

noodles from 2 packages chicken-flavor ramen noodles, crushed
1/2 cup sliced almonds
2 tablespoons sesame seeds
1 large head napa cabbage
1 small onion, chopped
Slaw Vinaigrette (below)

Spread the noodles from the ramen noodle packages with the almonds and sesame seeds on a shallow baking sheet. Toast under the broiler just until light brown, tossing occasionally. Cool slightly.

Slice the cabbage crosswise 1/2 inch thick. Combine with the noodle mixture and onion in a salad bowl and toss to mix well. Add the hot Slaw Vinaigrette and toss to mix.

Serves 6 to 8

Slaw Vinaigrette

seasoning packets from 2 packages chicken-flavor ramen noodles
1 cup vegetable oil
6 tablespoons apple cider vinegar
1/2 cup sugar
salt and pepper to taste

Combine the seasoning packets from the noodle packages with the vegetable oil, vinegar, sugar, salt and pepper in a small saucepan and bring to a boil.

Serves 6 to 8

Nashville serves as the capital of Tennessee, so naturally the state flag can be seen flying high above government buildings in the area. The flag, which has a solid red field edged with white and blue, also features a center circle with three stars. The flag's designer, LeRoy Reeves of the Third Regiment, Tennessee Infantry, said of his design, "The three stars are of pure white, representing the three grand divisions of the state. They are bound together by the endless circle of the blue field, the symbol being three bound together in one—an indissoluble trinity." This describes well the state, which is comprised of three diverse regions: the western Delta, the central Cumberland Valley, and the mountainous east. In essence, the stars represent the "Three States of Tennessee."

Sunflower Slaw

Sweet-and-Sour Vinaigrette

seasoning packets from 2 packages
  beef-flavor ramen noodles
3/4 cup vegetable oil
1/4 cup cider vinegar
1/2 cup sugar

Slaw

1 (16-ounce) package coleslaw mix
2 bunches green onions, chopped
1 stem broccoli, chopped
1 cup slivered almonds
1 cup sunflower seeds
noodles from 2 packages beef-flavor
  ramen noodles, crushed

To prepare the vinaigrette, combine the seasoning packets from the noodle packages, vegetable oil, vinegar and sugar in a bowl and whisk to mix well. Chill, covered, for 2 hours or longer.

To prepare the slaw, combine the coleslaw mix, green onions, broccoli, almonds and sunflower seeds in a large salad bowl. Add the vinaigrette and noodles at serving time and toss to coat well.

Serves 10 to 12

Southern Belle Salad

Light and lovely!

Dijon Vinaigrette

3 tablespoons white wine vinegar
5 tablespoons olive oil
1 teaspoon Dijon mustard
sugar and salt to taste

Salad

4 cups arugula leaves
4 cups torn Bibb lettuce
3 ripe peaches or red pears, sliced
1 cup crumbled bleu cheese (optional)
1/2 cup toasted pecans

To prepare the vinaigrette, combine the vinegar, olive oil, Dijon mustard, sugar and salt in a bowl and mix well.

To prepare the salad, combine the arugula and Bibb lettuce in a bowl and mix well. Spoon onto salad plates and arrange the peaches over the greens. Sprinkle with the cheese and pecans. Drizzle with the vinaigrette.

Serves 4

Strawberry and Spinach Salad

2 bunches fresh spinach, or 1 (10-ounce) package fresh spinach
1 quart strawberries
Sesame Seed Dressing (below)
1/4 cup toasted slivered almonds

Tear the spinach into bite-size pieces. Cut the strawberries into halves and toss with the spinach in a salad bowl. Add the Sesame Seed Dressing and toss to coat well. Top with the slivered almonds.

You may add 1/2 cup crumbled bleu cheese if desired.

Serves 6

Sesame Seed Dressing

2 tablespoons sesame seeds
1 tablespoon poppy seeds
1/2 cup olive oil
1/4 cup white wine vinegar
1/2 cup sugar
1 tablespoon minced onion
1/4 teaspoon Worcestershire sauce
1/4 teaspoon paprika

Combine the sesame seeds, poppy seeds, olive oil, vinegar, sugar, onion, Worcestershire sauce and paprika in a bowl and whisk until well mixed. Chill, covered, until serving time.

You may substitute raspberry vinegar for the white wine vinegar and omit the sesame seeds if you prefer.

Serves 6

Historical

If you are looking for elegant, historical, and breathtakingly sumptuous accommodations in Nashville, look no further than the glorious Hermitage Hotel, first opened in 1910. Nashville's first million-dollar hotel was named after Andrew Jackson's estate and is located downtown across from the Tennessee Performing Arts Center, within a stone's throw of the State Capitol. Featuring the very finest of materials, such as Italian sienna marble, Russian walnut wall panels, and sparkling cut glass, the hotel is an architectural jewel. The guest list is most impressive: Presidents Johnson, Kennedy, Nixon, Roosevelt, Taft, and Wilson all stayed there. Other notable guests include Gene Autry, Tallulah Bankhead, Al Capone, Bette Davis, and Al Jolson, to name a few. Minnesota Fats made the hotel his home for eight years, and had his own pool table on the mezzanine above the lobby. Currently undergoing a $15 million renovation, the hotel will reopen as one of the finest preservation efforts in the South.

Spinach and Gorgonzola Salad

Add sliced strawberries for a touch of summer color.

Gorgonzola Croutons and Bacon Curls
2 tablespoons crumbled Gorgonzola cheese
1/2 tablespoon butter, softened
2 (1/2-inch) slices sourdough country bread
4 to 6 slices bacon

Salad
8 ounces fresh baby spinach, trimmed and torn
1/3 red onion, thinly sliced and separated into rings
1 hard-cooked egg, cut into quarters
Creamy Dressing (below)

To prepare the croutons, blend the cheese and butter with a fork in a small bowl. Spread the mixture on 1 side of each slice of bread and cut into 1-inch pieces. Arrange the pieces cheese side up on a baking sheet. Twist each bacon slice into a tight spiral and arrange on the rack of a broiler pan. Place the croutons on the upper rack and the bacon on the center rack of an oven heated to 375 degrees. Bake for 15 minutes or until the croutons are golden brown and the bacon is crisp. Remove the bacon to paper towels to drain.

To prepare the salad, toss the spinach with the onion and egg in a bowl. Add the croutons and bacon and toss gently. Drizzle with the Creamy Dressing and serve immediately.

Serves 2

Creamy Dressing

1/2 garlic clove
1/8 teaspoon salt
1 tablespoon red wine vinegar
1 teaspoon honey
2 tablespoons mayonnaise
1 tablespoon olive oil

Crush the garlic with the salt in a bowl to a paste consistency. Process the garlic paste, vinegar, honey, mayonnaise and olive oil in a blender until smooth.

Serves 2

Cobb Salad

3 cups torn green leaf lettuce
1 cup chopped roasted turkey breast
2 medium tomatoes, chopped
1 avocado, chopped
1/2 cup crumbled bleu cheese
6 slices bacon, crisp-fried and crumbled
3 hard-cooked eggs, chopped
3 green onions, sliced
1/2 cup Old-Fashioned French Dressing (below)

Spread the lettuce evenly on a large platter. Sprinkle the turkey in a vertical strip over the lettuce. Sprinkle the tomatoes, avocado, bleu cheese, bacon and eggs in separate strips over the lettuce. Sprinkle the green onions in 2 diagonal strips over the top. Drizzle with the Old-Fashioned French Dressing at the table and toss to serve.

Serves 4 to 6

Old-Fashioned French Dressing

2 tablespoons each red wine vinegar and water
1 tablespoon fresh lemon juice
1/2 teaspoon Worcestershire sauce
1/2 teaspoon minced garlic
1/4 teaspoon sugar
1/8 teaspoon dry English mustard
1/2 teaspoon salt
1/8 teaspoon freshly ground pepper
1/3 cup vegetable oil
2 tablespoons olive oil

Combine the first nine ingredients in a bowl and whisk to mix well. Blend the oils in a measuring cup. Add to the vinegar mixture and whisk until smooth.

Makes 3/4 cup

Marinated Strawberry Chicken Salad

Dijon Marinade

1/4 cup whole-grain Dijon mustard
3 tablespoons water
1 tablespoon raspberry wine vinegar
1 teaspoon olive oil
2 garlic cloves, minced
2 tablespoons brown sugar
1/4 teaspoon pepper

Salad

4 skinless boneless chicken breasts
1 head red leaf lettuce, torn
4 ounces bleu cheese, crumbled
1/4 cup toasted walnuts
1 pint strawberries, sliced
Raspberry Maple Vinaigrette (below)

To prepare the marinade, combine the Dijon mustard, water, vinegar, olive oil, garlic, brown sugar and pepper in a sealable plastic bag and mix well.

For the salad, add the chicken to the marinade and turn to coat well. Marinate in the refrigerator for 2 hours or longer; drain. Grill the chicken for 7 minutes on each side or until cooked through. Cut diagonally into thin slices.

Arrange the lettuce on serving plates. Sprinkle the bleu cheese, walnuts and strawberries over the lettuce. Arrange the chicken slices over the top. Add the Raspberry Maple Vinaigrette and toss to coat well.

Serves 4

Raspberry Maple Vinaigrette

1/4 cup raspberry wine vinegar
2 tablespoons pure maple syrup
2/3 cup vegetable oil

Combine the vinegar, maple syrup and vegetable oil in a jar and shake to blend well.

Serves 4

Chicken Salad with Grapes

3¹/2 pounds skinless boneless chicken breasts, cooked
5 ribs celery, chopped
1¹/2 cups seedless red grape halves
1¹/2 teaspoons each tarragon or thyme and garlic powder
salt and pepper to taste
3 cups mayonnaise
¹/2 cup toasted slivered almonds

Cut the chicken into bite-size pieces, discarding any tough membranes. Combine with the celery and grapes in a large bowl. Season with the tarragon, garlic powder, salt and pepper.

Add the mayonnaise and toasted almonds and toss to coat well. Chill, covered, for 1 hour or longer before serving.

Serves 6 to 8

Chilled Broccoli Salad

8 slices bacon, crisp-fried and crumbled
florets and tender stem portions of 1 bunch broccoli, chopped
¹/2 cup each finely chopped red onion and celery
¹/2 cup raisins
¹/2 to ³/4 cup cashews or pecans
³/4 cup mayonnaise
¹/4 cup sugar
3 tablespoons red wine vinegar

Garnish
crumbled crisp-fried bacon

Combine the bacon with the broccoli, onion, celery, raisins and cashews in a large bowl and mix well.

Mix the mayonnaise, sugar and vinegar in a small bowl. Add to the broccoli mixture and mix well. Chill, covered, for 1 hour or longer before serving. Garnish with additional bacon.

Serves 6 to 8

Corn Bread Salad

A beautiful and unusual twist on a tasty southern favorite.

Salad

1 recipe corn bread, cooled and
    crumbled
1 (14 ounce) can black beans, drained
1 (14-ounce) can Shoe Peg corn,
    drained
1 medium red onion, chopped
3 large tomatoes, chopped
8 ounces (2 cups) shredded Cheddar
    cheese
1 (2-ounce) jar real bacon bits
1 small bunch green onions, chopped

Ranch Dressing

1 cup mayonnaise
1 cup sour cream
1 envelope ranch salad dressing mix

To prepare the dressing, combine the mayonnaise, sour cream and salad dressing mix in a small bowl and mix well.

To prepare the salad, layer the corn bread, beans, corn, onion and tomatoes 1/2 at a time in a large glass salad bowl. Spread the dressing over the layers. Sprinkle with the cheese, bacon and green onions.

Serves 8 to 10

Confetti Summer Salad

1 small zucchini, chopped
1 medium yellow bell pepper, chopped
1 medium red bell pepper, chopped
1 (16-ounce) can whole kernel corn,
    drained

1 tomato, seeded and chopped
1/2 cup Italian salad dressing
1/2 cup fresh salsa

Combine the zucchini, bell peppers, corn and tomato in a large salad bowl and mix gently. Add the salad dressing and salsa and toss to coat well. Chill, covered, for 24 hours, stirring occasionally.

Serves 6 to 8

Tomato Mozzarella Salad

15 Roma tomatoes, or 7 vine-ripened tomatoes
1½ pounds fresh mozzarella cheese balls
⅓ cup slivered basil leaves
¼ cup chopped flat-leaf Italian parsley
Italian Dressing (below)

Garnish
basil leaves

Cut the tomatoes into quarters and cut each quarter into 3 pieces. Cut each mozzarella cheese ball into quarters. Combine the tomatoes, cheese, basil and parsley in a bowl and mix gently.

Add the Italian Dressing to the tomato mixture and toss to coat well. Chill, covered, until serving time. Toss again before serving. Garnish with basil leaves.

Serves 6

Italian Dressing

¼ cup olive oil
⅓ cup red wine vinegar
1 tablespoon balsamic vinegar
2 teaspoons granulated garlic
1 tablespoon kosher salt
1 tablespoon mixed ground red, white and black peppercorns

Combine the olive oil, wine vinegar, balsamic vinegar, garlic, salt and pepper mixture in a small bowl and whisk until smooth.

Serves 6

Historical

When I rode down Broadway with my granddaddy on his way to work, we would pass the old Nashville Union Station. Entering the massive old Romanesque building with him was mesmerizing: The ceiling soared with vaults and arches, light glittered through stained glass, and our footsteps echoed off stone and wood. We went all the way down those long escalators to the platform, and Granddaddy told me about all the people who bustled through here on their travels, taking trains like the Dixie Limited and the Southwind. As I looked around, I was filled with both awe and sadness, because the space was completely empty except for us. The next day, we read in the paper that the station, which had served Nashville since 1900, had closed its doors for good. For years we lamented the sad empty space, and we were thrilled when, in 1986, it was magnificently preserved as a National Historic Landmark and reopened as the Union Station Hotel.

Summer Corn Salad

Salad

3 cups cooked fresh white corn kernels
2 tomatoes, chopped
1 green bell pepper, chopped
1 small purple onion, chopped
1 cucumber, peeled and chopped

Summer Salad Dressing

$1/2$ cup sour cream
$1/4$ cup mayonnaise
2 tablespoons white vinegar
2 teaspoons sugar
$1/2$ teaspoon celery seeds
$1/2$ teaspoon dry mustard
2 teaspoons salt
$1/2$ teaspoon pepper

For the dressing, combine the sour cream, mayonnaise, white vinegar, sugar, celery seeds, dry mustard, salt and pepper in a bowl and mix well.

For the salad, combine the corn, tomatoes, bell pepper, onion and cucumber in a bowl and mix gently. Add the salad dressing and toss to coat well. Chill, covered, until serving time.

Serves 8

Cavatappi Salad

$1/4$ cup minced sun-dried tomatoes
1 teaspoon minced dried garlic
2 tablespoons balsamic vinegar
1 tablespoon red wine vinegar
$1/4$ cup olive oil
2 teaspoons mixed ground red, white
    and black peppercorns

$1/4$ cup hot water
16 ounces uncooked cavatappi or
    other corkscrew pasta
1 teaspoon salt
$1/4$ cup grated Parmesan cheese
2 tablespoons chopped fresh flat-leaf
    Italian parsley

Combine the sun-dried tomatoes, garlic, balsamic vinegar, red wine vinegar, olive oil, pepper mixture and hot water in a bowl and mix well. Let stand for 30 minutes. Cook the pasta al dente with the salt, using the package directions; rinse and drain. Cool to room temperature. Combine the pasta with the sun-dried tomato mixture and toss to coat well. Spoon into serving bowls and sprinkle the servings with the cheese and parsley.

Serves 10

Chicken Pasta Salad

Great as a side salad or entrée.

16 ounces uncooked angel hair pasta
2 tablespoons olive oil
4 teaspoons red wine vinegar
1/2 cup olive oil
1/2 cup vegetable oil
2 teaspoons Dijon mustard
1 tablespoon salt
1/2 teaspoon pepper
6 cups chopped cooked chicken
1/4 cup prepared vinaigrette dressing
1 1/4 cups mayonnaise
1/4 cup chopped fresh parsley
1/4 cup chopped green onions
1/4 teaspoon dried basil
garlic salt to taste

Garnish

toasted almonds

Cook the pasta with 2 tablespoons olive oil using the package directions; rinse with cold water and drain. Combine the vinegar, 1/2 cup olive oil, vegetable oil, Dijon mustard, salt and pepper in a bowl and mix well. Add the pasta and toss to coat well. Chill, covered, for 8 hours or longer.

Add the chicken, vinaigrette, mayonnaise, parsley, green onions, basil and garlic salt to the pasta and mix gently. Adjust the seasonings. Garnish with toasted almonds.

You may add black olives, cherry tomatoes and/or chopped artichoke hearts to the salad if desired.

Serves 12

Couscous with Lime and Curry Vinaigrette

1¹/2 cups water
1¹/2 cups quick-cooking couscous
1 medium carrot, finely chopped
2 tablespoons water
1 medium yellow squash, finely chopped
1 medium zucchini, finely chopped
¹/4 cup raisins
¹/4 cup slivered almonds
Lime and Curry Vinaigrette (below)

Bring 1¹/2 cups water to a boil in a saucepan or microwave and pour over the couscous in a bowl. Let stand, covered, for 5 to 10 minutes or until the water is absorbed; fluff with a fork. Combine the carrot with 2 tablespoons water in a microwave-safe bowl and microwave, covered, on High for 1 minute or until the carrot is tender-crisp; drain.

Add the carrot, yellow squash, zucchini, raisins and almonds to the couscous and mix well. Add the Lime and Curry Vinaigrette and toss to coat well. Serve chilled or at room temperature.

Serves 6 to 8

Lime and Curry Vinaigrette

2 tablespoons white wine vinegar
2 tablespoons fresh lime juice
1 teaspoon grated or finely chopped lime zest
1 garlic clove, minced
¹/4 teaspoon curry powder
¹/4 teaspoon ground ginger
¹/4 teaspoon salt
cayenne pepper to taste
¹/2 cup olive oil

Combine the vinegar, lime juice, lime zest, garlic, curry powder, ginger, salt and cayenne pepper in a bowl and mix well. Add the olive oil and whisk until smooth.

Makes ³/4 cup

Come-Back Dressing

2 garlic cloves
1/2 medium onion, coarsely chopped
1 cup mayonnaise
1/2 cup ketchup
1/2 cup vegetable oil
1 teaspoon Worcestershire sauce
1 to 11/2 teaspoons mustard
juice of 1 lemon
11/2 teaspoons paprika
hot sauce to taste
salt to taste

Combine the garlic and onion in a blender and process until smooth. Add the mayonnaise, ketchup, vegetable oil, Worcestershire sauce, mustard, lemon juice, paprika, hot sauce and salt and process to mix well. Spoon into an airtight container and chill for 8 hours or longer before serving.

Makes 23/4 cups

Herbed Croutons

5 slices bread
1/2 cup olive oil
2 tablespoons herbes de Provence
1/2 teaspoon salt, or to taste
1/2 teaspoon pepper, or to taste

Cut the bread into 3/4-inch cubes. Combine with the olive oil in a bowl and mix to coat well. Add the herbes de Provence, salt and pepper. Spread in a single layer on a baking sheet. Broil on the lowest oven rack for 5 to 10 minutes or until brown on both sides, turning once. Store in an airtight container.

Makes 5 cups

Vegetables and Sides

Vegetables and Sides

True to its early designation as the "Athens of the South," Nashville has a dedication to education that is reflected in the nearly twenty accredited universities and colleges in the Nashville area.

From Belmont University to Fisk University, from Meharry Medical College to Vanderbilt University, and every collegiate discipline in-between, Nashville is a college town. With a college population of 80,000 plus, Nashville draws students from around the country and the world. Purchased by two women from Philadelphia in 1890, Belmont Mansion was reborn as a school for women. It later merged with Nashville's old Ward School and was renamed Ward-Belmont, serving as an academy and junior college for women. Today's Belmont University began as Belmont College in 1951 when the Tennessee Baptist Convention purchased Ward-Belmont and opened a co-ed liberal arts school offering both undergraduate and graduate degrees. Belmont's initial liberal arts focus has broadened to include, among other disciplines, the Mike Curb School of Music Business. In addition to taking regular business courses, these students complete additional studies in four main areas relevant to the music industry: general music business knowledge, music publishing, intellectual properties, and recording studio principles.

Fisk University, another outstanding liberal arts school and Nashville's oldest university, was founded in January 1866 and held its first classes in Union Army barracks near present-day Union Station. In 1871 the world-famous Fisk Jubilee singers started as a talented nine-member traveling troupe hoping to raise enough money through their performances of spiritual music to save the school from debt. Not only did the Jubilee Singers succeed in keeping Fisk University's doors open, they also opened the ears of the world to the music of the slaves. During a second tour of Europe, Queen Victoria of England was so impressed with the now eleven-member ensemble that she commissioned a floor-to-ceiling portrait of the singers as a gift to the University. The portrait currently hangs in Jubilee Hall, a National Historic Landmark. Fisk University is one of the nation's most prominent providers of education in the African-American community.

Another standout in the nation's African-American educational community, and indeed any educational community, is Meharry Medical College. The nation's first and today the nation's largest private medical education facility for African-Americans, Meharry Medical College was founded in Nashville in 1876. First a department of Central Tennessee College (later Walden University), the name was changed to Meharry Medical College of Walden University to honor the family that generously gave to ensure its financial support. In 1915 the State of Tennessee granted Meharry a separate charter. In 1931 Meharry moved from its original downtown location to today's present 26-acre campus in northwest Nashville. The college has grown to encompass four schools: Medicine, Dentistry, Graduate Studies and Research, and Allied Health Professions. In order to help Meharry keep abreast of the rapid changes in today's ever-evolving medical educational environment, a strategic alliance was formed with Vanderbilt University in June of 1999. This alliance covers six collaborative areas: Academic Support, Biomedical Research and Training, Clinical Science Training, Cultural Diversity, Health Services, and The Institute for Community Health. Vanderbilt University benefits equally with Meharry in the alliance. Vanderbilt University was founded in 1873 when Commodore Cornelius Vanderbilt donated a million dollars to build a school that would "contribute to strengthening the ties which should exist between all sections of our common country." His initial donation has resulted in a campus comprised of 220 buildings covering 326 acres, encompassing 10 schools and over 10,000 students. Vanderbilt facilities also include the Vanderbilt University Medical Center and The Freedom Forum First Amendment Center. Combined, the Vanderbilt network has become the largest private employer in Middle Tennessee. From the Peabody College of Education to the School of Medicine, Vanderbilt is one of the most highly regarded universities in the country.

Roasted Asparagus with Peanut Sauce

1 1/2 pounds fresh thin asparagus spears, trimmed
2 tablespoons vegetable oil or peanut oil
2 garlic cloves, minced
2 tablespoons smooth peanut butter
1 1/2 teaspoons soy sauce
1 1/2 teaspoons lemon juice
1/4 teaspoon red pepper flakes
2 to 3 teaspoons water

Arrange the asparagus in a shallow baking pan. Mix the oil and garlic in a small bowl. Pour over the asparagus, turning the asparagus to coat evenly. Roast at 450 degrees for 12 to 15 minutes or until tender, turning once or twice. Transfer to a serving dish.

Combine the peanut butter, soy sauce, lemon juice and red pepper flakes in a bowl. Add enough of the water to make a thin pouring consistency. Drizzle over the asparagus, coating well. Serve immediately.

Serves 6

Green Beans with Herbs and Feta Cheese

2 pounds fresh green beans, trimmed
2 tablespoons butter or margarine
2 tablespoons minced garlic
1/2 medium-large onion, chopped
1 tablespoon dried basil
1 tablespoon dried rosemary
1 cup crumbled feta cheese

Cut the green beans into bite-size pieces. Combine with enough water to cover in a saucepan and bring to a boil. Cook for 10 minutes; drain most of the water.

Add the butter, garlic, onion, basil and rosemary and mix well. Reduce the heat and simmer for 10 minutes or until the onion is tender, stirring frequently. Sprinkle the servings with the feta cheese.

You may adjust the amounts of the ingredients to suit your tastes.

Serves 4 to 6

Dilled Fresh Green Beans

Great to serve when green beans are in season.

1¹/2 pounds fresh green beans, trimmed
¹/2 cup olive oil
2 tablespoons each lemon juice and Dijon mustard
1 tablespoon cider vinegar
2 tablespoons sugar
³/4 cup minced green onions
3 tablespoons minced fresh dill
1 tablespoon chopped fresh parsley
salt and pepper to taste
¹/3 cup each chopped radishes and toasted walnuts

Cut the green beans into 1¹/2-inch pieces. Combine with a small amount of water in a saucepan and bring to a boil. Cook, covered, for 6 to 8 minutes or until tender-crisp; drain and cool.

Combine the olive oil, lemon juice, Dijon mustard, vinegar, sugar, green onions, dill, parsley, salt and pepper in a covered jar and shake well. Combine with the beans in a bowl and mix well.

Chill, covered, for 8 hours or longer. Add the radishes and walnuts at serving time and mix well.

Serves 8

Garlic Vinaigrette for Green Beans or Asparagus

3 garlic cloves
juice of 1 lemon
¹/4 cup olive oil
¹/8 teaspoon hot sauce
salt to taste

Mash the garlic with the lemon juice in a small bowl. Whisk in the remaining ingredients.

Makes ¹/2 cup

Green Beans with Roquefort and Walnuts

The bite of the cheese and the sweetness and crunch of the walnuts are perfect accents for fresh green beans.

1 pound fresh green beans, trimmed
4 (1/4-inch-thick) slices bacon
4 ounces Roquefort cheese or feta cheese, crumbled
1 1/2 cups toasted walnut halves
freshly ground pepper to taste

Add the green beans to a saucepan of boiling water and reduce the heat. Simmer for 3 minutes or until tender-crisp. Rinse under cold water and drain.

Fry the bacon in a skillet over medium heat from 5 to 7 minutes or until crisp. Remove to paper towels to drain and cool; crumble.

Add the green beans to the drippings in the skillet and cook over medium heat for 2 minutes, stirring frequently. Add the Roquefort cheese and toss for 30 seconds or just until the cheese begins to melt.

Spoon into a serving bowl and sprinkle with the walnuts, bacon and pepper. Serve immediately.

Serves 4

Carrot Soufflé

1 pound carrots, sliced
salt to taste
1/2 cup (1 stick) butter, melted
3 tablespoons White Lily flour
1 teaspoon baking powder
3 eggs
1/2 cup sugar
1 tablespoon vanilla extract

Combine the carrots with enough salted water to cover in a saucepan and cook, covered, until tender; drain. Combine with the butter in a blender or food processor and process until smooth. Add the flour, baking powder, eggs, sugar and vanilla and process until well mixed.

Spoon into a greased 1-quart baking dish. Bake at 350 degrees for 45 minutes or until set.

Serves 6

Corn and Scallion Pancakes

3 ears of corn
1/4 cup chopped scallions
1/2 jalapeño pepper, seeded and chopped
1 tablespoon unsalted butter
1 tablespoon dry white wine
1/4 cup milk
2 teaspoons honey
3/4 cup White Lily flour
1/4 cup yellow cornmeal
1/2 teaspoon baking powder
1/2 teaspoon salt
1/2 teaspoon pepper
3 large eggs, beaten

Blanch the corn briefly in boiling water in a saucepan. Grate the corn from the cobs through the large holes of a grater, collecting the pulp in a bowl; discard the cobs.

Sauté the scallions and jalapeño pepper in the heated butter in a skillet over high heat for 30 seconds or until the scallions wilt. Add the corn, wine and milk and cook over low heat for 3 minutes or until the corn is tender. Remove the skillet from the heat and stir in the honey. Cool the mixture slightly.

Combine the flour, cornmeal, baking powder, salt and pepper in a mixing bowl and mix well. Add the eggs to the cooled corn mixture and stir the corn mixture into the dry ingredients, mixing just until moistened.

Heat a griddle or cast-iron skillet over medium-high heat and oil lightly. Ladle the batter onto the griddle and cook until the edges appear set. Turn the pancakes and cook for 2 minutes longer or until golden brown. Serve immediately.

Serves 8

Corn Puddings on Broiled Tomatoes

A more sophisticated version of a traditional dish that is perfect for individual servings on a buffet. This eye-catching treat is wonderful with sweet summer corn and fresh tomatoes. Broiling the tomatoes brings out their natural sweetness and offsets the saltiness of the pudding.

1 cup fresh corn kernels
4 eggs, beaten
1¼ cups milk
½ teaspoon salt

red pepper to taste
2 small to medium firm tomatoes, cut
into 6 (½-inch) slices

Combine the corn with the eggs, milk, salt and red pepper in a bowl and mix well. Spoon into buttered muffin cups, filling ½ to ¾ full. Place the muffin pan in a larger pan with 1 inch hot water. Bake at 350 degrees for 20 minutes or until set.

Arrange the tomato slices in a broiler pan. Broil just until the slices are tender but still hold their shape. Place on a serving tray.

Invert the muffin cups to remove the puddings and place 1 pudding on each broiled tomato slice.

Serves 6

Marinated Onions

Vidalia onions make this recipe from Encore *even better.*

3 cups white vinegar
2 cups water
3 tablespoons sugar
3 or 4 white or red onions, thinly
   sliced and separated into rings

½ cup mayonnaise
1 teaspoon celery seeds (optional)
Tabasco sauce to taste
salt and freshly ground pepper to taste

Combine the vinegar, water and sugar in a medium saucepan and heat until the sugar dissolves, stirring frequently. Let stand to cool. Add the onions. Marinate, covered, in the refrigerator for 8 hours or longer; drain. Combine the mayonnaise, celery seeds, Tabasco sauce, salt and pepper in a bowl and mix well. Add the onions and mix gently.

Serves 6

Cinderella's Golden Potato Casserole

A popular recipe from Encore.

6 potatoes
8 ounces (2 cups) shredded Cheddar cheese
1/4 cup (1/2 stick) butter or margarine
2 cups sour cream
1/3 cup chopped green onions
1 teaspoon salt
1/4 teaspoon white pepper
2 tablespoons butter or margarine

Cook the potatoes in enough water to cover in a saucepan until tender. Drain and cool to room temperature. Peel the potatoes and shred coarsely.

Combine the cheese with 1/4 cup butter in a saucepan and cook until the cheese melts, stirring to blend well. Remove from the heat and stir in the sour cream, green onions, salt and white pepper. Add the potatoes and toss to coat well.

Spoon into a buttered 2-quart baking dish and dot with 2 tablespoons butter. Bake at 350 degrees for 25 minutes or until golden brown.

Serves 8

Twice-Baked Potatoes with Bleu Cheese

6 (10-ounce) russet potatoes
1/4 cup sour cream
1/4 cup crumbled bleu cheese
1/4 cup (1/2 stick) butter, softened
1 1/2 teaspoons minced garlic
1 1/2 teaspoons chopped fresh rosemary
salt and pepper to taste
6 tablespoons sour cream
6 teaspoons crumbled bleu cheese

Pierce the potatoes with a fork and place directly on the oven rack. Bake at 400 degrees for 1 1/4 hours or until tender. Remove to a baking sheet and cool for 5 minutes. Slice the top 1/3 from the long side of each potato. Scoop the pulp from the potatoes into a bowl, reserving 1/4-inch shells. Scoop the pulp from the tops into the bowl and discard the tops.

Add 1/4 cup sour cream, 1/4 cup bleu cheese, butter, garlic and rosemary to the potato pulp and mash until smooth. Season with salt and pepper. Spoon into a pastry bag fitted with a large star tip. Pipe into the reserved potato shells.

Bake for 25 minutes or just until heated through and golden brown. Top each potato with 1 tablespoon sour cream and 1 teaspoon bleu cheese.

Serves 6

Potatoes Gratin Dauphinois

1 garlic clove, cut into halves
2 pounds potatoes, peeled
4 ounces (1 cup) finely chopped Gruyère or Cheddar cheese
1 egg
1/4 cup (1/2 stick) butter, melted
1 teaspoon salt
1 teaspoon pepper
1 cup milk, boiling

Rub an earthenware baking dish with the cut sides of the garlic and butter the baking dish. Cut the potatoes into 1/8-inch slices and pat dry with a towel. Arrange half the potatoes in the prepared baking dish.

Combine the cheese, egg, butter, salt and pepper in a bowl and mix well. Spread half the mixture over the potatoes. Repeat the layers using the remaining ingredients. Pour the boiling milk over the layers.

Bake at 350 degrees on the upper oven rack for 20 to 30 minutes or until the potatoes are tender and the top is golden brown.

Serves 8

Notable

Influential in the Nashville community for decades, the Frist family made an impact in the medical field nationwide when they took their hospital management company, Hospital Corporation of America, or HCA, public in 1969. Dr. Thomas Frist, Sr., Jack C. Massey, and Dr. Thomas Frist, Jr., founded HCA in 1968 to manage Park View Hospital and to provide capital for expansion and maintenance of the latest in medical technology. By the time HCA went public, ten more hospitals were under HCA's management. At the end of 1969, there were 26 hospitals and 3000 beds under the management of HCA. One of the nation's leading providers of healthcare services, HCA manages more that 200 hospitals and 70 outpatient surgery centers in 24 states, England, and Switzerland.

Hot Potato Casserole

8 to 10 small new red potatoes with skins
2 tablespoons butter
2 large garlic cloves, crushed
8 ounces (2 cups) shredded sharp Cheddar cheese
8 ounces (2 cups) shredded mixed Cheddar cheese and Monterey Jack cheese
1 small bunch green onions, chopped
8 ounces (1 cup) sour cream
4 ounces cream cheese or Neufchâtel cheese, softened
salt and hot Hungarian paprika or cayenne pepper to taste

Cook the potatoes in enough water to cover in a saucepan until tender; drain. Combine with the butter and garlic in a bowl; break up the potatoes with a fork, mixing in the butter and garlic.

Reserve 1/4 cup of the Cheddar cheese, 1/4 cup of the Cheddar/Monterey Jack cheese mixture and a few of the green onions for the topping. Add 1 cup of each of the remaining shredded cheeses to the potatoes and mix well. Add the sour cream, cream cheese, remaining green onions and remaining 3/4 cup of each of the shredded cheeses gradually, mixing well. Season with salt and paprika.

Spoon into a greased baking dish. Top with the reserved cheeses and green onions. Sprinkle with additional paprika. Bake at 350 degrees until the potatoes are heated through and the cheese melts.

Serves 8

Rosemary Potatoes

3 tablespoons butter or olive oil
1 pound small red potatoes with skins
1 tablespoon chopped fresh rosemary, or 1 teaspoon crushed dried rosemary
1/2 teaspoon salt, coarse salt or kosher salt
1/4 teaspoon pepper

Melt the butter in a 9×13-inch baking dish. Cut the unpeeled potatoes into 3/4-inch pieces. Add the potatoes, rosemary, salt and pepper to the butter in the baking dish and toss to coat well.

Bake at 425 degrees for 25 to 35 minutes or until the potatoes are tender and golden brown.

Serves 4

Spinach with a Kick

Even people who think they don't like spinach will like this.

*3 pounds fresh spinach, or 1 to 2 (10-ounce) packages frozen
    chopped spinach, cooked and drained*
1/4 cup (1/2 stick) butter
1 teaspoon hot sauce
1/2 teaspoon salt
4 ounces cream cheese, softened
2 tablespoons milk
2/3 cup bread crumbs

Cook the fresh spinach in a small amount of water in a large saucepan just until tender and drain. Combine with the butter, hot sauce and salt in a bowl and mix well.

Combine the cream cheese with the milk in a small bowl and mix until smooth. Add to the spinach mixture and mix well. Spoon into a baking dish and top with the bread crumbs. Bake at 375 degrees for 10 minutes.

Serves 4

Garlic Spinach Sauté

2 garlic cloves, sliced
2 teaspoons olive oil
*2 (5-ounce) packages fresh baby spinach,
    or 1 (16-ounce) bunch of spinach*
salt to taste

Sauté the garlic in the heated olive oil in a skillet until tender but not brown. Remove the garlic with a slotted spoon. Add half the spinach and sauté until the spinach wilts. Add the remaining spinach and the garlic and season with salt. Cook just until the spinach is tender, stirring constantly.

Serves 2 to 4

Aunt's Favorite Squash

From Aunt Pitty Pat's Porch in Atlanta.

3 pounds yellow summer squash, chopped	*1 tablespoon sugar*
1/2 cup chopped onion	*1 teaspoon salt*
2 eggs	*1/2 teaspoon pepper*
1/4 cup (1/2 stick) butter	*1/4 cup (1/2 stick) butter, melted*
1/2 cup bread crumbs	*1/2 cup bread crumbs*

Cook the squash with the onion in a small amount of water until tender; drain. Remove to a bowl and mash until smooth. Add the eggs, 1/4 cup butter, 1/2 cup bread crumbs, sugar, salt and pepper and mix well. Spoon into a baking dish. Drizzle with the melted butter and sprinkle with 1/2 cup bread crumbs. Bake at 375 degrees for 1 hour or until golden brown.

Serves 8

Spaghetti Squash with Tomatoes and Basil

A light and flavorful squash recipe.

1/2 (3-pound) spaghetti squash that has been cut into halves lengthwise	*1 cup thinly sliced grape tomatoes*
1/4 cup water	*salt and pepper to taste*
2 tablespoons olive oil	*1 tablespoon grated Parmesan cheese*
1/4 cup shredded basil leaves	
1/4 teaspoon dried oregano	**Garnish**
2 tablespoons grated Parmesan cheese	*fresh basil leaves*

Place the squash cut side down in a microwave-safe dish. Pour the water around the squash and cover tightly with plastic wrap. Microwave on High for 12 minutes or until tender. Let stand, covered, for 3 minutes. Combine the olive oil, basil, oregano and 2 tablespoons Parmesan cheese in a large bowl and whisk until smooth. Stir in the tomatoes and season with salt and pepper.

Scrape the strands of the spaghetti squash from the shell with a fork and add to the tomato mixture; toss until evenly coated. Sprinkle with 1 tablespoon Parmesan cheese and garnish with basil leaves. Serve immediately.

Serves 2

Summer Squash Fantasy

Served by dear friends at a beachside picnic in California, this recipe had been handed down from a family in North Carolina. It's a delicious and refreshing side, which travels and translates well from coast to coast.

5 medium yellow squash
5 medium zucchini
1/2 cup thinly sliced red onion
1/2 cup sliced celery
1/2 cup seeded and sliced tomato
Vegetable Marinade (below)

Cut the yellow squash and zucchini into very thin slices. Combine with the onion, celery and tomato in a bowl and mix well. Add the Vegetable Marinade and toss to coat well. Marinate, covered, in the refrigerator for 2 to 12 hours. Drain the marinade to serve.

Serves 8

Vegetable Marinade

1/3 cup canola oil or extra-light olive oil
2/3 cup cider vinegar
1/2 cup sugar
2 garlic cloves, crushed
1 teaspoon freshly ground pepper

Combine the canola oil, vinegar, sugar, garlic and pepper in a bowl and mix well.

Makes 1 cup

Acorn Squash with Cranberries

No fat and delicious—not just for the holidays.

2 small acorn squash
1¹/₂ cups fresh cranberries
¹/₄ cup water
¹/₂ cup sugar
¹/₈ to ¹/₄ teaspoon coriander, or ¹/₈ teaspoon cinnamon

Cut the acorn squash into halves, discarding the seeds. Place cut side down in a microwave-safe dish. Microwave on High for 8 minutes or until tender.

Combine the cranberries with the water and sugar in a saucepan and cook over medium heat until the cranberries are tender and begin to pop. Stir in the coriander and adjust the sugar if necessary.

Place the squash cut side up in a baking dish and spoon the cranberry mixture into the cavities. Bake at 350 degrees for 10 minutes.

You may add chopped apple or orange to the cranberries if desired.

Serves 4

Rosemary and Garlic Yams

5 sweet potatoes, peeled
10 garlic cloves, crushed
¹/₄ cup olive oil
¹/₂ tablespoon rosemary
¹/₄ teaspoon salt
¹/₈ teaspoon pepper

Cut the sweet potatoes into 1-inch slices and cut each slice into quarters. Combine with the garlic, olive oil, rosemary, salt and pepper in a shallow baking pan and stir to coat well. Bake at 450 degrees for 30 minutes or until the sweet potatoes are tender, stirring every 10 minutes.

Serves 8

Sweet Potato Puff

A Thanksgiving tradition that everyone enjoys.

3 cups cooked and mashed sweet potatoes, or
     1 (40-ounce) can sweet potatoes, drained and mashed
1/2 cup (1 stick) butter, melted
2 eggs
1 cup sugar
1 teaspoon pumpkin pie spice
1 teaspoon vanilla extract
1 cup drained crushed pineapple
1/2 cup raisins
Pecan Topping (below)

Combine the sweet potatoes with the butter, eggs, sugar, pumpkin pie spice and vanilla in a bowl and mix well. Stir in the pineapple and raisins. Spoon into a greased baking dish.

Sprinkle the Pecan Topping over the sweet potatoes. Bake at 325 degrees for 30 minutes or until golden brown.

Serves 8

Pecan Topping

    1 cup packed brown sugar
    1/3 cup White Lily flour
    1/3 cup butter, melted
    1 cup chopped pecans

Mix the brown sugar, flour, butter and pecans in a bowl until crumbly.

Serves 8

Notable

Senator Bill Frist, M.D., born and raised in Nashville, is a fourth-generation Tennessean whose great-great-grandfather was one of Chattanooga's original founders. After completing medical training both here and abroad, Dr. Frist joined the teaching faculty at Vanderbilt University Medical Center in 1985. He founded and directed the Vanderbilt Transplant Center, which became, under his leadership, a world-renowned center for multi-organ transplantation. In 1994 Dr. Frist became Senator Frist and the first practicing physician elected to the Senate since 1928. Having saved many lives during his private practice, Senator Frist put his medical training to good use when he revived a tourist who had suffered a heart attack during a visit to the capitol.

Roasted Root Vegetables

An Herb Society luncheon favorite, this unusual and flavorful dish is especially nice for large fall and winter gatherings. Serve with red wine, and don't be intimidated by the sweet and delicious parsnips!

2 parsnips
4 large or 6 medium carrots
2 sweet potatoes, with or without skins
2 small yellow onions
2 small red onions
1 head garlic
4 small red potatoes, with or without skins
1 to 2 tablespoons extra-virgin olive oil
pepper to taste
2 teaspoons tomato paste
1/4 cup water
2 large sprigs of fresh rosemary
3 sprigs of fresh thyme

Soak a clay baker in cold water for 30 minutes. Cut the parsnips, carrots and sweet potatoes into similar sizes and shapes. Cut the onions into quarters. Separate the garlic into cloves, but do not peel. Combine the prepared vegetables with the potatoes, olive oil and pepper in a large bowl and mix well.

Spoon the vegetables into the clay baker. Mix the tomato paste with the water in a small bowl. Pour over the vegetables. Add the rosemary and thyme. Cover the baker and place in an unheated oven; place a large pan or baking sheet below the baker to prevent spills in the oven.

Set the oven at 425 degrees and bake for 1 hour or until the vegetables are tender, basting after 30 minutes. Serve in the cooking juices.

You may bake the vegetables in a large roasting pan covered with foil if you do not have a clay baker.

Serves 8

Golden Curried Couscous

1 small onion, finely chopped
2 tablespoons olive oil
2 garlic cloves, minced
1 teaspoon curry powder
cayenne pepper to taste
1 1/2 cups chicken broth
1 cup uncooked couscous
1/4 cup golden raisins
1/4 cup toasted slivered almonds or pine nuts

Sauté the onion in the heated olive oil in a medium skillet over medium heat for 10 minutes or until tender. Add the garlic, curry powder and cayenne pepper and cook until the garlic is tender. Let cool for 3 to 4 minutes.

Bring the chicken broth to a boil in a medium saucepan. Stir in the couscous and raisins and remove from the heat. Cover and let stand for 5 minutes or until the chicken broth is absorbed.

Fluff the couscous with a fork and add the onion mixture and almonds. Adjust the seasoning. Serve warm.

Serves 4

Couscous with Peas and Feta Cheese

1½ cups water
1 cup uncooked couscous
¼ cup olive oil
1 tablespoon fresh lemon juice
1 teaspoon grated lemon zest
⅛ teaspoon Tabasco sauce

¾ teaspoon salt
¼ purple onion, thinly sliced
¾ cup frozen green peas, thawed
½ cup crumbled feta cheese
¼ cup chopped fresh mint
2 tablespoons toasted pine nuts

Bring the water to a boil in a saucepan and stir in the couscous. Remove from the heat and let stand, covered, for 10 minutes.

Combine the olive oil, lemon juice, lemon zest, Tabasco sauce and salt in a large bowl and whisk until smooth. Add the couscous and mix with a fork. Add the onion, peas, feta cheese and mint and toss to mix well.

Chill, covered, for 2 hours or longer. Stir in the pine nuts just before serving.

Serves 4

Polenta with Green Chiles

2 cups milk
1 cup water
¾ cup yellow cornmeal
2 garlic cloves, minced
1 teaspoon salt
½ cup freshly grated Parmesan cheese
pepper to taste

2 (4-ounce) cans chopped green chiles,
    drained
⅔ cup chopped fresh cilantro
8 ounces (2 cups) shredded Monterey
    Jack cheese
¼ cup whipping cream

Combine the milk and water in a medium saucepan. Whisk in the cornmeal, garlic and salt. Cook over medium heat for 10 minutes or until the water is absorbed and the mixture thickens, whisking constantly. Remove from the heat and whisk in the Parmesan cheese and pepper; adjust the salt if necessary.

Layer the cornmeal mixture, green chiles, cilantro and Monterey Jack cheese ½ at a time in a greased 8×8-inch baking dish. Pour the whipping cream over the layers. Bake at 400 degrees for 25 to 30 minutes or until puffed and golden brown. Cut into squares to serve.

Serves 9

Wild Rice Dressing

Authentic American fare.

1 (6-ounce) package wild rice
4 cups water
1¹/2 cups chopped pecans
1 cup chopped onion
1 cup chopped celery
¹/2 cup (1 stick) butter
8 ounces mushrooms, sliced
salt and pepper to taste

Rinse and drain the wild rice. Combine with the water in a 3-quart saucepan and bring to a boil. Reduce the heat and simmer, loosely covered, for 45 to 60 minutes or until the rice is tender; drain any remaining water.

Sprinkle the pecans into a skillet and cook over low heat until toasted. Sauté the onion and celery in the butter in a large saucepan until tender. Add the mushrooms, salt and pepper and sauté for 5 minutes longer. Stir in the wild rice and pecans.

Spoon into a baking dish and bake at 350 degrees for 20 minutes or until heated through.

You should serve this dish within 2 hours of preparing it to preserve the crunchiness of the pecans.

Serves 8 to 10

Cultural

The Carl Van Vechten Gallery of Fine Arts at Fisk University opened in 1949 and was named for Carl Van Vechten, president of Fisk's Fine Arts Commission in the 1940s and 1950s. A photographer, novelist, art critic, and philanthropist, Van Vechten was also a friend of American artist Georgia O'Keefe and her husband, photographer Alfred Stieglitz. Their friendship led to the donation by O'Keefe of a portion of her late husband's art collection, the Alfred Stieglitz Collection of Modern Art. This permanent exhibit is showcased in Gallery 2, while Gallery 1 houses traveling and temporary art exhibits. In addition to works by O'Keefe and Stieglitz, the Van Vechten Gallery also houses a variety of works by masters such as Renoir, Picasso, and Cezanne, and African-American artists Jacob Lawrence, Aaron Douglas, and Stephanie Pogue.

Wild Mushroom and Sausage Stuffing

8 ounces bulk pork sausage
1/2 cup (1 stick) margarine
1 large onion, chopped
1 bunch green onions, sliced
16 ounces chanterelle mushrooms, sliced
16 ounces shiitake mushrooms, sliced
16 ounces enoki mushrooms, sliced
2 cups chicken broth
1 (8-ounce) package herb-flavor stuffing mix
1 tablespoon chopped fresh thyme, or 1 teaspoon dried thyme
1 tablespoon chopped fresh sage, or 1 teaspoon dried sage
1 tablespoon chopped fresh rosemary, or 1 teaspoon dried rosemary
salt and pepper to taste

Brown the sausage in a skillet, stirring until crumbly; drain. Melt the margarine in a large heavy saucepan. Add the onion and green onions and sauté until tender. Add the mushrooms and sauté until tender.

Add the sausage, chicken broth, stuffing mix, thyme, sage, rosemary, salt and pepper and mix well. Spoon into a greased 9×13-inch baking dish. Bake at 350 degrees for 45 to 60 minutes or until golden brown.

You may also stuff the mixture into a turkey to bake.

Serves 8 to 10

Fried Bananas

A great accompaniment for a spicy dish such as grilled Lime Pork Loin Chops on page 168.

4 firm bananas
1/3 cup strained fresh orange juice
1/3 cup yellow cornmeal
vegetable oil for deep-frying
1/2 teaspoon kosher salt or salt
hot sauce to taste

Cut the peeled bananas into 1/2-inch slices. Dip the slices into the orange juice and coat with the cornmeal. Heat 4 inches vegetable oil to 360 to 370 degrees in a deep fryer. Add the banana slices a few at a time and fry until golden brown; remove to a rack with a slotted spoon to drain and blot with paper towels. Sprinkle with the salt and hot sauce.

You may also serve this as an appetizer.

Serves 4

Cinnamon Pineapple

2 cups fresh pineapple chunks
1 cup pineapple juice
1/2 cup sugar
2 cinnamon sticks
10 whole cloves

Combine the pineapple, pineapple juice, sugar, cinnamon sticks and cloves in a saucepan and bring to a boil. Cook for 10 minutes. Chill, covered, for up to 12 hours. Drain the fruit, discarding the cinnamon and cloves. Serve chilled.

Serves 4

Entrées

Entrées

*The heart of any grand meal is the entrée
and the heart of Nashville is her music.
After all, Nashville is known as The Music City
with just cause. From the Ryman Auditorium and Music
Row, to Printer's Alley and Tootsie's Orchid Lounge,
Nashville resonates with her southern song.*

No trip to Nashville would be complete without visiting the
Country Music Hall of Fame. Located in the heart of downtown Nashville's
entertainment district, the Hall of Fame and Museum has a brand new
37-million-dollar state-of-the-art facility that provides visitors with the
opportunity to "Honor Thy Music" in a shrine-like setting. The Museum
houses rare music memorabilia and features multimedia touch screens
and listening stations, as well as three films commissioned especially
for the Hall of Fame.

Go from a state-of-the-art museum to a National Historic Landmark
when you visit the "Mother Church of Country Music," Nashville's Ryman
Auditorium. Built in 1892 by riverboat Captain Tom Ryman, the auditorium

became famous as a home to the Grand Ole Opry show in 1943. Although the show moved to its own facility in 1974, the Ryman remains one of the premier stages in the world of entertainment. After a major renovation in 1994, the Ryman has been beautifully preserved as a National Landmark. Widely renowned for its acoustic quality, which is said to be second only to that of the Mormon Tabernacle, the stage has hosted a veritable who's-who of entertainment legends, from W. C. Fields to Bob Dylan, Katherine Hepburn to Dolly Parton, and John Phillip Sousa to Bruce Springsteen. As diverse as the Ryman's performers, the sounds of the Music City run the gamut from Opry to Opera and Rhythm and Blues to Gospel.

While country music will always be the center stone, Nashville wears a variety of musical gems in her crown. Showcasing these gems is the Tennessee Performing Arts Center (TPAC) located in downtown Nashville. TPAC was dedicated in 1980 and built to serve as a home for the arts in Tennessee's capital. As downtown real estate is precious, the state agreed to share with the center a space that was already earmarked for state offices. With the valiant efforts of Nashville philanthropist Martha Ingram, the space went vertical, with the performance center at its base and the office space above. Inside the center is the Tennessee State Museum, as well as three varied theater spaces: Jackson Hall, Polk Theater, and Johnson Theater. These theaters serve as home to The Nashville Symphony, the Nashville Ballet, Circle Players, and the Nashville Opera Association. TPAC also hosts an annual series of Broadway Productions. A varied repertoire of performances by the Tennessee Repertory Theatre appears here as well. Visitors to TPAC can enjoy music and theater on a grand scale, or enjoy an intimate one-performer show. Whether you choose Country, Opera, Bluegrass, or Broadway (or anything in-between), Nashville is music to your ears.

Bourbon Beef Tenderloin

Bourbon Marinade
1 large yellow onion, chopped
2 large carrots, chopped
2 ribs celery, chopped
6 garlic cloves, chopped
2 tablespoons vegetable oil
1 cup bourbon
5 tablespoons tomato paste
2 cups chicken stock
2 cups beef stock
4 sprigs of fresh thyme
2 teaspoons pepper

Tenderloin
1 (4-pound) beef tenderloin, trimmed
1/2 cup White Lily flour
1 sprig of fresh rosemary, chopped
2 tablespoons pepper
1 tablespoon vegetable oil
2 tablespoons butter
1/4 cup White Lily flour

Garnish
parsley

To prepare the marinade, sauté the onion, carrots, celery and garlic in the vegetable oil in a 3-quart saucepan. Add the bourbon and bring to a simmer. Add the tomato paste, chicken stock, beef stock, thyme and pepper and mix well. Bring to a boil and remove from the heat. Cool and strain the mixture, reserving the vegetables and strained marinade. Store the vegetables and strained marinade in the refrigerator until time to reheat.

To prepare the tenderloin, combine the beef with the strained marinade in a shallow dish, turning to coat well. Marinate, covered, in the refrigerator for 8 hours or longer. Drain, reserving the marinade.

Mix 1/2 cup flour, rosemary and pepper together. Coat the tenderloin with the mixture. Brown on all sides in the vegetable oil in a roasting pan on the stovetop. Insert a meat thermometer into the thickest portion of the tenderloin and add 1/2 cup of the reserved marinade to the roasting pan. Roast at 325 degrees for 1 hour or to 145 degrees on the meat thermometer.

Melt the butter in a saucepan and blend in 1/4 cup flour. Cook until bubbly. Add 2 cups of the reserved marinade and cook until thickened, stirring constantly. Spoon into a serving bowl.

Reheat the reserved vegetables with a small amount of the reserved marinade in a saucepan. Slice the tenderloin as desired. Spoon the chutney of reserved vegetables into a serving bowl and place in the center of a serving platter. Arrange the sliced tenderloin around the vegetables and garnish with parsley. Serve with the gravy.

Serves 6

Salt-Encrusted Beef Tenderloin

2¹/2 cups White Lily flour
¹/4 cup mixed minced fresh herbs, such as rosemary, oregano,
    thyme and Italian parsley
1¹/2 cups kosher salt
2 tablespoons freshly ground pepper
2 egg whites
³/4 cup water
2 tablespoons olive oil
thicker end portion of 1 (1¹/2-pound) beef tenderloin, trimmed
¹/4 cup mixed minced fresh herbs
salt to taste

Mix the flour, ¹/4 cup mixed herbs, kosher salt and pepper in a large bowl. Beat the egg whites in a medium bowl just until foamy. Add 10 tablespoons of the water gradually, mixing well. Add to the flour mixture and mix with a wooden spoon until the mixture begins to form a ball. Knead for 4 minutes or until a firm moist dough forms, adding the 2 remaining tablespoons water if necessary for the desired consistency. Shape into a ball and wrap with plastic wrap. Let stand at room temperature for 4 to 24 hours.

Heat the olive oil in a large heavy skillet over medium-high heat. Add the beef and cook for 5 minutes or until brown on all sides; remove to a platter.

Roll the dough to a 10×13-inch rectangle on a lightly floured surface. Place the beef in the center of the rectangle and sprinkle with ¹/4 cup mixed herbs. Bring up the edges of the dough to enclose the beef completely and press the edges to seal. Place seam side down on a baking sheet. Insert a meat thermometer through the dough into the thickest portion of the beef.

Roast at 400 degrees for 25 minutes or to 120 degrees on the meat thermometer for rare. Let stand for 30 to 60 minutes; beef will continue to cook. Place the beef on a work surface; cut away and discard the crust. Cut the beef into thick slices and arrange on a serving platter. Sprinkle with salt to taste.

Serves 4

Notable

Martha Ingram was the 1999 recipient of the Association of Junior Leagues International Inc. (AJLI) Mary Harriman Award given for community leadership, which honors the founder of the Junior League. She has also served as the chairman of the boards of Ingram Industries and Vanderbilt University and has been a board member of TPAC, the Tennessee Repertory Theater, the Nashville Opera Association, and the Nashville Ballet. Her passion for a performing arts center in Tennessee began during her appointment to the advisory board of the Kennedy Center for the Performing Arts in 1972. This passion resulted TPAC and its endowment that has grown to $20 million. More than 100,000 school-children are brought every year to performances at TPAC as a result of the endowment. AJLI has said of her "Martha Ingram has demonstrated her love for her family, for the community, and for the Junior League through her tireless efforts to improve the quality of life and make Nashville a better place to live and work."

Meat Loaf Wellington

1 egg
1/2 cup milk
1 1/2 pounds ground beef
3 slices bread, crusts removed, torn
  into 1/4-inch pieces
1 cup peeled and chopped tomato
3/4 onion, chopped
1 cup chopped celery
1/2 cup pine nuts

1 teaspoon poultry seasoning
2 teaspoons salt
1/4 teaspoon pepper
2 sheets frozen puff pastry, thawed
1/2 cup sliced mushrooms
1/4 cup sliced green onions
4 ounces (1 cup) shredded Cheddar
  cheese
1 egg, beaten with 2 tablespoons water

Beat 1 egg with the milk in a large bowl. Add the ground beef, bread, tomato, onion, celery, pine nuts, poultry seasoning, salt and pepper; mix well. Shape into a loaf and place in a greased 5×9-inch loaf pan. Bake at 375 degrees for 1 1/4 hours. Cool and remove from the loaf pan.

Let the pastry stand at room temperature for 15 minutes. Shape the pastry into a ball and roll into a 12×18-inch rectangle on a lightly floured surface. Sauté the mushrooms in a nonstick skillet until tender. Combine the mushrooms, green onions and cheese in a bowl and mix well.

Spread the mushroom mixture in the center of the pastry. Place meat loaf on top. Bring up the edges of the pastry to enclose the meat loaf and topping completely. Brush the edges of the pastry with the egg wash and press to seal. Place seam side down on an ungreased baking sheet and brush the top and sides with the egg wash. Increase the oven temperature to 400 degrees. Bake for 30 to 40 minutes or until golden brown. Let stand for 10 minutes before slicing.

Serves 10 to 12

Leg of Lamb

1 garlic bulb, separated into cloves
1 (5-pound) boned leg of lamb, rolled
  and tied

1 cup dry vermouth
1/4 cup each fresh rosemary and thyme

Insert the garlic cloves into slits in the roast. Place in a shallow roasting pan and pour in the vermouth. Rub with the rosemary and thyme. Insert a meat thermometer into the thickest portion. Roast at 325 degrees for 20 minutes per pound or to 135 to 145 degrees on the meat thermometer for medium. Let rest for 10 minutes before carving.

Serves 10

Almond Pork Tenderloin Steaks

12 ounces pork tenderloin
1 teaspoon crumbled dried tarragon
1 teaspoon garlic salt
3 tablespoons butter
1 tablespoon White Lily flour
3/4 cup dry white wine
1 chicken bouillon cube, crushed
1 tablespoon Dijon mustard
1/4 cup whipping cream
1/2 cup toasted slivered almonds
1/4 cup sliced green onions

Cut the pork tenderloin into 1/2-inch steaks. Pound 1/8 to 1/4 inch thick between sheets of waxed paper. Rub with a mixture of the tarragon and garlic salt. Let stand for 1 hour.

Heat 1 tablespoon of the butter in a skillet. Add the pork in batches and cook for 3 to 4 minutes or until brown on both sides. Remove to a serving platter and keep warm.

Melt the remaining 2 tablespoons butter in the pan drippings in the skillet and stir in the flour. Cook until bubbly. Add the wine, chicken bouillon and Dijon mustard. Bring to a boil and cook for 1 minute or until thickened, stirring constantly. Stir in the cream and cook just until heated through; do not boil. Stir in 3/4 of the almonds and green onions. Spoon the sauce over the pork and top with the remaining almonds and green onions.

Serves 4

Nashville's Grand Ole Opry has helped bring the best of country music to the world since 1925. Originally known as the WSM Barn Dance, it was renamed the Grand Ole Opry three years later, and the legend began. The Opry airs on Friday and Saturday nights and is hosted by a mix of regular cast members and special guest hosts who vary from show to show. It features the best of live country and bluegrass, intermingled with down home comedy. After moving several times to accommodate the growing crowds, the Opry made its home at the Ryman Auditorium in 1943. Thirty years later the Opry outgrew the Ryman, and in 1974 it relocated to the Grand Ole Opry House, where it remains today. In country music, to play the Opry is to reach the top.

Mandarin Pork Roast

A good dish to make in advance for entertaining.

Pork Roast
2 tablespoons Dijon mustard
1 (4-pound) boneless pork loin
1/2 teaspoon garlic powder
1 teaspoon salt
1/4 teaspoon pepper

Orange Sauce
1 (11-ounce) can mandarin oranges
1/4 cup packed light brown sugar
1/4 cup vinegar
1 tablespoon soy sauce
1/2 cup water
1 chicken bouillon cube
2 tablespoons cornstarch
1 medium onion, chopped
1/3 cup chopped green bell pepper

To prepare the roast, spread the Dijon mustard over the pork and sprinkle with the garlic powder, salt and pepper. Place in a heavy roasting pan and insert a meat thermometer into the thickest portion. Roast at 325 degrees for 2 1/2 to 3 hours or to 170 degrees on the meat thermometer.

To prepare the sauce, drain the oranges, reserving the liquid. Combine the reserved liquid with the brown sugar, vinegar, soy sauce, water, bouillon cube, cornstarch and onion in a saucepan and mix well. Cook, covered, over medium heat until thickened and smooth, stirring constantly. Remove from the heat and stir in the bell pepper and oranges.

Spoon the orange sauce over the pork and roast, uncovered, for 30 minutes longer, basting occasionally. Slice to serve.

Serves 6 to 8

Glazed Ginger Pork Roast

An easy dish for entertaining. Just cook it ahead of time and serve it cold.

1/4 cup soy sauce
1/4 cup dry red or white wine
2 tablespoons honey
1 garlic clove, minced
1 tablespoon freshly grated gingerroot
1 (3-pound) boneless pork roast
3/4 cup currant jelly or apple jelly

Combine the soy sauce, wine, honey, garlic and ginger in a covered container and mix well. Add the pork roast and turn to coat well. Marinate, covered, in the refrigerator for 8 hours or longer, turning several times. Drain, reserving the marinade.

Place the pork on a rack in a shallow roasting pan and insert a meat thermometer into the thickest portion. Roast at 300 degrees for 2 hours or to 175 degrees on the meat thermometer, basting several times with the reserved marinade.

Combine 3 to 4 tablespoons of the reserved marinade with the jelly in a small saucepan. Cook over low heat until the jelly dissolves and the mixture is bubbly. Cool to room temperature.

Spoon the currant glaze over the pork and serve immediately or chill until serving time. Slice very thin when ready to serve and serve with sweet mustard and assorted breads.

Serves 8 to 10

ntertainment

Tootsie's Orchid Lounge is the infamous stomping ground of such country legends as Willie Nelson and Kris Kristofferson. It was featured in "Sweet Dreams," the movie about the life of Patsy Cline. Look for the purple neon sign as you stroll down Broadway.

Pork Tenderloin with Sautéed Peppers

Great for supper club or special guests.

Pork Tenderloin
1/2 green bell pepper, finely chopped
1 small onion, finely chopped
1 rib celery, finely chopped
1 tablespoon minced garlic
3 tablespoons margarine
1 tablespoon vegetable oil
1 teaspoon paprika
1 teaspoon dried thyme
1/2 teaspoon dry mustard
1 1/2 teaspoons salt
1 teaspoon cayenne pepper
2 teaspoons black pepper
4 pounds pork tenderloins

Sautéed Peppers
1/4 cup extra-virgin olive oil
2 tablespoons balsamic vinegar
1 red bell pepper, thinly sliced
1 yellow bell pepper, thinly sliced
1 orange bell pepper, thinly sliced
1 green bell pepper, thinly sliced
salt and pepper to taste

To prepare the pork, sauté the bell pepper, onion, celery and garlic in the margarine and vegetable oil in a large skillet until tender. Stir in the paprika, thyme, dry mustard, salt, cayenne pepper and black pepper.

Place the pork tenderloins fat side up on a work surface and cut several slits in each. Stuff the slits with some of the vegetable mixture and spread the remaining vegetable mixture over the surface of the pork.

Place the pork in a roasting pan and insert a meat thermometer into the thickest portion. Roast at 275 degrees for 1 1/2 hours or to 160 degrees on the meat thermometer. Increase the oven temperature to 425 degrees and roast for 15 minutes longer or until brown.

To prepare the peppers, heat the olive oil and balsamic vinegar in a large skillet. Add the red, yellow, orange and green peppers and sauté until tender-crisp. Season with salt and pepper. Spoon around the pork on a large platter to serve.

Serves 8 to 10

Fettuccini with Prosciutto and Bleu Cheese Sauce

1/2 cup pine nuts
2 (9-ounce) packages refrigerated fettuccini
1 cup crumbled bleu cheese
8 ounces cream cheese, chopped
1 1/2 cups half-and-half
6 ounces prosciutto, chopped
2 cups thinly sliced and packed fresh spinach
1/4 cup chopped fresh parsley
1/4 teaspoon salt
1/2 cup crumbled bleu cheese

Sprinkle the pine nuts in a single layer on a baking sheet. Bake at 350 degrees for 7 minutes or until toasted. Cook the pasta using the package directions; keep warm.

Combine 1 cup bleu cheese, cream cheese and half-and-half in a heavy saucepan. Cook over medium heat until the cheeses melt, stirring constantly until smooth.

Combine the pasta, prosciutto, spinach, parsley and salt in a large bowl and mix gently. Add the bleu cheese mixture and toss to coat well. Sprinkle with the pine nuts and 1/2 cup bleu cheese. Serve immediately.

You may substitute sun-dried tomatoes for the prosciutto for a vegetarian dish.

Serves 8

Notable

Nashville's Printer's Alley is home to the Nashville institution Hatch Show Print. Some call it art; some call it Americana. Call it what you will, but since the late 1800s, Hatch Show Print has been hammering out advertising posters in their signature style for an amazing variety of clients and venues. Simplistic images, clean lines, and balanced text, all from the distinct hand-carved woodblock process of letterpress printmaking, combine to form these brilliant prints. Entertainment was completely dependent on these show posters for successful advertising. But with the variety of media and technologies available today, the fact that Hatch Show Print is still around is a testament to its unique style. From Hank Williams and Louis Armstrong to Shania Twain and Bob Dylan to Nike and the Oxford University Press, the unique glimpse of yesterday provided by Hatch Show Print never loses its appeal.

Chicken Breasts Lombardy

Chicken

1 cup sliced fresh mushrooms
2 tablespoons butter or margarine
8 skinless boneless chicken breasts
1/3 cup White Lily flour
1/3 cup butter or margarine

Wine Sauce

1/2 cup marsala
1/3 cup chicken broth
1/4 teaspoon salt
1/8 teaspoon pepper
2 ounces (1/2 cup) shredded fontina
    cheese or mozzarella cheese
1/2 cup grated Parmesan cheese
1/4 cup chopped green onions

To prepare the chicken, sauté the mushrooms in 2 tablespoons butter in a large skillet until tender. Cut each chicken breast into halves lengthwise. Pound 1/8 inch thick between sheets of heavy-duty plastic wrap.

Coat the chicken lightly with the flour. Melt 1 to 2 tablespoons of the remaining butter in a large skillet over medium heat. Add the chicken to the skillet in batches and cook for 3 to 4 minutes on each side or until golden brown, adding additional butter to the skillet with each batch. Remove each batch to a lightly greased 9×13-inch baking dish, overlapping the edges if necessary; reserve the pan drippings. Sprinkle the mushrooms over the chicken.

To prepare the sauce, add the wine and chicken broth to the drippings in the skillet, stirring to deglaze the skillet. Bring to a boil and reduce the heat. Simmer for 8 minutes, stirring occasionally. Stir in the salt and pepper. Pour over the chicken.

Combine the fontina cheese, Parmesan cheese and green onions in a small bowl. Sprinkle over the chicken. Bake at 375 degrees for 20 minutes. Broil 6 inches from the heat source with the oven door partially open for 1 to 2 minutes or until golden brown.

Serves 8

Chicken with Sun-Dried Tomatoes and Artichokes

4 skinless boneless chicken breasts
1/2 teaspoon salt
1/4 cup White Lily flour
2 tablespoons olive oil
1/3 cup chablis or other white wine
1 1/2 teaspoons arrowroot or cornstarch
1 (14-ounce) can reduced-sodium chicken broth
1 (6-ounce) jar marinated artichoke hearts, drained
8 ounces oil-pack sun-dried tomatoes, drained
1 tablespoon chopped fresh parsley
freshly ground pepper to taste

Sprinkle the chicken with the salt and coat with the flour. Sauté in the heated olive oil in a large skillet for 3 to 4 minutes on each side or until cooked through and golden brown. Add the wine to the skillet and cook for 30 seconds. Remove the chicken to a plate and cover to keep warm.

Blend the arrowroot with 2 tablespoons of the chicken broth in a small bowl. Add the remaining chicken broth to the skillet, stirring to deglaze the skillet. Add the artichokes and sun-dried tomatoes and bring to a boil.

Stir in the arrowroot mixture and cook for 4 to 5 minutes or until thickened, stirring constantly. Pour the sauce over the chicken and sprinkle with the parsley and pepper.

Serves 4

If you're looking for a quiet evening of acoustic music at its best, go where the natives go—The Bluebird Café. Since 1982, Amy Kurland's Bluebird, located in Green Hills, has hosted a wide array of the area's songwriters, singers, and musicians in an intimate setting. While the food is tasty, it definitely takes a back seat to the music. "Writer's Night," "Open Mic," and "In The Round" performances are some of the best in town. Here you will find the famous, the almost famous, and the as-yet-unknown, all under the bright blue awning. Come experience the venue where legends are made, but "Shhhhhhhhhhhh"—no talking, please!

Chicken with Cherry Tomato Sauce

Great way to use up all those cute little tomatoes in the spring and summer. It's also pretty with a mixture of yellow pear tomatoes and grape tomatoes.

Chicken
4 skinless boneless chicken breasts
salt and pepper to taste
White Lily flour
1¹/2 tablespoons butter
1¹/2 tablespoons vegetable oil

Cherry Tomato Sauce
¹/4 cup minced onion
1¹/2 teaspoons ground cumin
¹/8 teaspoon ground red pepper
1 teaspoon sugar
2 tablespoons cider vinegar
6 tablespoons orange juice (juice of about 2 oranges)
1 tablespoon lime juice
1 cup cherry tomato halves
¹/4 cup chopped fresh cilantro
salt and freshly ground black pepper to taste

To prepare the chicken, pat the chicken dry, season generously with salt and pepper and coat with flour. Heat the butter and vegetable oil in a heavy skillet over medium-high heat until the foam subsides. Add the chicken and sauté until golden brown on both sides. Remove to a plate and cover to keep warm.

To prepare the sauce, add the onion, cumin and red pepper to the drippings in the skillet and sauté over medium heat until the spices are fragrant. Add the sugar and cook until the onion caramelizes, stirring constantly. Stir in the vinegar, orange juice and lime juice. Increase the heat and bring to a boil, scraping to deglaze the skillet. Add the tomatoes and cilantro and remove from the heat. Season with salt and black pepper. Spoon over the chicken and serve immediately.

Serves 4

Chicken Scaloppine

1/4 cup fine dry bread crumbs
1/4 cup grated Parmesan cheese
2 tablespoons chopped parsley
1 teaspoon salt
1/4 teaspoon pepper
1 egg
1 tablespoon water
4 skinless boneless chicken breasts
1/4 cup vegetable oil
2 tablespoons butter
8 fresh mushrooms, sliced
1/4 cup white wine
1 tablespoon lemon juice
1 tablespoon chopped parsley
hot cooked angel hair pasta

Garnish
lemon slices

Mix the bread crumbs, Parmesan cheese, 2 tablespoons parsley, salt and pepper in a bowl. Beat the egg with the water in a small bowl. Dip the chicken into the egg mixture, then coat with the bread crumb mixture.

Pound the chicken flat between sheets of plastic wrap. Sauté in the heated vegetable oil in a skillet over medium heat until brown on both sides. Remove to a plate and cover to keep warm.

Melt the butter in the drippings in the skillet and add the mushrooms. Sauté for 1 minute. Return the chicken to the skillet and add the wine and lemon juice; sprinkle with 1 tablespoon parsley. Simmer, covered, for 10 to 15 minutes or until cooked through.

Serve over pasta and garnish with lemon slices.

Serves 4

Notable

With the increasing popularity of artists such as Michael W. Smith, Steven Curtis Chapman, Yolanda Adams, and Sixpence None the Richer, gospel music has taken the country by storm. In 2001, gospel music sales rose an astonishing 13.5 percent, while the rest of the music industry declined. Gospel music, or contemporary Christian music, as some refer to it, finds its home in Nashville. The Gospel Music Association (GMA) has its headquarters here, as do the industry's largest labels: EMI Christian Music Group, Provident Music Group, and Word Entertainment. Many of the industry's most popular artists, such as Amy Grant, Newsboys, Jars of Clay, dcTalk, Steven Curtis Chapman, and Michael W. Smith, live right here in Davidson or neighboring Williamson County.

Chicken Paprikash

A great meal for cold nights and definitely worth the wait.

1 cup White Lily flour
2¼ teaspoons paprika
¼ teaspoon ginger
¼ teaspoon basil
nutmeg to taste
2½ teaspoons salt
¼ teaspoon cayenne pepper
¼ teaspoon black pepper
3 pounds chicken tenderloins
3 tablespoons butter

3 tablespoons vegetable oil
2½ cups chicken broth
2 cups sour cream
½ cup sherry
3 tablespoons chili sauce
2 tablespoons Worcestershire sauce
1 garlic clove, crushed
1 (8-ounce) can sliced water chestnuts,
    drained

Mix the flour with the paprika, ginger, basil, nutmeg, salt, cayenne pepper and black pepper in a shallow dish. Add the chicken to the flour mixture and turn to coat as heavily as possible. Brown the chicken on both sides in the heated butter and vegetable oil in a skillet. Remove the chicken to a 9×13-inch baking dish.

Add the chicken broth to the pan drippings, stirring to deglaze the skillet. Stir in the sour cream, sherry, chili sauce, Worcestershire sauce, garlic and water chestnuts. Cook until heated through. Spoon over the chicken.

Cover the chicken and bake at 325 degrees for 1 hour or until cooked through. Serve with rice.

Serves 8

Linguini Chicken and Oranges

The squeeze of orange juice adds a surprising dimension to the simple flavors of this dish.

1/2 cup (1 stick) butter
1 medium onion, thinly sliced
2 garlic cloves, minced
1 tablespoon shredded fresh basil
3/4 teaspoon crushed dried red pepper flakes
8 chicken thighs (2 to 2 1/2 pounds)
8 ounces uncooked linguini
2 (10-ounce) packages frozen chopped spinach, thawed and
*   drained*
1 cup grated Parmesan cheese
1 small orange, cut into 4 wedges

Melt the butter in a 12×15-inch baking pan in a 400-degree oven. Stir the onion, garlic, basil and pepper flakes into the butter. Arrange the chicken skin side up in the prepared pan. Bake at 400 degrees for 45 minutes or until well browned; remove to a plate and cover to keep warm.

Cook the linguini in 4 inches boiling water in a 3- to 4-quart saucepan for 10 minutes or until al dente; drain and keep warm.

Add the spinach to the liquid in the baking pan, stirring to deglaze the pan. Add the linguini and Parmesan cheese, tossing to mix well.

Spoon the pasta onto serving plates and top each serving with 2 pieces of chicken. Add an orange wedge to each plate to squeeze over the chicken and pasta.

Serves 4

Culinary

To cook 8 ounces of pasta al dente, add it to 6 cups of boiling water and 4 teaspoons salt. Cook it for 2 minutes, stirring to separate, and remove it from the heat to stand, covered, for 10 minutes. Rinse and drain well to serve. A good rule of thumb is that macaroni will double in volume when cooked, but noodles increase by 1/3.

Chicken and Mushroom Crepes

1 cup shiitake or other wild
    mushrooms
5 tablespoons butter
6 tablespoons White Lily flour
1 cup chicken broth, heated
1½ cups half-and-half, heated
salt to taste

1 teaspoon hot pepper sauce
¼ cup sherry
2 cups chopped cooked chicken
1 tablespoon minced onion
Crepes (below)
grated Parmesan cheese
sliced almonds

Sauté the mushrooms in 1 tablespoon of the butter in a skillet; remove with a slotted spoon. Melt the remaining 4 tablespoons butter in the skillet. Blend in the flour and cook for 5 minutes, stirring frequently. Stir in the chicken broth and half-and-half. Cook until thickened, stirring constantly.

Stir in the salt, hot sauce and sherry. Add the chicken, onion and sautéed mushrooms and mix well.

Spoon 1 spoonful of the chicken mixture into the center of each crepe and roll to enclose the filling. Arrange the filled crepes in a baking dish. Spoon the remaining chicken mixture over the top and sprinkle with Parmesan cheese. Broil just until golden brown and sprinkle with almonds.

Serves 4 to 6

Crepes

1 cup White Lily flour
salt to taste
3 eggs
¾ cup milk

3 tablespoons heavy cream
1 tablespoon butter, melted
vegetable oil

Mix the flour and salt in a mixing bowl. Add the eggs, milk, cream and butter and mix until smooth. Heat a small crepe pan or cast-iron skillet and wipe lightly with vegetable oil. Spoon in just enough batter to form a very thin layer, tilting the pan to spread evenly.

Cook until light brown on the bottom and turn to brown the other side. Repeat the process with the remaining batter, stacking the crepes between layers of waxed paper.

Serves 4 to 6

Italian Fried Chicken

Serve this with a pasta salad and sautéed zucchini and summer squash sprinkled with Parmesan cheese for a simple and pretty luncheon or supper.

4 skinless boneless chicken breasts
1 egg
1 cup Italian bread crumbs or seasoned bread crumbs
2 to 3 tablespoons olive oil
1 garlic clove, crushed

Pound the chicken flat between sheets of plastic wrap with a meat mallet. Dip in the egg, then coat with the bread crumbs. Heat the olive oil with the garlic in a skillet. Add the chicken and sauté for 5 to 7 minutes or until golden brown and cooked through, turning once.

Serves 4

Chicken and Vegetable Pasta

A great dish for a busy day. Serve with bread and a salad.

1 teaspoon olive oil
2 garlic cloves, minced
6 ounces (or more) boneless chicken, cut into bite-size pieces
1/2 cup frozen green peas, thawed
1/3 cup shredded carrot
1/2 cup chicken broth
2 tablespoons cream cheese
2 cups cooked farfalle
3 tablespoons grated Parmesan cheese
1/2 teaspoon grated lemon zest
1/8 teaspoon salt
1/8 teaspoon pepper

Heat a skillet sprayed with nonstick cooking spray over medium heat and add the olive oil. Add the garlic and sauté for 15 seconds. Add the chicken and sauté for 1 minute. Stir in the peas and carrot and sauté for 1 minute. Remove from the heat.

Combine the chicken broth and cream cheese in a saucepan and cook over medium heat for 3 minutes or until the cream cheese melts, whisking to blend well. Add the chicken mixture, pasta, Parmesan cheese, lemon zest, salt and pepper and mix well. Cook for 1 minute. Serve with additional Parmesan cheese.

You may use low-fat or fat-free cream cheese for a lighter version of this dish.

Serves 4

Red Snapper with Toasted Pecan Butter

1/2 cup White Lily flour
4 teaspoons paprika
2 teaspoons garlic powder
1/4 teaspoon thyme
1 1/2 teaspoons salt
1/4 teaspoon ground red pepper
4 red snapper fillets
1/2 cup milk
1/4 cup peanut oil
2/3 cup chopped pecans
1/8 teaspoon white pepper
1/8 teaspoon ground red pepper
1/4 cup (1/2 stick) butter
1 tablespoon fresh lemon juice
2 tablespoons finely chopped parsley

Mix the flour, paprika, garlic powder, thyme, salt and 1/4 teaspoon red pepper in a bowl. Dip the fish fillets in the milk and coat with the flour mixture.

Heat the peanut oil in a 12-inch skillet and add the fish fillets. Cook for 6 minutes or until golden brown on both sides, turning once. Remove to serving plates and keep warm.

Toss the pecans with the white pepper and 1/8 teaspoon red pepper. Cook in the heated butter in a skillet for 3 minutes or until toasted. Remove from the heat and stir in the lemon juice and parsley. Spoon over the fish fillets. Serve immediately.

Serves 4

Culinary

Remember the following fish substitutions when the fish called for in your recipe is not available.

Flounder: sole, yellowtail, turbot, lemon sole

Pompano: red snapper, redfish, bluefish, mackerel, halibut, turbot

Redfish: broiled sole, striped bass, brook trout, whitefish, baked haddock, swordfish, turbot, red snapper

Red snapper: yellowtail, gray snapper

Speckled trout: bass, brook trout, perch, scampi

Crab Cakes with Spicy Thai Emerald Sauce

16 ounces cooked crab meat
1/4 cup minced red onion
2 tablespoons minced red bell pepper
2 large eggs, beaten
1 cup sourdough bread crumbs
1/4 cup chopped fresh cilantro
1/2 teaspoon Tabasco sauce

2 teaspoons black sesame seeds, toasted
1/4 teaspoon allspice
1/2 teaspoon salt
1/4 teaspoon white pepper
olive oil or vegetable oil for frying
Spicy Thai Emerald Sauce (below)

Flake the crab meat and pulse in the food processor 2 or 3 times to chop. Combine with the onion, bell pepper, eggs, bread crumbs, cilantro, Tabasco sauce, sesame seeds, allspice, salt and white pepper in a bowl and mix well.

Shape by 1/4 cupfuls into patties. Fry in 1/4 inch hot olive oil in a skillet until golden brown on both sides. Serve immediately with the Spicy Thai Emerald Sauce.

You may prepare the patties in advance, freeze on a baking sheet sprayed with nonstick cooking spray and store in sealable plastic bags in the freezer until time to fry and serve.

Serves 6 to 8

Spicy Thai Emerald Sauce

5 tablespoons lime juice
1 tablespoon fish sauce
2 1/2 tablespoons loosely packed
   chopped cilantro

2 or 3 small Thai chiles, thinly sliced
6 garlic cloves, coarsely chopped
1/4 cup packed brown sugar

Combine the lime juice, fish sauce, cilantro, chiles, garlic and brown sugar in a blender and process until smooth. Spoon into a serving dish.

Serves 6 to 8

Bourbon-Glazed Salmon

6 tablespoons bourbon
1 cup packed brown sugar
1/4 cup reduced-sodium soy sauce
2 tablespoons lime juice
2 garlic cloves, crushed
2 teaspoons ginger
1/2 teaspoon salt
1/4 teaspoon pepper
8 (6-ounce) salmon fillets
4 teaspoons sesame seeds
1/2 cup thinly sliced green onions

Combine the bourbon, brown sugar, soy sauce, lime juice, garlic, ginger, salt and pepper in a large sealable plastic bag. Add the salmon fillets and seal the bag, turning to coat the salmon well. Marinate in the refrigerator for 30 minutes, turning once. Drain, discarding the marinade.

Arrange the salmon fillets on a rack sprayed with nonstick cooking spray in a broiler pan. Broil for 11 minutes or until the fish flakes easily when tested with a fork. Sprinkle with the sesame seeds and green onions and serve immediately.

Serves 8

Occasions

Nashville is a celebrity town with plenty of opportunities for stargazing, but none so unique and personal as Fan Fair. Each summer Music City gets a star-studded kick-off in June when fans get a chance to enjoy good food, great music, and a chance to get an autograph and a photo snapped with some of the industry's greats. The brainchild of the Country Music Association (CMA) and the Grand Ole Opry, Fan Fair was created in 1972 as a benefit for the Country Music industry, its fans, the artists, and the artists' favorite charities. The net proceeds are divided, with half going to the CMA, which uses the funds for the advancement and development of country music, research, the Hall of Fame, and many other arenas. The other half goes to charities, which are chosen by the artists who participate. The celebrities love the venue, for it is a rare opportunity to get up close and personal with the people who helped make their careers. The fans . . . well, they just can't seem to get enough.

Martini Scallops

1/4 cup olive oil
2 pounds sea scallops
1 tablespoon minced shallot
2 large garlic cloves, minced
1/4 cup dry vermouth
1/4 cup vodka
1/2 cup slivered and drained sun-dried
    tomatoes

1/8 teaspoon cayenne pepper
1 cup cream
1/2 teaspoon salt
1/2 teaspoon black pepper
hot cooked rice or angel hair pasta

Heat the olive oil in a large saucepan and add the scallops. Sauté for 2 to 3 minutes or until opaque; remove with a slotted spoon.

Add the shallot and garlic to the saucepan and sauté for 3 minutes. Stir in the vermouth, vodka, sun-dried tomatoes and cayenne pepper. Cook over high heat for 5 to 10 minutes or until reduced to a syrupy consistency. Stir in the cream, salt and black pepper.

Return the scallops to the sauce and cook for 1 minute or until heated through. Serve over rice or pasta.

Serves 4 to 6

Oven-Baked Shrimp Stroganoff

8 ounces uncooked medium egg
    noodles
8 ounces (1 cup) sour cream or
    reduced-fat sour cream
1 (10-ounce) can cream of mushroom
    soup

1 pound cooked and peeled shrimp
1/4 cup sliced green onions
1 teaspoon dried dill
4 ounces (1 cup) shredded Cheddar
    cheese

Cook the noodles using the package directions; drain. Combine the sour cream, soup, shrimp, green onions, dill and half the Cheddar cheese in a bowl and mix well. Add the noodles and mix gently.

Spoon into a greased shallow 2-quart baking dish. Bake, covered, at 350 degrees for 30 minutes. Sprinkle with the remaining 1/2 cup cheese and bake, uncovered, for 5 minutes longer.

Serves 6 to 8

Shrimp and Feta Pasta alla Grecque

1 pound unpeeled shrimp
1 package crab boil
salt to taste
8 ounces feta cheese, drained and coarsely crumbled
1 cup sliced scallions
1 cup tomato sauce
1/2 cup olive oil
1/4 cup fresh lemon juice
1 tablespoon chopped fresh parsley
1 tablespoon chopped fresh basil
1 tablespoon chopped fresh dill
1/2 teaspoon salt
1/4 teaspoon pepper
16 ounces uncooked fettuccini or other flat pasta

Bring a large saucepan of water to a boil and add the shrimp, crab boil and salt. Cook for 5 minutes; drain. Cool and peel the shrimp.

Combine the shrimp with the feta cheese and scallions in a large bowl. Add the tomato sauce, olive oil, lemon juice, parsley, basil, dill, 1/2 teaspoon salt and pepper and mix well. Chill, covered, for 1 hour.

Cook the pasta using the package directions; drain. Add to the shrimp mixture and toss to mix well.

Remember that overcooked seafood becomes tough. Cooked shellfish can be frozen, but reheat just to serving temperature to prevent it from becoming mushy or tough.

Serves 6

Pasta with Artichokes

A great picnic dish.

3 or 4 garlic cloves, chopped
1/2 teaspoon red pepper flakes
1 teaspoon salt
2 tablespoons olive oil
2 (6-ounce) jars marinated artichoke hearts
1 medium onion, chopped
1 (28-ounce) can crushed tomatoes
1 teaspoon dried basil
1 teaspoon dried oregano
16 ounces uncooked penne, rotini or ziti
1/3 cup grated Parmesan cheese

Sauté the garlic, red pepper flakes and salt in the olive oil in a 10- or 12-inch skillet over medium heat for 3 to 4 minutes or until the garlic is tender. Drain the artichokes, reserving the liquid. Add the reserved liquid and onion to the skillet and cook for 10 minutes or until the onion is translucent, stirring frequently.

Add the tomatoes and bring to a simmer. Simmer over low heat for 20 minutes, stirring occasionally. Add the artichokes, basil and oregano and cook for 10 minutes.

Cook the pasta using the package directions; drain. Add to the skillet with the Parmesan cheese. Cook until heated through and the flavors blend. Serve immediately or chill until serving time and serve at room temperature.

Serves 6

Creamy Penne Pomodoro

Add cooked shrimp or chicken for a one-dish meal.

16 ounces uncooked penne
coarse salt to taste
2 tablespoons olive oil
1 to 2 teaspoons minced garlic
3 or 4 fresh basil leaves, slivered, or 1 teaspoon dried basil
4 cups chopped tomatoes
salt and freshly ground pepper to taste
1/2 cup heavy cream
3/4 cup freshly grated Parmesan cheese

Cook the pasta al dente with coarse salt to taste in boiling water in a saucepan; drain and keep warm.

Heat a skillet over medium heat for 1 minute. Add the olive oil and heat for several seconds. Add the garlic, basil and tomatoes and sauté for 8 minutes, stirring frequently. Season with salt and pepper. Remove from the heat and stir in the cream.

Combine the tomato mixture with the pasta in a large bowl and toss to mix well. Sprinkle with the Parmesan cheese.

Serves 6

Culinary

For a variation on penne pasta toss with Pesto. To prepare Pesto, combine 2 cups loosely packed fresh basil leaves, 2 medium garlic cloves, 3/4 to 1 cup extra-virgin olive oil, 6 tablespoons unsalted butter and 1 teaspoon salt with 3 ounces pine nuts, walnuts or pecans in a food processor and process until smooth. Serve immediately or store in the refrigerator or freezer. You may freeze the Pesto in muffin cups if desired and remove the amount needed. Serve with pasta, shrimp or chicken.

Four Fabulous Chutneys

Add chutney to wild rice to dress up a standard side dish to serve with pork tenderloin. These are favorites from Encore.

2 lemons, finely chopped and seeded
2 garlic cloves, minced
6 cups peeled and chopped apples or pears
8 ounces raisins
2¼ cups packed brown sugar
2 cups cider vinegar
¾ cup chopped crystallized ginger, or 2 teaspoons ground ginger
1½ teaspoons salt
¼ teaspoon cayenne pepper

Combine the lemons, garlic, apples, raisins, brown sugar, vinegar, ginger, salt and cayenne pepper in a large saucepan. Cook until the fruit is very tender, adding water if necessary for the desired consistency. Spoon into hot sterilized jars, leaving ½ inch headspace. Seal with 2-piece lids.

Makes 4 pints

For Fresh Tomato Chutney, combine 1 cup chopped tomato, ½ cup chopped green bell pepper, ¼ cup chopped red bell pepper, ¼ cup chopped onion and ½ cup lemon juice in a bowl. Let stand at room temperature for 1 hour, stirring frequently. Makes 2½ cups.

For Mango Chutney, combine 5 pounds sliced green mangoes, 2 chopped large onions, 2 chopped green bell peppers, 1 peeled and chopped lime, 1 cup seedless raisins and 2 minced garlic cloves in a large saucepan. Add 4 ounces chopped crystallized ginger, 3 cups packed brown sugar, 4 cups white wine vinegar, 1 tablespoon cinnamon, 1 teaspoon ground cloves, 1 teaspoon allspice, 2 teaspoons salt and ¼ teaspoon cayenne pepper and mix well. Bring to a boil and simmer for 1 hour, stirring frequently. Seal in jars as above. Makes 6 pints.

For Peach Chutney, grind 4 pounds chopped peaches, 1 cup chopped crystallized ginger and 8 ounces seedless raisins in a meat grinder or blender. Combine with ¼ cup chopped onion, 1½ pounds sugar, 3 cups tarragon vinegar, 2 tablespoons mustard seeds, 1 tablespoon chili powder and 1 tablespoon salt in a large saucepan. Bring to a boil and simmer for 2 to 3 hours or until the desired consistency. Seal in jars as above. Makes 6 pints.

Avocado Sauce

1 medium avocado
1 or 2 garlic cloves
1 tablespoon chopped fresh cilantro
1/2 cup olive oil
1/4 cup canola oil
1/4 cup reduced-fat sour cream
1/4 cup fresh orange juice
2 tablespoons lime juice
2 tablespoons red wine vinegar
salt and pepper to taste

Combine the avocado, garlic, cilantro, olive oil, canola oil, sour cream, orange juice, lime juice, vinegar, salt and pepper in a blender and process at high speed until smooth and creamy. Serve immediately to prevent separation. Serve with grilled chicken or fish.

Serves 4

Blender Hollandaise Sauce

3 egg yolks
2 tablespoons fresh lemon juice
1/2 cup (1 stick) butter or margarine, chopped, softened
1/2 teaspoon salt
1/8 teaspoon pepper
1/2 cup boiling water

Combine the egg yolks, lemon juice, butter, salt and pepper in a blender and process until smooth. Add the boiling water gradually, processing constantly. Pour into a double boiler and cook over hot water until thickened, stirring constantly.

Makes 1 cup

Grilling and Game

Grilling and Game

With fourteen lakes in Middle Tennessee,
catfish, smallmouth bass, trout, and sunfish are just a
few of the catches available to fishermen of all ages and
skills in the Nashville area. Over twenty state parks
located within easy driving distance provide Nashville
residents and visitors with many outdoor opportunities.
From rock climbing to caving, from hunting
to nature photography, and from biking to boating,
if it has to do with nature, you can find it here.

The Metro Parks System is comprised of 92 parks and covers over 9,200 acres. The largest of Nashville's municipal parks are the Warner Parks. Separated only by Old Hickory Boulevard, the Percy Warner and Edwin Warner Parks encompass over 2,680 acres. Found within the Warner Parks system is Nashville's oldest model airplane flying field and the Warner Park Nature Center, which has a full schedule of programs for children and adults alike. Area outdoor enthusiasts also enjoy traditional park

amenities such as two public golf courses, miles of horseback riding and jogging trails, baseball diamonds, and picnic shelters.

Several portions of the historic Natchez Trace Parkway are also located within the Warner Parks' boundaries. The 445-mile trail was used for hundreds of years as a main artery of transportation—first for wildlife roving between salt licks, next for the Native Americans moving along a southwest-to-northeast route, and then for the 1800s' boatmen traveling between their Nashville area homes and the Mississippi River, where they floated downstream to Natchez or New Orleans to sell crops and goods. Today, "the Trace" is a popular destination spot for dedicated bicyclists, equestrians, and picnic lovers alike.

Picnicking of a different sort, also known as tailgating, takes place in the parking lots around the area, including Vanderbilt University's Dudley Field and the coliseum, home to the Tennessee Titans and the Tennessee State University Tigers. Aficionados come early and stay late to make the most of their team's efforts in battle. Here, tailgate parties come in every shape and size, and you'll find a beach towel and a cooler for two in the back of a pickup truck right next to linen tablecloths and fine china in antique wicker baskets ready to serve a party of twelve. From a bucket of juicy fried chicken to a fire-grilled perfectly marinated flank steak, all flavors and varieties of food are welcomed with open arms and big appetites. From the novice weekend burger flipper to the expert chef de barbeque, Nashville tailgaters have their grills fired up!

Grilled Sage Polenta

1³/₄ cups chicken broth
1³/₄ cups water
³/₄ cup uncooked polenta
1 teaspoon minced garlic
¹/₃ cup chopped fresh sage
1 ounce (¹/₄ cup) shredded Monterey Jack cheese
1 ounce (¹/₄ cup) grated Parmesan cheese

Bring the chicken broth and water to a boil in a saucepan. Add the polenta, garlic and sage. Cook until thickened, stirring frequently. Stir in the cheeses and remove from the heat. Spoon the mixture into a loaf pan lined with waxed paper. Chill for 8 hours or longer.

Invert the polenta onto a cutting board and cut into 1/2-inch slices. Cut holes in a large sheet of foil and place on a grill rack over very hot coals. Arrange the polenta slices on the foil and grill for 2 minutes on each side.

You may also cook in 2 tablespoons heated vegetable oil or olive oil in a skillet for 5 minutes on each side or until golden brown.

Serves 6

Grilled Rustic Bread

1 loaf rustic Italian bread
3 tablespoons olive oil
3 tablespoons butter
4 garlic cloves, cut into halves
1/2 teaspoon Tabasco sauce

Cut the bread into 1/2-inch slices. Heat the olive oil and butter in a saucepan over low heat. Add the garlic and Tabasco sauce. Cook just until the garlic is tender, stirring frequently.

Spread the mixture on the bread slices. Place on a grill rack. Grill over medium indirect heat until each side is lightly toasted.

Serves 8

Wild Duck Gumbo

3 large ducks
2 small onions, cut into quarters
3 ribs celery, cut into halves
3 links smoked sausage, sliced
1 cup vegetable oil
1 cup White Lily flour
2 onions, chopped
2 green bell peppers, chopped
3 ribs celery, chopped
6 to 8 teaspoons chopped garlic

Combine ducks with the onion quarters, large celery pieces and enough water to cover in a large saucepan. Cook for 2 to 3 hours or until the meat is falling from the bones. Strain and reserve the broth. Let the ducks stand until cool and cut the meat into bite-size pieces, discarding the skin and bones.

Brown the sausage in a large saucepan; remove the sausage with a slotted spoon. Add the vegetable oil to the drippings in the saucepan and blend in the flour. Cook for 45 minutes or until medium-dark brown, stirring constantly; do not burn.

Add the chopped onions and cook until tender. Add the bell peppers, chopped celery and garlic and cook for 10 minutes or until tender, stirring constantly; mixture will be thick.

Stir in the duck broth, duck meat and sausage. Simmer for 1 hour. Garnish with thinly sliced green onions.

You may need to add a small amount of additional flour to adjust for the fact that the sausage drippings are being used in addition to the vegetable oil.

Serves 8

Historical

Radnor Lake first came into private use in 1914 to provide water for the engines and livestock of the Louisville and Nashville Railroad Company at Radnor Yards. When migrating birds began to include the lake on their annual journey, the Tennessee Ornithological Society asked that it be named a wildlife sanctuary. In 1923, L&N complied with this request, and all other uses of the lake were halted. Plans for a housing development nearly robbed the area of the lake in 1962, but local reaction resulted in the area being turned into a park. Through the combined efforts of the federal government and concerned residents, the state purchased Radnor Lake in 1973 and designated it as the first state natural area.

Seared Duck Breast with Wilted Greens

Shallot Vinaigrette
1/2 cup olive oil
1/2 cup cider vinegar
1 tablespoon balsamic vinegar
1 shallot, sliced
2 teaspoons Dijon mustard
1/4 teaspoon Tabasco sauce

Salad
2 wild duck breasts
salt and freshly ground pepper
1 1/2 tablespoons butter
mixed greens

To prepare the vinaigrette, combine the olive oil, cider vinegar, balsamic vinegar, shallot, Dijon mustard and Tabasco sauce in a bowl and whisk until smooth.

To prepare the salad, place the duck on a work surface and slice horizontally to make 4 thinner slices. Sprinkle generously with salt and pepper. Heat the butter in a skillet until very hot. Add the duck and sear for about 1 1/2 minutes on each side; duck will be slightly pink in the center.

Combine the mixed greens with the desired amount of the vinaigrette and spoon onto serving plates. Place 2 hot pieces of duck on each salad. Serve immediately.

Serves 2

Grilled Asparagus

1 pound asparagus, trimmed
coarse sea salt
1 tablespoon olive oil

Sprinkle the asparagus with the salt and combine with the olive oil in a sealable plastic bag; turn to coat well. Place in a vegetable grilling basket and grill over medium heat for 6 to 8 minutes or until done to taste, turning frequently.

You may also prepare this on the stovetop in a ridged grilling skillet.

Serves 4

Grilled Corn on the Cob

4 ears of corn
3 tablespoons butter or olive oil
salt and pepper to taste

Peel back the corn husks, leaving the husks intact on the stem. Remove and discard the corn silks. Soak the corn in cool water in a large bowl for 1 hour; drain. Brush the kernels with the butter and sprinkle with salt and pepper. Bring the husks up to cover the kernels and tie with kitchen twine. Place on a grill rack. Grill for 45 minutes or until tender.

Serves 4

Grilled Eggplant

Great for zucchini or summer squash also.

1 (1-pound) eggplant
3 tablespoons olive oil
salt and pepper to taste

Cut the eggplant lengthwise $1/2$ inch thick. Brush both sides with the olive oil and season with salt and pepper. Place on a grill rack. Grill over medium coals for 5 to 10 minutes on each side or until tender.

Serves 4 to 6

Grilled vegetables are an easy way to add a taste of summer to any meal. Do not try to grill vegetables individually unless they are big enough to avoid falling through the grill rack. Instead, use metal or wooden skewers soaked in water, or a grilling basket or tray to keep the vegetables intact. You might also try marinating the vegetables in a raspberry vinaigrette for a change of taste.

Marinated Flank Steak with Horseradish Sauce

Easy and great for entertaining, and the leftovers make wonderful sandwiches.

1/2 cup soy sauce
1/2 cup dry white wine
2 tablespoons olive oil
1/2 onion, chopped
2 garlic cloves, chopped
3 tablespoons chopped fresh rosemary
1 (2-pound) flank steak, trimmed
pepper to taste
Horseradish Sauce (below)

Combine the soy sauce, wine, olive oil, onion, garlic and rosemary in a shallow dish and mix well. Add the steak and turn to coat well. Marinate, covered, for several hours in the refrigerator; drain, reserving the marinade.

Bring the reserved marinade to a boil in a small saucepan and boil for 1 minute. Season the steak generously with pepper. Grill the steak on a rack over hot coals for 6 minutes on each side for rare, basting frequently with the marinade.

Let the steak stand for 15 minutes before serving. Cut diagonally across the grain into thin slices. Line a serving platter with romaine. Arrange the steak slices on the prepared platter. Serve with the Horseradish Sauce.

You can prepare this as much as 2 hours in advance and serve at room temperature.

Serves 6

Horseradish Sauce

1/2 cup sour cream
4 teaspoons prepared horseradish
2 green onions, chopped
pepper to taste

Combine the sour cream, horseradish, green onions and pepper in a bowl and mix well. Store in the refrigerator for up to 24 hours.

Makes 1/2 cup

Stuffed Beef Tenderloin

Tastes great with boursin cheese, too.

10 to 12 medium mushrooms, sliced
2 green onions, finely chopped
1 garlic clove, crushed
4 to 5 sprigs of fresh parsley, chopped
1/4 cup (1/2 stick) butter
1 (3-pound) beef tenderloin, trimmed
1/4 cup crumbled bleu cheese
melted butter

Sauté the mushrooms, green onions, garlic and parsley in 1/4 cup butter in a skillet for 10 minutes or until the mushrooms and green onions are tender.

Cut a horizontal pocket in the beef tenderloin, cutting to but not through the bottom of 1 side. Spread the sautéed vegetables on the bottom half and sprinkle with the bleu cheese. Replace the top half and secure with wooden picks or kitchen twine.

Brush the tenderloin with melted butter and place on a grill rack. Grill until medium-rare or until done to taste. Let stand, covered, for 5 minutes before slicing.

Serves 6

Bleu Cheese Burgers

1 pound ground chuck
2 teaspoons salt
1 teaspoon pepper
4 sesame seed hamburger buns, split
4 (1/2-inch) slices Bleu Cheese Butter

Combine the ground chuck, salt and pepper in a bowl and mix well. Shape into 4 patties 1 inch thick. Place on a grill rack. Grill over medium-hot coals until done to taste, placing the buns on the grill to warm during the last few minutes of the grilling time. Place 1 slice Bleu Cheese Butter on each burger and place the burgers in the buns to serve.

Serves 4

Bleu Cheese Butter

1 cup (2 sticks) unsalted butter, softened
1/2 cup crumbled bleu cheese
2 teaspoons pepper

Combine the butter, bleu cheese and pepper in a food processor and pulse until well mixed. Shape into a log and wrap in foil. Freeze for 45 minutes or until firm.

Makes 1 1/2 cups

For Herbed Burgers, add 2 teaspoons chopped fresh thyme or 1 teaspoon dried thyme, 1 crushed garlic clove and 1 tablespoon finely chopped onion to the ground chuck. Serve with butter flavored with garlic and parsley.

For Spicy Burgers, add 1/2 teaspoon Tabasco sauce, 1 tablespoon Worcestershire sauce and 1 teaspoon Dijon mustard to the ground chuck. Serve with butter flavored with cilantro and chili powder.

Provençale Lamb Chops

Great with fresh spring asparagus.

2 garlic cloves, minced
2 tablespoons olive oil
2 teaspoons grated lemon zest
1 tablespoon chopped fresh rosemary, or 1 teaspoon crumbled
   dried rosemary
1/2 teaspoon dried thyme
1 teaspoon coarse salt
pepper to taste
8 (4-ounce) lamb chops

Garnish
fresh rosemary sprigs
lemon slices

Crush the garlic against the side of a mixing bowl with the back of a spoon. Add the olive oil, lemon zest, rosemary, thyme, salt and pepper and mix well. Rub the mixture over both sides of the lamb chops and place in a shallow dish. Marinate, covered, in the refrigerator for 15 to 60 minutes.

Place the lamb chops on a grill rack 4 inches above very hot coals. Grill for 5 minutes on each side for medium-rare. Garnish with fresh rosemary and lemon slices.

You may substitute pork chops for the lamb chops and grill until cooked through.

Serves 4

Lime Pork Loin Chops

1/2 cup olive oil
1/3 cup fresh lime juice
2 tablespoons soy sauce
6 large garlic cloves, chopped
2 tablespoons grated fresh gingerroot

2 teaspoons Dijon mustard
salt, cayenne pepper and black pepper
  to taste
4 (12-ounce) pork tenderloins,
  trimmed

Process the first 9 ingredients in a blender or food processor. Combine with the pork in a large sealable plastic bag and place in a shallow dish. Marinate in the refrigerator for 24 to 48 hours, turning occasionally. Let stand at room temperature for 30 minutes; drain. Place on an oiled grill rack over hot coals 5 to 6 inches from the heat source. Grill for 10 minutes or until cooked through, turning once. Let stand for 5 minutes. Slice to serve.

Serves 12 to 16

Jamaican Pork Tenderloin

1 tablespoon Jamaican jerk seasoning
1 tablespoon olive oil
1 (1-pound) pork tenderloin, trimmed
1 cup chopped onion
1 green bell pepper, chopped
1 red bell pepper, chopped
2 teaspoons minced garlic
1/4 cup apple juice

1 teaspoon cornstarch
1 tablespoon Jamaican jerk seasoning
1 cup orange juice
1/4 teaspoon ground cumin
1/2 teaspoon ground red pepper
1/4 teaspoon salt
1/4 cup thinly sliced green onions

Combine 1 tablespoon jerk seasoning with the olive oil in a small bowl. Rub over the pork, coating evenly, and place in a shallow dish. Marinate, covered, in the refrigerator for 1 hour.

Grill the pork over hot coals for 3 minutes on each side or until brown. Remove to a baking pan and insert a meat thermometer into the thickest portion. Roast in a 350-degree oven for 25 to 30 minutes or to 155 degrees on the meat thermometer.

Combine the onion, bell peppers, garlic and apple juice in a saucepan. Cook over low heat for 5 minutes, stirring constantly. Blend the cornstarch with 1 tablespoon jerk seasoning and the orange juice in a bowl. Add to the vegetables in the saucepan and stir in the cumin, ground red pepper and salt. Bring to a boil and cook for 3 minutes or until thickened, stirring constantly. Slice the pork and arrange on a serving plate. Spoon the vegetable mixture over the top. Sprinkle with the green onions.

Serves 4

Loin of Venison with Red Currant Bordelaise

Make the deer hunter in your family proud!

1 tablespoon dried juniper berries
1 tablespoon dried allspice
1 tablespoon peppercorns
1 boneless backstrap saddle of venison
4 shallots, minced
1 bottle of dry red wine
2 cups game stock
3 tablespoons red currant jelly
2 teaspoons corn oil

Combine the juniper berries, allspice and peppercorns in a spice grinder and process to a powder. Rub the mixture over the venison. Marinate, covered, in the refrigerator for several hours.

Combine the shallots and red wine in a saucepan and bring to a boil. Reduce the heat and simmer for 45 minutes or until reduced by 3/4. Add the game stock and bring to a boil. Reduce the heat and cook for 30 minutes or until reduced by 1/2; the sauce should be thick enough to coat the back of a spoon. Stir in the jelly.

Drain the venison. Brown on all sides in the heated corn oil in a large skillet. Remove to a roasting pan. Roast at 400 degrees for 6 to 8 minutes per pound. Let stand for 10 minutes to cool. Remove to a cutting board and slice diagonally. Serve with the sauce.

Serves 4

otable

The Tennessee Conservation League accepts fresh venison to distribute to agencies, soup kitchens, and shelters across the state. In a partnership with hunters and participating processors, Hunters for the Hungry donated more than 59,000 pounds of fresh venison during the 2000–2001 season alone. The service not only provides fresh meat for those in need who might otherwise have gone without, but it also helps keep the area's burgeoning deer population in check. Think about it the next time you are in the woods.

Venison Cannelloni

1 cup finely chopped onion
2 tablespoons olive oil
4 garlic cloves, crushed
1 (10-ounce) package fresh spinach, or 1 (10-ounce) package frozen creamed spinach
butter
16 ounces ground venison or ground beef
16 ounces venison sausage, casings removed, or mild pork sausage
3/4 cup grated Parmesan cheese
3 tablespoons cream
3 eggs, lightly beaten
2 teaspoons chopped fresh oregano
2 teaspoons chopped fresh basil
1 teaspoon Cajun seasoning
1/2 teaspoon Tabasco sauce
1 1/2 (14-count) packages cannelloni or manicotti shells
4 cups tomato sauce
1/4 cup grated Parmesan cheese
2 tablespoons butter (optional)

Sauté the onion in the heated olive oil in a heavy saucepan for 3 minutes. Add the garlic and sauté for 10 minutes. Add the spinach and cook for 5 minutes. Remove to a bowl with a slotted spoon.

Melt a small amount of butter in the same saucepan and add the ground venison and sausage. Cook until light brown, stirring until crumbly; drain. Stir in the spinach mixture, 3/4 cup Parmesan cheese, cream, eggs, oregano, basil, Cajun seasoning and Tabasco sauce.

Cook the pasta using the package directions; drain. Spoon the venison mixture carefully into the pasta shells. Spread half the tomato sauce in a shallow baking dish. Arrange the stuffed shells in a single layer in the prepared dish and top with the remaining tomato sauce. Sprinkle with 1/4 cup Parmesan cheese and dot with 2 tablespoons butter.

Bake at 275 degrees for 30 minutes. Broil just until light brown before serving.

You may freeze the stuffed shells until time to bake if desired.

Serves 10

Can Can Chicken

2 (3-pound) chickens
1 tablespoon brown sugar
1 tablespoon sweet paprika
2 teaspoons chili powder
1 teaspoon oregano
1/2 teaspoon garlic powder
1 teaspoon salt
1/4 teaspoon cayenne pepper
1 teaspoon black pepper
2 (12-ounce) cans beer
1 small onion, chopped
2 garlic cloves, chopped

Rinse the chickens inside and out and pat dry; trim off any fat. Mix the brown sugar, paprika, chili powder, oregano, garlic powder, salt, cayenne pepper and black pepper in a small bowl. Rub 1 teaspoon of the mixture in the cavity of each chicken and rub the remaining spice mix on the outsides.

Open the cans of beer and pour out half the beer from each can. Stuff the onion and garlic into the cans. Stand 1 chicken on each can with the feet on either of the can.

Scatter hickory chips over coals heated to medium-hot. Place the chicken and beer cans on the grill rack. Close the lid, leaving the vents open. Grill for 1 1/2 to 2 hours or until the wings move easily, adding 6 to 8 briquettes to the grill every 30 minutes.

Serves 8

Entertainment

The Nashville Superspeedway, opened in April of 2001, plays host to some of the best racing in the country, including NASCAR, Busch, Craftsman Truck, and Indy Racing. The $125 million, 1.33-mile superspeedway accommodates 50,000 enthusiastic racing fans and boasts a track that features fourteen-degree banking in the turns, nine-degree banking on the backstretch, five-degree banking on the front stretch, and ranges in width from 55 to 60 feet. Come on out, grill up some Can Can Chicken, and join race fans of all ages in welcoming a new level of racing to Nashville.

Grilled Citrus Chicken with Papaya Salsa

Citrus Oil
1/2 cup olive oil
grated zest of 1 lemon
grated zest of 1 lime
grated zest of 1 orange

Chicken
4 skinless boneless chicken breasts
salt and pepper to taste
Papaya Salsa (below)

To prepare the citrus oil, combine the olive oil, lemon zest, lime zest and orange zest in a small container. Chill, covered, in the refrigerator for 24 hours.

To prepare the chicken, combine it with the desired amount of the citrus oil in a shallow dish and sprinkle with salt and pepper. Marinate, covered, in the refrigerator for 1 hour.

Insert a meat thermometer in the thickest portion of 1 piece of chicken. Place the chicken across the grill rack over medium-hot coals. Grill for 5 minutes, changing the angle of the chicken on the rack to form a crisscross pattern. Grill for 5 minutes. Turn the chicken over and cook to 165 degrees on a meat thermometer.

Remove the chicken to serving plates and top with the Papaya Salsa.

Use only the colored part of the citrus when zesting it, avoiding the white pith.

Serves 4

Papaya Salsa

1 papaya
1/2 jalapeño pepper
1/4 bunch fresh cilantro, finely
   chopped

2 tablespoons fresh lime juice
1 tablespoon honey
1/8 teaspoon salt
1/4 teaspoon cayenne pepper

Peel the papaya and cut it into halves, discarding the seeds. Chop it into 1/2-inch pieces. Mince the jalapeño pepper, discarding the seeds. Combine the papaya and jalapeño pepper with the cilantro, lime juice, honey, salt and cayenne pepper in a medium bowl and mix well. Chill, covered, in the refrigerator for 1 hour. You may also serve the salsa with grilled fish or as an appetizer with fried plaintain chips or tortilla chips.

Makes 1 cup

Chicken Teriyaki Skewers

It's just not summer until you've had this for dinner on your back porch.

4 skinless boneless chicken breasts
Teriyaki Marinade (below)
12 slices bacon, cut crosswise into halves
1 large green bell pepper, cut into squares
1 large red bell pepper, cut into squares
1 (16-ounce) can pineapple chunks
8 ounces fresh whole mushroom caps

Cut each chicken breast into halves lengthwise and then crosswise 2 times to form 6 cubes. Add to the Teriyaki Marinade and marinate, covered, for 1 to 12 hours.

Drain the chicken and wrap each piece in bacon. Thread on 4 skewers, alternating with the bell peppers, pineapple and mushroom caps and beginning and ending with chicken. Grill for 10 minutes on each side or until the bacon is crisp and the chicken is cooked through.

Serves 4

Teriyaki Marinade

1/2 cup vegetable oil
1/4 cup soy sauce
3 to 4 tablespoons dry sherry
juice of 1 lemon
1 or 2 garlic cloves, minced
1/2 teaspoon ground ginger

Combine the vegetable oil, soy sauce, sherry, lemon juice, garlic and ginger in a nonmetallic bowl and mix well.

Makes 1 cup

Honey Mustard Chicken Drumsticks

1/3 cup honey
1/4 cup Dijon mustard
1/4 cup soy sauce
juice of 2 lemons

10 to 12 garlic cloves, minced
2 teaspoons pepper
16 to 18 chicken drumsticks
salt to taste

Combine the honey, Dijon mustard, soy sauce, lemon juice, garlic and pepper in a bowl and whisk until smooth. Cut several deep slits to the bone in each drumstick. Add to the honey mustard mixture and marinate, covered, in the refrigerator for 1 to 6 hours, turning occasionally.

Drain the chicken and place on a grill over medium-hot coals. Grill, covered, for 15 to 20 minutes or until the chicken is cooked through, turning every 3 to 6 minutes. Season with salt.

Serves 8 to 10

Stuffed Cornish Game Hens

1/2 cup cottage cheese
1 garlic clove, minced
1/2 teaspoon grated lemon zest
1/2 teaspoon sage

1/2 teaspoon tarragon
salt and lemon pepper to taste
2 (1 1/2-pound) Cornish game hens
1 tablespoon olive oil

Combine the cottage cheese, garlic, lemon zest, sage, tarragon, salt and lemon pepper in a bowl and mix well.

Ask the butcher to split the game hens into halves. Place flat skin side up on a work surface and loosen the skin over the breast portion of each half to form pockets. Spoon the cottage cheese mixture into the pockets.

Place skin side up in a roasting pan and rub with the olive oil. Season with salt and lemon pepper. Roast at 400 degrees for 1 hour or until the juices run clear. Let stand for 5 minutes before serving.

You may substitute crumbled feta cheese, ricotta or cream cheese for the cottage cheese in this recipe.

Serves 4

Fried Dove

1/2 cup White Lily flour
1/2 teaspoon salt
1/8 teaspoon pepper
12 dove breasts
1/4 cup (1/2 stick) butter
1 tablespoon shortening
1/2 cup boiling water
1/4 cup (1/2 stick) butter
1 tablespoon White Lily flour
1 cup boiling water

Mix 1/2 cup flour, salt and pepper together. Coat the dove well with the flour mixture. Heat 1/4 cup butter with the shortening in a skillet. Add the dove and cook over high heat to seal in the juices, turning often.

Reduce the heat and add 1/2 cup boiling water. Simmer, covered, until the dove are very tender and the water has evaporated, adding additional water if necessary. Remove the dove to a plate.

Melt 1/4 cup butter in the skillet over low heat. Return the dove to the skillet skin side down and cook until golden brown. Remove the dove to a serving plate and keep warm.

Stir 1 tablespoon flour into the drippings in the skillet and cook until bubbly. Add 1 cup boiling water and cook until thickened, stirring constantly. Adjust the seasonings and serve with the dove.

Serves 6

Duck Rolls

1/2 cup (1 stick) butter
1/2 cup olive oil
juice of 1 lime
Tabasco sauce to taste
6 large or 12 small boneless duck
   breasts

Greek seasoning to taste
6 or 12 jalapeño peppers
6 slices hickory smoked bacon, cut into
   halves

Melt the butter with the olive oil, lime juice and Tabasco sauce in a small saucepan over low heat for the basting sauce.

Pound the duck breasts between 2 sheets of plastic wrap to flatten. Sprinkle lightly with the Greek seasoning. Place 1 jalapeño pepper in the center of each duck breast and roll to enclose the pepper. Wrap 2 half slices of bacon around each roll and secure with a wooden pick.

Grill over hot coals for 10 to 20 minutes or until done to taste, turning occasionally and brushing with the basting sauce; duck should be slightly pink in the center.

Serves 6

Parmesan Duck Breasts

Basting Sauce
1/4 cup (1/2 stick) butter
1/4 cup olive oil
5 garlic cloves, crushed
1/2 teaspoon Tabasco sauce

Duck
2 eggs
1/2 teaspoon Tabasco sauce
freshly ground pepper to taste
1 cup Italian bread crumbs
1/4 cup grated Parmesan cheese
12 boneless duck breasts
White Lily flour

To prepare the basting sauce, melt the butter with the olive oil, garlic and Tabasco sauce in a small saucepan over low heat. Cook until the garlic is tender.

To prepare the duck, beat the eggs with the Tabasco sauce and pepper in a small bowl. Mix the bread crumbs with the Parmesan cheese in a shallow dish. Pound the duck breasts between 2 sheets of plastic wrap to flatten. Coat with flour, dip into the egg mixture and roll in the crumb mixture, coating well. Grill over medium-hot coals for 4 minutes on each side or until done to taste, brushing with the basting sauce; duck should be slightly pink in the center.

Serves 6

Grilled Catfish

1/4 cup chopped onion
2 teaspoons olive oil
1 cup mayonnaise
1 (2-ounce) jar chopped pimento, drained
4 teaspoons capers
1 tablespoon chopped parsley
1 tablespoon lime juice
1/4 teaspoon Tabasco sauce
1/2 teaspoon salt
6 (6- to 7-ounce) catfish fillets
1 teaspoon lemon pepper
1/2 teaspoon dillweed

Garnish
lime slices

Sauté the onion in the olive oil in a saucepan until tender. Remove from the heat. Stir in the mayonnaise, pimento, capers, parsley, lime juice, Tabasco sauce and salt. Reserve half the mixture.

Sprinkle the catfish with lemon pepper and dillweed. Brush the remaining mayonnaise mixture over the fillets.

Grill the fillets over medium coals for 7 to 8 minutes on each side or until the fish flakes easily. Remove to a serving plate. Garnish with lime slices and serve with the reserved mayonnaise mixture.

Serves 6

ntertainment

Savannah, Tennessee, has held the title of "Catfish Capital of the World" since the early 1950s, when it was added to the city's cancellation postmark. The titled mark now holds a patent from the U.S. Patent Office. Visit nearby Savannah in the summer and cook what you catch in the World Championship Catfish Cook-Off during their annual National Catfish Derby.

Grilled Salmon with Thai Curry Sauce and Basmati Rice

Minted Vegetables

3 cups finely shredded green cabbage
*3/4 cup julienned strips of peeled and
   seeded cucumber*
3 tablespoons minced fresh cilantro
3 tablespoons minced fresh mint
1 tablespoon soy sauce
3 tablespoons rice vinegar

Basmati Rice

2 tablespoons unsalted butter
1 cup uncooked basmati rice
1 1/2 cups water

Salmon

4 (6-ounce) pieces salmon fillet
olive oil
salt and pepper to taste
Thai Curry Sauce (below)
1/4 cup roasted peanuts

To prepare the vegetables, combine the cabbage, cucumber, cilantro, mint, soy sauce and rice vinegar in a bowl and toss to coat well.

To prepare the rice, bring the butter, rice and water to a boil in an ovenproof dish with a lid. Place on the center rack in a 400-degree oven and bake for 12 minutes. Keep warm.

To prepare the salmon, brush the fillet pieces with olive oil and season with salt and pepper. Place on an oiled grill rack 5 to 6 inches above hot coals and grill for 5 minutes on each side.

To serve, spoon the rice onto 4 serving plates. Place the salmon on the rice and top with the vegetables. Drizzle with the Thai Curry Sauce and top with the peanuts.

Serves 4

Thai Curry Sauce

1 1/8 teaspoons minced fresh gingerroot
1 1/8 teaspoons minced garlic
2 1/4 teaspoons peanut oil
1 1/2 teaspoons curry powder
1 1/2 teaspoons Thai red curry paste
1 1/2 teaspoons paprika

3/4 teaspoon ground coriander
3/4 teaspoon ground cumin
1 1/4 cups unsweetened coconut milk
3 tablespoons tomato purée
1 tablespoon soy sauce
1 1/2 tablespoons dark brown sugar

Sauté the gingerroot and garlic in the peanut oil in a heavy saucepan over medium-high heat until golden brown. Add the curry powder, curry paste, paprika, coriander and cumin and sauté for 1 minute or until fragrant. Stir the coconut milk and whisk into the saucepan with the tomato purée, soy sauce and brown sugar. Bring just to a boil and remove from the heat; keep warm.

Serves 4

Grilled Brown Sugar Salmon

The brown sugar brings out the flavor of the salmon.

1 (2¹/2- to 3-pound) salmon fillet
¹/4 cup packed brown sugar
2 tablespoons lemon juice
2 tablespoons butter, melted

Garnish
thinly sliced lemon
chopped fresh parsley

Place the fillet skin side down on a work surface and rub the cut side with the brown sugar; let stand for 30 minutes. Drizzle with the lemon juice and butter.

Place skin side down on heavy-duty foil on a grill rack. Grill over medium-low coals just until the fillet is opaque; do not turn.

Lift the fillet from the foil with 2 spatulas, dividing into 2 pieces if necessary and leaving the skin on the foil. Place on a serving platter and garnish with the lemon slices and parsley.

When buying fresh fish, look for fish that is firm and has no pronounced odor. Ask to find out what you are buying, since fish frozen in water for up to one year may be sold as fresh.

Serves 4 to 6

Barbecued Trout

A cooking method that is also great for other types of fish.

1/2 cup olive oil
1/4 cup (1/2 stick) butter
1/4 cup Worcestershire sauce
juice of 1 lime
1/2 teaspoon Tabasco sauce
1 tablespoon Greek seasoning
6 trout fillets

Combine the olive oil, butter, Worcestershire sauce, lime juice, Tabasco sauce and Greek seasoning in a saucepan. Heat until the butter melts, stirring to mix well. Brush some of the mixture over the trout fillets and let stand for 10 minutes.

Grill the trout over medium coals for 6 to 8 minutes on each side or until cooked through, brushing with the remaining olive oil mixture.

Serves 6

Grilled Ginger Tuna

1/4 cup teriyaki sauce
1/4 cup white wine
2 teaspoons chopped garlic
2 teaspoons chopped gingerroot
4 (4- to 8-ounce) tuna steaks

Combine the teriyaki sauce, wine, garlic and gingerroot in a sealable plastic bag. Add the tuna steaks and seal the bag, turning to coat well. Marinate in the refrigerator for up to 3 hours; drain.

Grill the fillets over medium coals for 4 minutes on each side or until cooked through.

Serves 4

Grilled Portobello and Arugula Burgers

Great on crusty bread, too.

4 large Portobello mushroom caps
2 tablespoons olive oil
4 teaspoons minced fresh rosemary
salt and pepper to taste
Rosemary Mayonnaise (below)
4 whole wheat buns, toasted
roasted red bell peppers, cut into $1/2$-inch strips
2 large bunches arugula

Brush the mushrooms with olive oil and sprinkle with the rosemary, salt and pepper. Place on a grill rack sprayed with nonstick cooking spray. Grill over medium-hot coals for 10 minutes on each side. Cut into $3/4$-inch slices.

Spread the Rosemary Mayonnaise over the cut sides of the buns. Arrange the mushrooms, roasted bell peppers and arugula on the bun bottoms and replace the bun tops.

Serves 4

Rosemary Mayonnaise

$1/2$ cup nonfat mayonnaise
2 teaspoons Dijon mustard
2 teaspoons minced fresh rosemary
1 garlic clove, minced

Combine the mayonnaise, Dijon mustard, rosemary and garlic in a small bowl and mix well.

Serves 4

Pizza Margherita on the Grill

2 teaspoons olive oil
1 garlic clove, minced
1/8 teaspoon salt
1/8 teaspoon pepper
1/4 cup thinly sliced fresh basil

2 tablespoons chopped fresh oregano
Pizza Pastries (below)
4 plum tomatoes, thinly sliced
4 ounces (1 cup) shredded mozzarella
   cheese

Mix the olive oil, garlic, salt and pepper in a small bowl. Mix the basil and oregano together.

Place the Pizza Pastries on a grill rack sprayed with nonstick cooking spray. Grill for 3 minutes or until puffed and golden brown, piercing the bubbles with a fork as they appear. Turn the pastries and brush with the olive oil mixture.

Top with the tomatoes, mozzarella cheese and herb mixture. Grill for 4 to 5 minutes longer or until the cheese melts and the crusts are light brown.

Serves 6

Pizza Pastries

2 cups White Lily bread flour
1 envelope quick-rising dry yeast
1/2 teaspoon sugar
1/2 teaspoon salt

1 tablespoon olive oil
3/4 cup warm (120- to 130-degree)
   water

Mix the flour, yeast, sugar and salt in a large bowl and make a well in the center. Combine the olive oil and warm water in a small bowl. Add to the well in the dry ingredients and mix to form a dough.

Knead on a lightly floured surface for 10 minutes. Place in a large bowl coated with nonstick cooking spray and turn to coat the surface. Let rise, covered, in a warm place for 45 minutes or until doubled in bulk.

Punch down the dough and divide into 2 equal portions. Let rest for 10 minutes. Shape into 2 circles on a surface sprinkled with cornmeal.

You may prepare the dough in the food processor by pulsing the dry ingredients. Add the olive oil mixture gradually while processing constantly. Knead 9 to 10 times. Proceed as above.

Makes 2 pastries

Glazed Pineapple

2 tablespoons dark rum
1 tablespoon fresh lime juice
2 tablespoons honey
1 fresh pineapple

Mix the rum, lime juice and honey in a small bowl. Cut the pineapple into quarters and cut away the core. Place on a grill rack. Grill the pineapple over medium-low coals for 5 to 10 minutes on each side or until tender, brushing with the rum mixture.

You may also cut the pineapple into $^{1}/_{2}$-inch slices.

Serves 4

Meat "Rub"-a-dub

An easy rub for ribs or chicken that keeps well in an airtight container.

2 tablespoons paprika
$1^{1}/_{2}$ teaspoons dark brown sugar
$1^{1}/_{2}$ teaspoons sugar
$^{1}/_{2}$ teaspoon dry mustard
$^{1}/_{2}$ teaspoon garlic powder
$^{1}/_{2}$ teaspoon onion powder
1 teaspoon salt
$^{1}/_{2}$ teaspoon celery salt
1 teaspoon cayenne pepper
$^{1}/_{2}$ teaspoon freshly ground black pepper

Combine the paprika, brown sugar, sugar, dry mustard, garlic powder, onion powder, salt, celery salt, cayenne pepper and black pepper in a small jar with a lid. Cover the jar and shake to mix well. Store in a cool dark place for up to 6 months.

Makes $^{1}/_{4}$ cup, or enough for 2 racks of ribs or 2 chickens

Historical

After the boundaries of the Warner Parks were mapped out, the Works Progress Administration (WPA) of the Franklin D. Roosevelt presidency took on many projects that enhanced the development of the parks. The seven limestone entrance gates, dry-stacked stone retainer walls, two stone bridges, hiking trails, and bridle paths are just some of the projects completed at the parks through the backbreaking efforts of the men of the WPA. The steeplechase course, also a WPA project, is the only racetrack built by the federal government.

Best-Ever Barbecue Sauce

1 onion, chopped
1/2 cup water
1/4 cup vinegar
1/4 cup (1/2 stick) butter
juice of 1/2 lemon
2 tablespoons sugar

1 tablespoon prepared mustard
11/2 teaspoons salt
1/4 teaspoon cayenne pepper, or to taste
1/2 teaspoon black pepper
1/2 cup ketchup
2 tablespoons Worcestershire sauce

Combine the onion, water, vinegar, butter, lemon juice, sugar, mustard, salt, cayenne pepper and black pepper in a saucepan and mix well. Simmer for 20 minutes, stirring occasionally. Stir in the ketchup and Worcestershire sauce and bring to a boil.

Use as a sauce for grilling chicken or meat.

Makes 21/4 cups

Pico de Gallo

2 pounds vine-ripened tomatoes, chopped
1 small yellow onion, chopped
1 bunch cilantro, finely chopped
2 bunches green onions, thinly sliced

1 tablespoon minced garlic
1 jalapeño pepper, seeded and minced
juice of 2 limes
2 tablespoons red wine vinegar
1 teaspoon salt

Combine the tomatoes, onion, cilantro, green onions, garlic and jalapeño pepper in a bowl. Add the lime juice, vinegar and salt and mix well. Chill, covered, for 1 hour or longer. Serve with grilled fajitas, chicken or fish or as a dip with tortilla chips.

Makes 5 cups

Cilantro Tartar Sauce

Also good as a dip with pita points.

¹/2 cup mayonnaise
¹/2 cup sour cream
¹/2 cup plain yogurt
1 tablespoon fresh lemon juice
1 tablespoon fresh lime juice
¹/2 cup minced onion
¹/4 cup minced sweet pickle relish
¹/4 cup chopped fresh cilantro
1 teaspoon granulated garlic
¹/2 teaspoon salt

Combine the mayonnaise, sour cream, yogurt, lemon juice and lime juice in a bowl and mix well. Stir in the onion, pickle relish, cilantro, garlic and salt. Chill, covered, for 4 hours or longer. Serve with fish.

Makes 2¹/2 cups

Lemon Caper Sauce

¹/2 cup mayonnaise
2 tablespoons lemon juice
1 tablespoon tiny whole capers or chopped large capers
1 tablespoon chopped fresh dill, or ¹/2 teaspoon dried dill
cayenne pepper to taste

Combine the mayonnaise and lemon juice in a bowl and mix well. Stir in the capers, dill and cayenne pepper. Serve with grilled salmon or other seafood.

Makes ³/4 cup

Desserts

Desserts

*Art in Nashville is like dessert to a five-course meal—
a fine way to wind down your tour of the
"Athens of the South." So dubbed in the 1800s due to the
city's prominence in arts, education, culture, and trade,
Nashville boasts the world's only full-scale replica
of the Athens Parthenon.*

Our Parthenon, located in Centennial Park, was constructed between 1895 and 1897 to house the Art Exhibition for the Tennessee Centennial Exposition and serve as a reflection of the city's nickname. The original structure, made of wood, brick, and plaster, was intended to be temporary. Popular demand interceded, however, and the building remained. Nashville's Parthenon has undergone two reconstructions, the first during the 1920s and a second one, completed in the fall of 2001, lasting ten years and costing over 12 million dollars. An art gallery sits in the base of the Parthenon and houses visiting exhibits and a permanent collection of fine works of art by 19th and 20th century American artists.

Museums in Nashville reached new heights with the renovation of the old main post office and, in the spring of 2001, the subsequent addition of the Frist Center for the Visual Arts to the city's art landscape.

The downtown Art Deco building, on the National Register of Historic Places since 1984, provides the perfect setting and location for a state-of-the-art museum. With nearly 24,000 square feet of gallery space dedicated to presenting the best of visual arts from around the region and the world, artists in a variety of mediums—textiles, sculpture, paint, and film to name a few—find ample space to display their works. The Frist Center also provides a myriad of hands-on experiences for even the youngest art enthusiast in the ArtQuest Gallery's exhibits and adjoining classrooms. Since education and outreach are two of the Frist Center's main commitments, the museum is striving to increase Nashville's knowledge and appreciation of art by keeping the Center accessible, affordable, and fun. Free admission to those 18 years old and younger is a part of this commitment and makes the Frist Center an especially educational, enjoyable, and inexpensive family outing.

No visit to Nashville would be complete without a visit to the Cheekwood Botanical Garden and Museum of Art. Originally the home and estate of the Leslie Owen Cheek family, Cheekwood sits on 55 beautifully landscaped acres and provides visitors with the unique chance to view works of art and works of nature in one setting. At most museums, rotating exhibits are only found indoors. At Cheekwood, however, exhibits change outdoors as well. From *Treehouses* to *Dave Rogers' Big Bugs*, Cheekwood makes the most of nature's canvas. Children are welcome here, and Saturday morning classes are intended for families, with only a nominal materials donation requested. Kids have a blast at Cheekwood and don't even realize they are learning about art as they silkscreen a T-shirt, mold a clay garden marker, or paint with watercolors. Summer camps are also available for all ages and levels of expertise. More than a dozen gardens grace the grounds in all seasons, allowing visitors to enjoy nature's beauty year-round. The annual spring Wildflower Fair provides visitors with the opportunity to not only see beautiful wildflowers but also to purchase them. Stop in for a first glimpse of spring color and leave with an armful of it!

Caramel Pecan Chocolate Cheesecake

Graham Cracker Crust

1²/3 cups graham cracker crumbs
1/4 cup sugar
6 tablespoons (3/4 stick) butter, melted

Filling

1 (14-ounce) package caramel candies
1 (5-ounce) can evaporated milk
1 cup toasted chopped pecans
16 ounces cream cheese, softened
1/2 cup sugar
2 eggs
1 teaspoon vanilla extract
3/4 cup semisweet chocolate chips, melted
pecan halves

To prepare the crust, combine the graham cracker crumbs, sugar and butter in a bowl and mix well. Press over the bottom and 1 inch up the side of a 9-inch springform pan. Bake at 350 degrees for 7 to 9 minutes or until light brown.

To prepare the filling, combine the candies with the evaporated milk in a heavy saucepan. Melt over low heat, stirring to blend well. Spread over the graham cracker crust and sprinkle with the toasted chopped pecans.

Beat the cream cheese at high speed in a mixing bowl until light. Add the sugar gradually, beating until fluffy. Beat in the eggs 1 at a time. Stir in the vanilla and melted chocolate. Spread evenly in the prepared springform pan.

Bake at 350 degrees for 30 minutes. Loosen the crust from the side of the pan with a knife. Cool on a wire rack. Chill, covered, for 8 hours or longer.

Place the cheesecake on a serving platter and remove the side of the pan. Arrange the pecan halves around the top edge of the cheesecake.

Serves 12

Almond Cheesecake

Cheesecake Crust

1 1/4 cups graham cracker crumbs
3 tablespoons sugar
1/3 cup butter, melted

Filling

16 ounces cream cheese, softened
3 eggs
1 cup sugar
3 cups sour cream
2 teaspoons vanilla extract
1/2 teaspoon almond extract
1/2 teaspoon salt

For the crust, combine the graham cracker crumbs, sugar and butter in a bowl and mix well. Press over the bottom of a springform pan with the back of a spoon.

For the filling, beat the cream cheese in a mixing bowl until light. Beat in the eggs 1 at a time. Add the sugar gradually, beating constantly until smooth. Stir in the sour cream, flavorings and salt.

Spoon into the prepared springform pan and bake at 375 degrees for 50 minutes or until the side of the filling appears set but the center is still soft. Cool on a wire rack.

Chill the cooled cheesecake, covered, until serving time. Place on a serving platter and remove the side of the pan. Decorate top of cheesecake with almond slices.

Serves 8 to 12

Notable

Formerly known as the HCA Foundation, the Frist Foundation was established to invest resources in various not-for-profit organizations in the Nashville Metropolitan area. It was renamed to recognize the philanthropic efforts of its founding directors, Dr. Thomas Frist, Sr., and Dr. Thomas Frist, Jr., current chairman of the board. Special programs and grants are funded by the foundation to help organizations improve the way in which they provide services to Nashville's citizens. To name a few, Frist Foundation grants have gone to the Nashville Zoo, the Warner Parks, and eleven area school principals to further their studies. The Frist family joined with the foundation to make a $25 million commitment to the Frist Center to ensure its facilities remain open and affordable to the community. The Frist family is dedicated to improving the lives of those with whom they share this great city.

Chocolate Raspberry Torte Cheesecake

Cookie Crust

2 cups finely crushed vanilla wafers
3 tablespoons butter, melted

Filling

24 ounces cream cheese, softened
1¹/2 cups sugar
3 eggs
1 cup sour cream
1 teaspoon vanilla extract
8 ounces cream cheese, softened
6 ounces (1 cup) semisweet chocolate chips
¹/2 cup seedless raspberry preserves

Raspberry Chocolate Topping

6 ounces (1 cup) chocolate chips
¹/4 cup whipping cream
¹/3 cup raspberry liqueur (optional)

To prepare the crust, mix the cookie crumbs and butter in a bowl. Press over the bottom and side of a 9-inch springform pan.

To prepare the filling, beat 24 ounces cream cheese with the sugar in a mixing bowl until light and fluffy. Beat in the eggs 1 at a time. Add the sour cream and vanilla and mix well. Spread evenly over the crust.

Combine 8 ounces cream cheese with the chocolate chips in a heavy saucepan and melt over low heat, stirring to blend well. Stir in the preserves. Drop by spoonfuls over the cream cheese layer in the pan.

Bake at 325 degrees for 1 hour and 20 minutes or until set. Loosen crust from the side of the pan with a knife. Cool on a wire rack. Remove the pan rim.

To prepare the topping, melt the chocolate chips in a heavy saucepan. Stir in the whipping cream and liqueur.

Spread the topping over the cooled cheesecake. Chill, covered, until serving time. Place on a serving platter and remove the side of the pan.

Serves 12

Margarita Cheesecake

24 ounces cream cheese, softened
1 cup sugar
4 large eggs
1/4 cup lime juice
1/4 cup tequila
1/4 cup Triple Sec
Pretzel Crust (below)
1 cup puréed strawberries

Combine the cream cheese and sugar in a mixing bowl and beat until light and fluffy. Beat in the eggs 1 at a time. Stir in the lime juice, tequila and Triple Sec. Spoon into the Pretzel Crust.

Reserve half the strawberry purée. Spread the remaining strawberry purée over the cream cheese filling. Bake at 325 degrees for 1 hour and 20 minutes.

Loosen the crust from the side of the pan with a knife. Turn off the oven and return the cheesecake to the oven. Leave in the oven for 30 minutes. Cool on a wire rack.

Place on a serving plate and remove the side of the pan. Slice to serve and top each serving with a dollop of the reserved purée.

Serves 12

Pretzel Crust

1 1/2 cups crushed pretzels
1/2 cup (1 stick) butter, melted

Mix the crushed pretzels and butter in a bowl. Press into a 9-inch springform pan. Bake at 325 degrees for 8 to 10 minutes or until light brown.

Serves 12

Occasions

For those needing a chocolate fix in February, get a ticket and drop in at the Incredible Edible Chocolate Festival. Taste your share of the 100,000 samples of one—or more—of the 150 varieties of chocolate available. Go ahead, you can taste test 25 samples before you'll eat more than your share.

Double-Chocolate Torte

Chocolate Cake
8 ounces bittersweet chocolate, chopped
1 cup (2 sticks) unsalted butter
1 cup sugar
5 large eggs
1 tablespoon vanilla extract
1/4 teaspoon salt
1/4 cup White Lily flour

Chocolate Mousse
1/2 cup (1 stick) unsalted butter
4 large egg yolks
1/4 cup whipping cream
1 tablespoon vanilla extract
8 ounces bittersweet chocolate, chopped
4 large egg whites
1/2 cup sugar
3/4 cup whipping cream
2 tablespoons sugar

Garnish
fresh raspberries

To prepare the cake, melt the chocolate with the butter in a large saucepan over low heat, stirring constantly. Cool to lukewarm. Whisk in the sugar and then the eggs, 1 at a time. Stir in the vanilla and salt. Add the flour and mix until smooth.

Spoon into a 10-inch springform pan that has been buttered and dusted with sugar. Bake at 325 degrees for 35 minutes; a tester will not come out clean. Cool in the pan on a wire rack. Chill, covered, in the refrigerator.

To prepare the mousse, melt the butter in a double boiler over simmering water. Combine the egg yolks, 1/4 cup whipping cream and vanilla in a bowl and mix well. Whisk into the melted butter. Cook for 6 minutes or to 150 degrees on a kitchen thermometer, whisking constantly. Remove from over the water. Add the chocolate and whisk until melted and blended.

Beat the egg whites with 1/2 cup sugar in a large bowl until medium-stiff peaks form. Whisk 1/4 of the egg white mixture into the chocolate mixture. Fold in the remaining egg white mixture.

Spread the mousse mixture evenly over the cake in the pan. Chill, covered, for 6 hours or more or until the mousse is set. Place on a serving plate and remove the side of the pan.

Beat 3/4 cup whipping cream with 2 tablespoons sugar in a mixing bowl until soft peaks form. Spread over the torte. Garnish with raspberries.

Serves 10

Chocolate Fondue

8 ounces German's sweet chocolate
1/2 cup (1 stick) butter
1 cup sugar
1/2 cup heavy whipping cream
3 tablespoons Grand Marnier or other liqueur
1/8 teaspoon salt

Combine the chocolate and butter in a small heavy saucepan or microwave-safe dish. Melt over low heat or microwave on High for 2 to 3 minutes or until melted.

Add the sugar, whipping cream, liqueur and salt. Cook over medium heat for 5 minutes or microwave on High for 2 to 4 minutes or until the mixture boils and the sugar is completely dissolved, stirring often.

Serve with banana chunks, pineapple chunks, apple wedges, pear wedges, pound cake pieces, maraschino cherries and/or strawberries.

You may prepare this in advance and reheat to serve as fondue or as hot fudge sauce. Do not use margarine in this recipe.

Makes 21/4 cups

Culinary

Caramel Sauce, a popular recipe from **Nashville Seasons,** *is a delicious alternative to chocolate sauces. Combine a 1-pound package of dark brown sugar with 4 teaspoons cornstarch and a pinch of salt in a medium saucepan. Add 2 cups milk and cook over medium heat until thick, stirring constantly. The mixture may appear to curdle but will become smooth as you continue to stir. Stir in 2 tablespoons butter and 1 teaspoon vanilla. This sauce tastes great served over ice cream or angel food cake, but we recommend it right off the spoon. Yum!*

Hot Fudge Sauce

1 (16-ounce) can chocolate sauce
1 (14-ounce) can sweetened condensed milk
1/2 cup (1 stick) butter
1/2 teaspoon vanilla extract

Combine the chocolate sauce, condensed milk, butter and vanilla in a double boiler. Cook until the butter melts, stirring to blend well. Serve over ice cream or pound cake and strawberries. Store the sauce in the refrigerator and reheat in the microwave to serve.

This makes enough for three 8-ounce gift jars with some left over for the cook. Do not use margarine in this recipe.

Makes 41/2 cups

Frozen Chocolate Delight

1 package ladyfingers
1/2 gallon vanilla ice cream, softened
1 (12-ounce) jar hot fudge sauce, or Hot Fudge Sauce (above)
1 (12-ounce) jar caramel or butterscotch sauce
6 to 8 toffee candy bars, crushed
12 ounces whipped topping

Line the bottom of a round glass bowl or 9×13-inch dish with the ladyfingers. Spread the ice cream over the ladyfingers. Drizzle with the fudge sauce, caramel sauce and half the crushed candy. Spread the whipped topping over the top and sprinkle with the remaining candy. Freeze until serving time.

You may substitute coffee ice cream for the vanilla ice cream and brush the ladyfingers with 1/4 cup Kahlúa for variety.

Serves 6 to 8

Peppermint Ice Cream

A must for family birthday celebrations.

4 eggs
2¼ cups sugar
1 quart whipping cream
5 cups milk
1 tablespoon vanilla extract
1½ teaspoons peppermint extract
¼ teaspoon salt
1½ cups crushed peppermint candy

Beat the eggs at medium speed in a mixing bowl until frothy. Add the sugar gradually and beat for 5 minutes or until thick and pale yellow. Add the whipping cream, milk, flavorings and salt and mix well. Stir in half the candy.

Pour into a 1-gallon ice cream freezer container. Freeze using the manufacturer's instructions, adding the remaining candy as the mixture begins to thicken. Let stand for 1 hour or longer before serving.

You may crush the candy in a food processor or by placing it in a plastic bag and crushing with a rolling pin.

Serves 15

Culinary

For a quick and festive Holiday Dessert, place small scoops of peppermint ice cream in wine glasses and add small scoops of dark chocolate cake; a dense, moist cake works best. Drizzle with Hot Fudge Sauce (page 196), dollop with fresh whipped cream and garnish with a small peppermint stick. They are lovely to look at and even better to eat!

Perfect Chocolate Cake

Cake

2 cups boiling water

1 cup baking cocoa

2³/₄ cups sifted White Lily flour

¹/₂ teaspoon baking powder

2 teaspoons baking soda

¹/₂ teaspoon salt

1 cup (2 sticks) butter or margarine,
    softened

2¹/₂ cups sugar

4 eggs

1¹/₂ teaspoons vanilla extract

Chocolate Frosting

6 ounces (1 cup) chocolate chips

¹/₂ cup half-and-half

1 cup (2 sticks) butter or margarine

2¹/₂ cups confectioners' sugar

Whipped Cream Filling

1 cup heavy whipping cream

¹/₄ cup confectioners' sugar

1 teaspoon vanilla extract

To prepare the cake, pour the boiling water over the baking cocoa in a medium heatproof bowl, whisking until smooth. Cool completely. Sift the flour, baking powder, baking soda and salt together.

Combine the butter, sugar, eggs and vanilla in a large mixing bowl and beat for 5 minutes or until smooth, scraping the bowl occasionally. Beat in the flour mixture ¹/₄ at a time at low speed, alternating with the cocoa mixture and beginning and ending with the dry ingredients; do not overmix.

Spoon into 3 greased and lightly floured 9-inch cake pans and smooth the tops. Bake at 350 degrees for 25 to 30 minutes or until the surface springs back when lightly touched. Cool in the pans for 10 minutes. Loosen from the sides of the pans with a spatula and remove to wire racks to cool completely.

To prepare the frosting, combine the chocolate chips, half-and-half and butter in a medium saucepan. Cook over medium heat until the chocolate chips and butter melt, stirring until smooth. Remove from the heat and whisk in the confectioners' sugar. Spoon into a bowl set into a larger bowl of ice and beat until of spreading consistency.

To prepare the filling, whip the heavy cream with the confectioners' sugar and vanilla in a mixing bowl until soft peaks form. Chill until time to assemble the cake.

To assemble the cake, place a cake layer top side down on a serving plate and spread with half the filling. Place the second cake layer top side down on the first layer and spread with the remaining filling. Top with the third cake layer top side up and spread the frosting over the top and side, swirling into a decorative pattern with a spatula. Chill for 1 hour or more before serving. Slice with a thin knife.

Serves 10 to 12

Almond Cake with Raspberry Sauce

Enjoyed in the Show House Tea Room.

Cake

3/4 cup sugar
1/2 cup (1 stick) butter, softened
7 to 8 ounces almond paste
3 large eggs
1 tablespoon kirsch
1/4 teaspoon almond extract
1/4 cup White Lily flour
1/3 teaspoon baking powder
confectioners' sugar

Raspberry Sauce

1 pint fresh raspberries, or 1 (12-ounce) package frozen
     raspberries, thawed
2 teaspoons sugar

To prepare the cake, combine the sugar, butter and almond paste in a mixing bowl and mix well. Beat in the eggs, liqueur and almond extract. Add the flour and baking powder and beat just until moistened; do not overmix.

Spoon into a buttered and floured 8-inch cake pan. Bake at 350 degrees for 35 to 40 minutes or until a tester inserted into the center comes out clean. Cool on a wire rack and invert onto a serving plate. Sprinkle with confectioners' sugar.

To prepare the sauce, reserve 8 raspberries. Combine the remaining raspberries with the sugar in a food processor and purée.

Slice the cake and spoon the sauce over the slices. Top each serving with 1 of the reserved raspberries.

For a more cake-like consistency, use up to 1 1/2 cups of White Lily flour.

Serves 8

Cultural

Local politician Phil Ponder is known around the country for his art. Painting began as a hobby in 1979 and became a second career in 1989. In 1994 his painting Atlanta USA *received the Griffin Memorial Watercolor Award. Best known for prints of famous buildings such as The Hermitage, Belle Meade Plantation, and the entire Nashville skyline, he also designed the twelve holiday ornaments for the Easter Seal Society. If you spot one of his works, snatch it up and take a bit of Nashville home for your wall.*

Carrot Cake Perfection

1 pound carrots, peeled and sliced
3 cups White Lily flour
2³/₄ cups sugar
1¹/₂ teaspoons baking powder
1¹/₂ teaspoons baking soda
2 teaspoons cinnamon
1 teaspoon salt
1¹/₃ cups vegetable oil
6 eggs
1 (8-ounce) can crushed pineapple, drained
1 tablespoon vanilla extract
1 cup chopped pecans
¹/₂ cup flaked coconut
Cinnamon Cream Cheese Frosting (page 201)
Praline Filling (page 201)
Candied Pecans (page 201)

Cook the carrots, covered, in enough boiling water to cover for 20 minutes or until tender; drain and cool slightly. Chop coarsely in a food processor or mash with a potato masher; mashed carrots should measure about 1¹/₂ cups.

Mix the flour, sugar, baking powder, baking soda, cinnamon and salt in a large mixing bowl and make a well in the center. Add the vegetable oil, eggs, pineapple and vanilla to the well and beat at low speed for 1 minute or just until smooth. Fold in the carrots, pecans and coconut.

Spread evenly in 3 greased and lightly floured 9-inch cake pans. Bake at 350 degrees for 35 to 40 minutes or until the layers test done. Cool in the pans for 10 minutes. Loosen from the sides of the pans with a knife and remove to a wire rack to cool completely.

Spoon the Cinnamon Cream Cheese Frosting into a pastry bag. Place 1 cake layer top side up on a cake plate. Pipe about 1 cup of the frosting around the edge of the layer and pipe about 2 tablespoons of the frosting into the center of the layer, leaving a ring between the two.

Spoon half the Praline Filling into the unfrosted ring. Add a second cake layer top side up and repeat the frosting and filling steps. Add the third cake layer top side up and frost the top and side of the cake with the remaining frosting. Garnish with Candied Pecans. Store in the refrigerator.

Serves 12

Cinnamon Cream Cheese Frosting

8 ounces cream cheese, softened
1/2 cup (1 stick) butter, softened
1 teaspoon cinnamon
1 teaspoon vanilla extract
5³/4 to 6¹/4 cups sifted confectioners' sugar

Combine the cream cheese, butter, cinnamon and vanilla in a large mixing bowl and beat at medium speed until light and fluffy. Add half the confectioners' sugar gradually, beating constantly until smooth. Add enough of the remaining confectioner's sugar gradually to make a frosting of a spreading consistency, beating constantly.

Frosts 1 cake

Praline Filling

3 tablespoons butter
3 tablespoons brown sugar
2 tablespoons whipping cream
1 teaspoon vanilla extract

Melt the butter in a small saucepan over medium heat. Stir in the brown sugar and cream. Bring to a boil, stirring constantly. Reduce the heat and simmer for 3 minutes, stirring occasionally. Stir in the vanilla. Cool to room temperature.

Makes 1/3 cup

ulinary

For Candied Pecans, mix 1/4 cup packed brown sugar with 1 tablespoon orange juice in a small bowl. Add 3/4 cup pecan halves and stir to coat well. Spread in a lightly greased 8×8-inch baking pan. Bake at 350 degrees for 12 minutes or until light brown, stirring once. Remove to a baking sheet and separate with forks. Cool on a wire rack.

Italian Cream Cake

A popular recipe from Encore.

Cake

1 cup buttermilk
1 teaspoon baking soda
1¹/2 teaspoons vanilla extract
¹/2 cup (1 stick) butter or margarine,
    softened
¹/2 cup shortening
2 cups sugar
5 egg yolks, beaten
2 cups White Lily flour
5 egg whites
1 cup coconut
1 cup chopped pecans

Cream Cake Frosting

12 ounces cream cheese, softened
³/4 cup (1¹/2 sticks) butter or
    margarine, softened
1¹/2 (1-pound) packages confectioners'
    sugar
1¹/2 teaspoons vanilla extract

To prepare the cake, mix the buttermilk, baking soda and vanilla in a bowl. Cream the butter, shortening and sugar in a large mixing bowl until light and fluffy. Beat in the egg yolks. Add the flour alternately with the buttermilk mixture, mixing well after each addition.

Beat the egg whites in a mixing bowl until soft peaks form. Fold into the batter. Fold in the coconut and pecans.

Spoon into 3 greased and floured 8-inch cake pans. Bake at 350 degrees for 30 minutes. Cool in the pans for 10 minutes. Remove to a wire rack to cool completely.

To prepare the frosting, beat the cream cheese and butter in a mixing bowl until smooth. Add the confectioners' sugar and vanilla and beat until smooth.

Spread the frosting between the layers and over the top and side of the cake. Chill, covered, until serving time and store in the refrigerator.

Serves 16

Red Velvet Cake

Cake

2¹/₂ cups White Lily cake flour
1 tablespoon baking cocoa
¹/₂ teaspoon salt
1 teaspoon baking soda
1 cup buttermilk
1 tablespoon white vinegar
¹/₂ cup shortening
1¹/₂ cups sugar
2 large eggs
1 (1-ounce) bottle of red food coloring
1¹/₄ teaspoons vanilla extract

Cream Cheese Frosting

8 ounces cream cheese, softened
¹/₂ cup (1 stick) butter or margarine, softened
1 (1-pound) package confectioners' sugar, sifted
1¹/₄ teaspoons vanilla extract

To prepare the cake, mix the flour, baking cocoa and salt together. Dissolve the baking soda in the buttermilk and vinegar in a 4-cup measure. Beat the shortening at medium speed in a mixing bowl until light. Add the sugar gradually, beating constantly until fluffy. Beat in the eggs 1 at a time. Add the food coloring and vanilla and mix well. Add the dry ingredients alternately with the buttermilk mixture, beginning and ending with the dry ingredients and beating constantly at low speed after each addition. Beat at medium speed for 2 minutes longer.

Spoon into 3 greased and floured 8-inch cake pans. Bake at 350 degrees for 25 minutes or until a wooden pick inserted in the center comes out clean. Cool in the pans on a wire rack for 10 minutes. Remove to the wire racks to cool completely.

To prepare the frosting, beat the cream cheese and butter in a mixing bowl until light. Add the confectioners' sugar gradually, beating at low speed until smooth. Beat in the vanilla. Spread the frosting between the layers and over the top and side of the cake.

Serves 12

Lemon-Filled Pound Cake

Bake an extra treat for yourself! Reserve some of the cake batter and bake it in a miniature loaf pan.

1¹/₂ cups (3 sticks) butter, softened
3 cups sugar
6 eggs
2 teaspoons vanilla extract
3 cups White Lily flour
¹/₄ teaspoon baking soda
¹/₄ teaspoon salt
1 cup sour cream
Lemon Curd Filling (page 205)
Cream Cheese Frosting (page 205)

Garnish
thin lemon slices, raspberries or edible flowers

Beat the butter in a large mixing bowl until light. Add the sugar gradually, beating constantly until fluffy. Beat in the eggs 1 at a time. Mix in the vanilla.

Sift the flour, baking soda and salt together. Add to the creamed mixture ¹/₃ at a time, alternating with the sour cream and mixing well after each addition. Spoon into 2 greased and floured 8-inch cake pans.

Bake at 300 degrees for 40 minutes or until the cake is golden brown and a tester inserted into the center comes out clean. Cool in the pans on wire racks for 10 minutes. Remove to the wire racks to cool completely.

Split the cake layers horizontally into 4 layers with a very sharp knife. Stack the layers on a cake plate, spreading the Lemon Curd Filling between the layers to within 1 inch of the edge. Spread the Cream Cheese Frosting over the top and side of the cake. Garnish with lemon slices, raspberries or edible flowers.

To make the cake layers easier to split evenly, freeze them until they are firm enough to be easily handled. You can also split cake layers with plain dental floss.

Serves 16

Lemon Curd Filling

2 tablespoons plus 1 teaspoon cornstarch
1/4 cup water
1 tablespoon butter, melted
1/4 cup fresh lemon juice
grated zest of 1 lemon
2/3 cup sugar
3 tablespoons water
3 egg yolks, beaten

Blend the cornstarch with 1/4 cup water in a double boiler. Add the butter, lemon juice, lemon zest, sugar and 3 tablespoons water and whisk until smooth. Place over 2 to 3 inches simmering water. Cook for 5 minutes or until thickened, whisking constantly. Reduce the heat and cover. Cook for 8 minutes without stirring.

Whisk a small amount of the hot mixture into the egg yolks; whisk the egg yolks into the hot mixture. Increase the heat and cook for 2 minutes over boiling water, whisking constantly. Remove from the heat and whisk for 3 minutes longer. Cool to room temperature. Chill, covered, in the refrigerator for up to 2 days.

Makes enough to fill 4 cake layers

Cream Cheese Frosting

6 tablespoons (3/4 stick) butter, softened
8 ounces cream cheese, softened
1 (1-pound) package confectioners' sugar, sifted
1 teaspoon vanilla extract
milk

Beat the butter and cream cheese in a mixing bowl until light and fluffy. Add the confectioners' sugar gradually, mixing well after each addition. Beat in the vanilla and add milk 1 teaspoon at a time if needed for the desired consistency.

Makes enough to frost a 4-layer cake

ulinary

Sugared edible flowers and leaves make an attractive garnish for homemade cakes and dress up cakes from the market. Violets, pansies, rose petals, and mint leaves are good choices, but make sure they have no insecticide residue. Use a pastry brush to coat each petal or leaf with lightly beaten egg white. Dip gently into granulated sugar and place on a plate liberally sprinkled with sugar. Sift additional sugar over the petals and place in a warm spot to dry for 8 hours or longer. Use within a few days or freeze between layers of paper towels in an airtight container for up to 6 months.

Sour Cream Orange Pound Cake

Even those who claim they don't like sweets seem to make an exception for this moist pound cake.

3 cups sifted White Lily flour
1/4 teaspoon baking soda
1/2 teaspoon salt
1 cup (2 sticks) butter, softened
2 3/4 cups sugar
6 eggs
1 cup sour cream
1/2 teaspoon vanilla extract
1/2 teaspoon orange extract
grated zest of 1 orange
Orange Glaze (below)

Sift the flour, baking soda and salt together. Cream the butter and sugar in a mixing bowl until light and fluffy. Beat in the eggs 1 at a time. Add the sifted dry ingredients alternately with the sour cream, mixing well after each addition. Beat in the flavorings and orange zest.

Spoon into a greased and floured bundt pan. Bake at 325 degrees for 1 to 1 1/2 hours or until a wooden pick comes out clean.

Pierce holes in the warm cake. Pour the Orange Glaze over the cake and let stand until cool. Remove to a serving plate.

Premeasure all the ingredients to make the task easier.

Serves 14 to 16

Orange Glaze

1/2 cup confectioners' sugar
1/4 cup orange juice

Mix the confectioners' sugar and orange juice in a small bowl.

Strawberry Cake

1 (2-layer) package strawberry cake mix
1 half-pint frozen strawberries in syrup, thawed
2 eggs
1/3 cup vegetable oil
1/3 cup water
Creamy Frosting (below)

Garnish
chocolate-covered strawberries

Combine the cake mix, strawberries, eggs, vegetable oil and water in a large mixing bowl and beat at medium speed until smooth.

Spoon into 2 greased 8-inch cake pans. Bake at 350 degrees for 25 minutes. Cool in the pans for 5 minutes and remove to a wire rack to cool completely.

Spread the Creamy Frosting between the layers and over the top and side of the cake. Garnish with the strawberries.

Serves 10

Creamy Frosting

1/2 cup (1 stick) butter, softened
8 ounces cream cheese, softened
1/2 cup shortening
1/2 teaspoon vanilla extract
1 (2-pound) package confectioners' sugar

Combine the butter, cream cheese and shortening in a mixing bowl and beat until light. Beat in the vanilla. Add the confectioners' sugar gradually and beat until fluffy.

Makes enough to frost a 2-layer cake

Cultural

The Nashville Parthenon was built to be an exact replica of the ancient Greek Parthenon, and it comes very close: its external measurements are within 1/8 inch of the original structure. At 41 feet and 10 inches, the Parthenon's central statue of Athena Parthenos is the world's largest indoor sculpture. Athena holds a six-foot-tall statue of Nike in the palm of her hand and the flagpole from a local McDonald's was used as the basis for her spear.

Easy Food Processor Pie Crust

1 cup White Lily flour
7 tablespoons unsalted butter, chilled,
    finely chopped

1/8 teaspoon salt
3 tablespoons (or more) ice water

Combine the flour, butter and salt in a food processor fitted with a metal blade. Process for 10 to 15 seconds or until crumbly. Add the ice water and pulse 8 to 10 times or just until the mixture begins to hold together; do not process until it forms a ball.

Shape into a 6-inch disk on plastic wrap, working in 1 tablespoon additional flour if the dough is too sticky to handle; wrap in the plastic wrap. Chill for 1 hour or longer.

Roll the dough to an 11-inch circle on lightly floured waxed paper. Fold into quarters and unfold into a pie plate or tart pan. Trim to fit the pan and crimp the edge. Bake as directed in the pie recipe.

Makes 1 (9-inch) pie shell or 1 (10-inch) tart shell

Best Blueberry Pie

An easy and delicious treat for family, new neighbors, or friends with new babies.

1 1/3 cups (or less) sugar
1/3 cup cornstarch
2 tablespoons orange juice
1 teaspoon lemon juice
1/2 teaspoon freshly grated nutmeg
1/4 teaspoon cinnamon

3 1/2 cups blueberries
1/2 teaspoon vanilla extract
1/2 teaspoon almond extract
1 recipe 2-crust pie pastry
3 tablespoons butter

Mix the sugar and cornstarch in a saucepan. Add the orange juice, lemon juice, nutmeg and cinnamon and mix well. Stir in the blueberries. Cook over low heat until the mixture is thickened, stirring occasionally. Cool to room temperature and stir in the flavorings.

Line a 9-inch pie plate with 1 of the pastries. Spoon the blueberry mixture into the pastry and dot with the butter. Top with the remaining pastry. Trim and seal the edge and cut vents in the top.

Bake at 450 degrees for 10 minutes. Reduce the oven temperature to 350 degrees and bake for 35 minutes longer.

Serves 8

Coconut Pie

1/2 cup (1 stick) margarine, melted
4 eggs, beaten
2 cups sugar
1 cup milk
2 teaspoons vanilla extract
1 (14-ounce) package flaked coconut
2 unbaked (9-inch) pie shells

Combine the margarine, eggs, sugar, milk and vanilla in a mixing bowl and mix well. Stir in the coconut. Spoon into the pie shells and bake at 350 degrees for 45 minutes or until set and golden brown. Cool on wire racks.

Makes 2 pies

Fresh Lemon Icebox Pie

Super easy and refreshing.

2 cups whipping cream
1 cup sugar
1 to 2 tablespoons grated lemon zest
1/2 cup fresh lemon juice

Garnish
lemon twists
whipped cream
fresh raspberries

Combine the whipping cream and sugar in a large bowl and stir to mix well. Add the lemon zest and lemon juice. Spoon into a round pan and freeze, covered, for 3 hours or longer. Cut into wedges to serve. Garnish the servings with a lemon twist and a dollop of whipped cream or fresh raspberries.

Serves 6 to 8

Culinary

Originally made by my great-great-grandmother's cook Sally, this recipe for coconut pie has been handed down through four generations. When my great-great-grandmother asked for the recipe for one pie, Sally told her that she couldn't make just one! True to the southern tradition of making food for our neighbors, the recipe has been handed down as is— for two pies. Make one for yourself and give the other to the neighbor who just moved in or take it to a holiday party. It's the holiday dessert for my family and now my husband's family as well. Enjoy!

Show House Chocolate Pecan Pie

A Show House Tea Room favorite for years.

*6 ounces (1 cup) semisweet chocolate
   chips*
1¼ cups chopped pecans
2 unbaked (9-inch) pie shells
½ cup (1 stick) butter, melted

1 cup sugar
1 cup light corn syrup
4 eggs, beaten
2 tablespoons whiskey

Sprinkle the chocolate chips and pecans in the pie shells. Combine the butter, sugar, corn syrup, eggs and whiskey in a bowl and mix well. Spoon into the prepared pie shells. Bake at 350 degrees for 45 to 50 minutes or until the filling is set and the crust is golden brown. Garnish with whipped cream and strawberries.

Makes 2 pies

Strawberry Rhubarb Pie

A southern classic.

*1 pound rhubarb, cut into ¼-inch
   slices (about 4 cups)*
2½ cups thinly sliced strawberries
1½ cups sugar
⅔ cup White Lily flour

¼ teaspoon nutmeg
1½ teaspoons cinnamon
1 recipe 2-crust pie pastry
2 tablespoons margarine or butter

Combine the rhubarb and strawberries in a bowl. Mix the sugar, flour, nutmeg and cinnamon in a bowl. Add to the rhubarb and strawberries and mix well. Let stand for 15 minutes, stirring occasionally.

Spoon into a pastry-lined pie plate and dot with the margarine. Cut the remaining pastry into strips and arrange in a lattice on top of the fruit. Bake in the lower third of the oven at 375 degrees for 35 to 40 minutes or just until the crust is golden brown.

Serves 8

Minnie Pearl's Chess Pie

A popular recipe from Encore.

1/2 cup (1 stick) butter or margarine
1 1/2 cups sugar
3 eggs, beaten
1 tablespoon cider vinegar
1 tablespoon vanilla extract
1/2 teaspoon salt
1 unbaked (8-inch) pie shell

Combine the butter and sugar in a saucepan and cook over medium heat until the butter melts, stirring until smooth. Remove from the heat and whisk a small amount of the hot mixture into the eggs; whisk the eggs into the hot mixture. Whisk in the vinegar, vanilla and salt.

Spoon into the pie shell and bake at 300 degrees for 50 minutes.

Serves 6

Minnie Pearl

Notable

The beloved Grand Ole Opry legend Sarah Cannon, also known as Minnie Pearl, was a passionate philanthropist with two primary causes—children and cancer. Diagnosed with breast cancer in 1983, Sarah lent her name in 1991 to a group of affiliated HCA hospitals located in middle Tennessee and southern Kentucky that are now known collectively as the Sarah Cannon Cancer Center. Her former home was the Decorators Show House for 2000 and raised hundreds of thousands of dollars for Junior League of Nashville charities, benefiting women, children, and families throughout the greater Nashville area. Minnie placed the recipe for Chess Pie in an earlier Junior League of Nashville cookbook, Encore, and we want to honor her by placing it in this one as well.

Summer Peach Pie

$1/4$ cup White Lily flour
$1/2$ cup sugar
$3/4$ teaspoon cinnamon
5 cups sliced peeled peaches
    (about 3 pounds)
1 unbaked deep-dish pie shell

1 tablespoon fresh lemon juice
$1/2$ cup packed light brown sugar
1 tablespoon sugar
$1/3$ cup rolled oats
$1/3$ cup White Lily flour
2 tablespoons butter

Mix $1/4$ cup flour, $1/2$ cup sugar and cinnamon in a large bowl. Add the peaches and toss gently to coat well. Spoon into the pie shell and drizzle with the lemon juice.

Mix the brown sugar, 1 tablespoon sugar, oats and $1/3$ cup flour in a small bowl. Cut in the butter until crumbly. Sprinkle over the peach mixture.

Bake at 375 degrees for 40 minutes or until light brown. Cool on a wire rack for 1 hour or longer before serving.

Serves 8

Springtime Lemon Tarts

A taste treat for visitors to the Show House Tea Room.

1 lemon
1 egg
$1/4$ cup sugar
salt to taste
3 eggs

$1^{3}/4$ cups sugar
$1/2$ cup (1 stick) butter or margarine,
    melted
12 to 16 tart shells

Slice the lemon, discarding the seeds. Combine the lemon slices, 1 egg, $1/4$ cup sugar and salt in a blender and process at high speed until puréed. Add 3 eggs, $1^{3}/4$ cups sugar and butter and process until smooth.

Arrange the tart shells on a baking sheet. Spoon the lemon mixture into the tart shells, filling almost to the tops. Bake at 350 degrees for 35 to 40 minutes or until golden brown. Cool on a wire rack.

You may freeze the baked tarts.

Makes 12 to 16

Chocolate Tartlets with Orange Cookie Crust

6 ounces bittersweet or semisweet chocolate, chopped
6 tablespoons (3/4 stick) unsalted butter
1/2 cup sugar
2 large eggs
2 large egg yolks
2 tablespoons Grand Marnier
1 teaspoon finely grated orange zest
1/4 teaspoon salt
1 tablespoon White Lily flour
Orange Cookie Tart Shells (at right)

Combine the chocolate and butter in a double boiler or wide metal bowl set in a larger saucepan; the bowl should not touch the water in the larger pan and should seal the larger pan so that no steam escapes to cause the chocolate to seize. Cook over simmering water until the chocolate and butter melt, stirring to blend well. Remove from the heat and cool for 10 minutes, stirring occasionally.

Combine the sugar, eggs, egg yolks, liqueur, orange zest and salt in a large standing mixer bowl and beat with the whisk attachment for 8 minutes or until a very thick ribbon forms when the whisk is lifted. Sift the flour over the mixture and fold in gently. Fold the mixture into the chocolate mixture.

Arrange the Orange Cookie Tart Shells on a baking sheet. Spoon the filling into the shells and bake at 350 degrees for 15 minutes or until the filling puffs and begins to crack.

You may freeze the unbaked tartlets for up to 1 week and bake frozen for 25 minutes.

Makes 8

For Orange Cookie Tart Shells, combine 13/4 cups White Lily flour, 3/4 cup softened unsalted butter, 2/3 cup confectioners' sugar, 1 tablespoon grated orange zest and 1/2 teaspoon salt in a food processor. Process just until a dough forms. Shape into a ball on a work surface and divide into 8 equal portions.

Press 1 portion of the dough evenly over the bottom and side of each of eight 43/4-inch tartlet pans with 3/4-inch sides and removable bottoms; prick with a fork. Chill until firm. Bake at 350 degrees for 18 minutes or until pale golden brown. Cool in the pans on a wire rack.

Chocolate Cappuccino Cookies

12 ounces (2 cups) semisweet or
    bittersweet chocolate chips
3 ounces unsweetened baking
    chocolate
1/2 cup (1 stick) butter
1/2 teaspoon vanilla extract
3 eggs
1 cup sugar

1 tablespoon instant coffee granules,
    crushed
1 cup White Lily flour
1 teaspoon baking powder
1/4 teaspoon salt
3/4 cup chopped pecans or walnuts
    (optional)
confectioners' sugar

Reserve 1 cup of the chocolate chips. Combine the remaining 1 cup chocolate chips with the unsweetened chocolate and butter in a medium microwave-safe bowl. Microwave on High for 1 1/2 minutes; stir to blend well. Microwave for 30 seconds longer if necessary to melt completely. Stir in the vanilla. Combine the eggs, sugar and instant coffee in a large mixing bowl. Beat at high speed for 3 minutes. Add the melted chocolate and mix well.

Sift the flour, baking powder and salt together. Add to the chocolate mixture and mix gently. Fold in the reserved chocolate chips and pecans. Drop by tablespoonfuls 2 inches apart on lightly greased cookie sheets. Bake at 350 degrees for 10 minutes; do not overbake. Sift confectioners' sugar onto the tops of the warm cookies. Cool on the cookie sheets.

Makes 2 dozen

Cranberry Cookies

3 cups sifted White Lily flour
1 teaspoon baking powder
1/4 teaspoon baking soda
1/2 teaspoon salt
1/2 cup (1 stick) butter or margarine,
    softened
1 cup sugar

3/4 cup packed brown sugar
1 teaspoon vanilla extract
1/3 cup milk
1 egg
1 tablespoon grated orange zest
2 1/2 cups coarsely chopped fresh
    cranberries or dried cranberries

Sift the flour, baking powder, baking soda and salt together. Cream the butter, sugar, brown sugar and vanilla in a mixing bowl until light and fluffy. Beat in the milk and egg. Add the sifted dry ingredients, orange zest and cranberries and mix well. Drop by 2 tablespoonfuls 2 inches apart on greased cookie sheets. Bake at 375 degrees for 15 to 18 minutes or until golden brown. Cool on the cookie sheets for 5 minutes and remove to a wire rack to cool completely.

Makes 3 1/2 dozen

Ginger Cookies

A recipe rumored to have come from the kitchen of the boyhood home of General Robert E. Lee.

4 cups White Lily flour
4 teaspoons baking soda
2 teaspoons cinnamon
1 teaspoon ginger
1 teaspoon ground cloves
1¹/2 cups (3 sticks) margarine
¹/2 cup molasses
2 cups sugar
2 eggs
sugar

For a quick and cool Summer Berry Treat, layer in your favorite clear goblet—lemon yogurt, fresh berries, crushed graham crackers, and whipped topping. Place in the freezer until chilled. Garnish with a berry and sprig of mint. It's lovely, delicious, and guilt-free!

Sift the flour, baking soda, cinnamon, ginger and cloves together. Melt the margarine in a saucepan and combine with the molasses, 2 cups sugar and eggs in a mixing bowl; beat until smooth. Add the sifted dry ingredients and mix well to form a dough. Chill, covered, for several hours.

Shape the dough into small balls and roll in additional sugar. Place on cookie sheets and bake at 350 degrees for 8 to 10 minutes or until firm and golden brown. Cool on the cookie sheets for 5 minutes and remove to wire racks to cool completely.

You may increase the recipe, shaping the chilled dough into a roll 1 inch in diameter. Cut into ³/4-inch pieces, dip the cut side into the sugar and bake as above.

Makes 5 dozen

Apricot Oat Squares

1¹/₂ cups White Lily flour, sifted
1 teaspoon baking powder
¹/₄ teaspoon salt
1¹/₂ cups quick-cooking oats

1 cup packed brown sugar
³/₄ cup (1¹/₂ sticks) butter
³/₄ cup apricot jam or other jam

Sift the flour, baking powder and salt into a bowl. Add the oats and brown sugar and mix well. Cut in the butter until crumbly.

Press ²/₃ of the crumb mixture into a 9×13-inch baking pan. Spread the apricot jam over the crumb mixture and sprinkle with the remaining crumb mixture. Bake at 375 degrees for 30 to 35 minutes or until light brown. Cool in the pan on a wire rack and cut into squares to serve.

Makes 16

Glazed Spice Bars

Whenever Grandma brings an assortment of cookies, these are the first to go!

Bars
1 cup sugar
³/₄ cup vegetable oil
¹/₄ cup honey
1 egg
2 cups White Lily flour
1 teaspoon baking soda
1 teaspoon cinnamon
¹/₂ teaspoon salt
1 cup chopped pecans

Spice Bar Glaze
1 cup confectioners' sugar
1 tablespoon mayonnaise
1 tablespoon water
1 teaspoon vanilla extract

To prepare the bars, combine the sugar, vegetable oil, honey and egg in a mixing bowl and mix well. Add the flour, baking soda, cinnamon and salt and mix well. Mix in the pecans; dough will be stiff. Press into an ungreased 9×13-inch baking pan. Bake at 350 degrees for 25 to 30 minutes or until golden brown.

To prepare the glaze, combine the confectioners' sugar, mayonnaise, water and vanilla in a bowl and mix until smooth. Spread over the hot baked layer.

Cool in the pan on a wire rack and cut into bars to serve.

Makes 3 dozen

Cinnamon Apple Streusel Bars

1¹/4 cups graham cracker crumbs
1¹/4 cups White Lily flour
¹/4 cup sugar
¹/2 cup packed brown sugar
1 teaspoon cinnamon
³/4 cup (1¹/2 sticks) butter or margarine, melted
2 cups chopped peeled apples (2 medium apples)
¹/4 cup packed brown sugar
¹/2 cup confectioners' sugar
1 tablespoon milk

Combine the graham cracker crumbs, flour, sugar, ¹/2 cup brown sugar and cinnamon in a large bowl. Add the butter and mix until crumbly. Reserve 1 cup of the crumb mixture.

Press the remaining crumb mixture over the bottom of a greased 9×13-inch baking pan. Bake at 350 degrees for 8 minutes.

Toss the apples with ¹/4 cup brown sugar until the brown sugar dissolves and the apples are evenly coated. Spread over the baked layer and sprinkle with the reserved crumb mixture.

Bake at 350 degrees for 30 to 35 minutes or until the apples are tender and the top is golden brown. Cool in the pan on a wire rack.

Blend the confectioners' sugar with the milk in a small bowl. Drizzle over the top and cut into bars.

Makes 3 dozen

Which apple for your pie or salad?

Best for all-around cooking, pies, sauces, and baking: Empire (firm and slightly tart), Golden Delicious (sweet, mellow flavor), Granny Smith (crisp and tart), Jonagold (tart and sweet), Jonathan (tart and spicy— also for caramel apples), and Rome Beauty (hard with rich flavor)

For scrumptious cobblers, crisps, and double-crust pies: Cortland (juicy and tart), McIntosh (juicy and crisp)

Great for spicy cider: Winesap (firm and aromatic)

For excellent sauces, salads, or just eating right out of your hand: Braeburn (sweet and tart), Fuji (crisp and spicy), Gala (crisp and sweet), Ginger Gold (sweet and tangy), and, of course, Red Delicious (sweet and juicy)

Irish Shortbread Toffee Squares

The contributor of this recipe received it while on vacation in Ireland. It was recited from memory as they sat by a wood-burning stove. It has been a favorite in Nashville for more than twenty years.

Shortbread

1/2 cup (1 stick) butter, softened
1/4 cup sugar
1 cup White Lily flour

Toffee and Chocolate Topping

1/2 cup (1 stick) butter
1/2 cup sugar
2 tablespoons maple syrup
1 (5-ounce) can sweetened condensed milk
6 ounces (1 cup) semisweet chocolate chips

To prepare the shortbread, cream the butter and sugar in a mixing bowl until light and fluffy. Add the flour and beat at low speed until crumbly. Press over the bottom of a 7×11-inch baking pan and bake at 350 degrees for 16 to 20 minutes or until light golden brown.

To prepare the topping, combine the butter, sugar, maple syrup and condensed milk in a saucepan. Cook over medium-high heat until the mixture leaves the side of the saucepan, stirring constantly and taking care not to let the mixture burn. Pour over the baked layer and cool completely on a wire rack.

Melt the chocolate chips in a small saucepan over low heat. Spread over the cooled toffee layer. Cool completely and cut into squares.

Serves 12

Pecan Pie Bars

2 cups White Lily flour
1/2 cup sugar
1/8 teaspoon salt
3/4 cup (1 1/2 sticks) butter, chopped
1 cup packed brown sugar
1 cup light corn syrup
1/2 cup (1 stick) butter
4 large eggs, beaten
2 1/2 cups chopped pecans
1 teaspoon vanilla extract

Mix the flour, sugar and salt in a large bowl. Cut in 3/4 cup butter with a pastry blender until crumbly. Press evenly over the bottom of a greased 9×13-inch baking pan. Bake at 350 degrees for 17 to 20 minutes or until light brown.

Combine the brown sugar, corn syrup and 1/2 cup butter in a saucepan and bring to a boil over medium heat, stirring gently. Remove from the heat. Stir a small amount of the hot mixture into the eggs; stir the eggs into the hot mixture. Stir in the pecans and vanilla. Pour over the baked layer.

Bake at 350 degrees for 34 to 35 minutes or until set. Cool in the pan on a wire rack and cut into squares to serve.

Makes 16

Cultural

Nashville in the round can be found at Red Grooms' Tennessee Fox Trot Carousel. A native of Nashville and an internationally renowned artist, Red Grooms' sculptures take visitors on a 3-D tour of some of Nashville's most famous citizens, past and present. Adelicia Acklen, Captain Thomas Ryman, Andrew Jackson, Wilma Rudolph, and the GooGoo Cluster are just a few of the area's icons to be transformed under Grooms' hand. The canopy's rounding board and inner structure's covering also depict area treasures, such as the Fisk Jubilee Singers, the Iroquois Steeplechase, and the Grand Ole Opry. Come take a spin through Tennessee's history—and you don't even have to be a kid to enjoy it!

Toffee Bars

Named "Best Cookie" at the Cookbook Committee holiday cookie swap.

15 graham crackers
1 cup (2 sticks) butter
1 cup packed brown sugar

1 cup chopped walnuts
12 ounces (2 cups) milk chocolate
  chips

Arrange the graham crackers in a single layer on a greased cookie sheet. Melt the butter in a small saucepan and add the brown sugar and walnuts. Bring to a boil and boil for 1 minute, stirring constantly.

Pour the hot mixture evenly over the graham crackers. Bake at 350 degrees for 12 minutes. Sprinkle the chocolate chips over the top and let melt. Spread the soft chocolate over the toffee carefully. Cool completely on a wire rack. Break into pieces.

Serves 12

Mint Crème Brownies

2 ounces unsweetened chocolate
1/2 cup (1 stick) margarine
2 eggs
1 cup sugar
1/2 cup White Lily flour
1 1/2 cups confectioners' sugar
1 1/2 tablespoons margarine, softened

1 1/2 tablespoons shortening
2 tablespoons milk
1/2 teaspoon peppermint extract
3 drops of green food coloring
1/2 cup semisweet chocolate chips
3 tablespoons margarine

Melt the unsweetened chocolate and 1/2 cup margarine in a small saucepan. Beat the eggs with the sugar in a mixing bowl until thick. Add the flour and chocolate mixture and mix well. Spread in an 8×8-inch baking pan and bake at 350 degrees for 25 minutes. Cool on a wire rack.

Sift the confectioners' sugar into a bowl. Add 1 1/2 tablespoons margarine, shortening, milk, peppermint extract and food coloring and mix until smooth. Spread over the cooled brownie layer. Chill, covered, for 1 hour. Melt the chocolate chips with 3 tablespoons margarine in a small saucepan, stirring to blend well. Spread over the peppermint layer. Chill for 20 minutes. Score into squares. Store in the refrigerator. Cut into squares to serve.

Makes 16

Layered Peppermint Bark

17 ounces white chocolate, chopped
30 red and white hard peppermint candies, coarsely chopped
7 ounces bittersweet chocolate, chopped
6 tablespoons whipping cream
3/4 teaspoon peppermint extract

Invert a 10×15-inch baking sheet and line with foil, securing the edges. Mark a 9×12-inch rectangle on the foil.

Place the white chocolate in a double boiler or metal bowl set in a larger saucepan; the bowl should not touch the water in the larger pan and should seal the larger pan so that no steam escapes to cause the chocolate to seize. Heat until the white chocolate melts and registers 110 degrees on a candy thermometer.

Spread 2/3 cup of the white chocolate onto the rectangle marked on the foil with a spatula. Sprinkle with 1/4 cup of the crushed peppermint candies. Chill for 15 minutes or until set.

Combine the bittersweet chocolate with the whipping cream and peppermint extract in a heavy medium saucepan and cook over medium-low heat just until melted, stirring to blend well. Cool for 5 minutes or until lukewarm. Drizzle in long lines over the chilled white chocolate layer and spread evenly with an icing spatula. Chill, covered, for 25 minutes or until firm.

Reheat the remaining white chocolate to 110 degrees on a candy thermometer over barely simmering water. Pour over the dark chocolate layer and spread quickly. Sprinkle immediately with the remaining crushed peppermint candies. Chill for 20 minutes or just until firm.

Lift the foil to a work surface. Trim the edges of the candy smooth and cut crosswise into 2-inch strips. Slice off the foil onto the work surface with a metal spatula. Cut each strip crosswise into 3 sections and cut each section diagonally into 2 triangles. Store in the refrigerator. Let stand at room temperature for 15 minutes before serving.

Serves 36

Notable

On the banks of the Cumberland River nineteen-year-old Howell Campbell founded the Standard Candy Company in 1901. His idea was simple: quality people and quality ingredients make quality candy. In 1912, he developed the GooGoo Cluster, "America's 1st Combination Candy Bar," a candy bar made with more than milk chocolate. The GooGoo originally came in one combination: milk chocolate, peanuts, marshmallow, and caramel. Today's lineup has two more GooGoos vying for attention— Peanut Butter and the Supreme, with pecans. For a true taste of the South, try a GooGoo.

Family Favorites

Family Favorites

Momma's fried chicken. Fresh, flavorful green beans.
Vine-ripened Tennessee tomatoes. Brown sugar–glazed carrots.
Homemade flour-dusted biscuits. Ahhh!
Southern comfort food at its finest—a meat 'n three.
If you've never heard of one, a meat 'n three is a meal
consisting of a meat, three vegetables, and bread.
What to drink with this family favorite?
Why the "house wine of the South" of course—sweet tea.
And be prepared—all tea will come sweetened
unless you specify otherwise!

Meat 'n three also denotes a type of restaurant found in the South—a place where comfort food is served with gusto and little regard for caloric or carbohydrate intake. Meat 'n threes are favorites with families around Nashville as they are a great way to serve a variety of vegetables to a variety of children, not to mention Mom and Dad.

Beloved local meat 'n threes that have stood the test of time include Rotier's on West End since 1945, Loveless Cafe off Highway 100 for about 50 years, the Satsuma Tea Room on Union Street for nearly 80 years, and Swett's Restaurant, family-owned for decades on Clifton Avenue.

A local family favorite for breakfast is the Pancake Pantry, which can be found in quaint, eclectic Hillsboro Village, just outside the Vanderbilt area. Hillsboro Village is a four-block neighborhood chock full of restaurants for differing tastes, unique specialty shops with everything from guitars to gowns and copper pots to Copperfield, and the 1925 Belcourt Theater, which plays revival films and hosts local theater and music. You can browse away the day here and have your pancakes, ice cream, and coffee without moving your car.

For family browsing of a different sort, check out the Nashville Zoo at Grassmere. Located on more than 200 acres, Grassmere brings Nashville face-to-face with the wild outdoors. There are elephants, gibbons, and white tigers (oh, my!!) and a 66,000-square-foot jungle gym for the young and young at heart. The Croft Center, which houses the Unseen World Exhibit, was named for the sisters who bequeathed their estate to the Adventure Science Center (formerly known as the Cumberland Science Museum and Sudekum Planetarium). An outing to the Adventure Science Center can turn a rainy day into an adventure under the stars. Overnight science adventure camp-ins, dinosaur birthday parties, the Stars over Tahiti, and preschooler hands-on workshops are just a few of the possibilities that await guests at the Museum and Planetarium, along with visiting exhibits that change just often enough to keep the museum fresh and new and the locals coming back time and again!

Banana Blueberry Smoothie

1 cup apple juice
1 banana, coarsely chopped
1 cup frozen blueberries
1 medium apple, coarsely chopped
1/2 teaspoon lime juice

Combine the apple juice, banana, blueberries, apple and lime juice in a blender. Process until smooth. Serve in 5-ounce glasses.

Serves 4

Bacon and Cheddar Pinwheels

This unusual combination of ingredients always leaves everyone asking for the recipe.

20 slices white sandwich bread, crusts trimmed
1 (14-ounce) can sweetened condensed milk
1/4 cup prepared mustard
1 teaspoon Worcestershire sauce
1 1/2 pounds sliced bacon
8 ounces (2 cups) shredded sharp Cheddar cheese

Flatten the bread slices with a rolling pin or by hand. Combine the condensed milk, mustard and Worcestershire sauce in a bowl and mix well. Cut the entire block of bacon into halves and separate the slices.

Arrange 3 bacon halves side by side on a work surface. Place 1 flattened piece of bread on the bacon and spread with 1 tablespoon of the condensed milk mixture. Top with 1 tablespoon cheese. Roll the bacon to enclose the bread and secure with wooden picks. Repeat with the remaining ingredients. Cut each roll into 3 pinwheels, cutting between the bacon slices.

Arrange the pinwheels on a baking sheet and bake at 350 degrees for 45 to 50 minutes or until golden brown and crisp.

Makes 5 dozen

Toasted Cream Cheese and Apple Pockets

Works well as a breakfast treat for families on the go.

34 slices fresh whole wheat bread
8 ounces reduced-fat cream cheese, softened
1 Golden Delicious apple, peeled and chopped
1/4 cup confectioners' sugar
1/8 teaspoon cinnamon
1 tablespoon butter, melted
2 tablespoons sugar
1/8 teaspoon cinnamon

Cut a 3-inch round from the center of each bread slice with a cookie cutter or biscuit cutter. Arrange half the rounds on a lightly greased baking sheet.

Combine the cream cheese, apple, confectioners' sugar and 1/8 teaspoon cinnamon in a bowl and mix until smooth. Spoon about 1 tablespoon of the cream cheese mixture into the center of each bread round and top with the remaining bread rounds. Crimp the edges of the pockets with a fork to seal. Brush the tops with butter.

Mix the sugar and 1/8 teaspoon cinnamon in a small bowl. Sprinkle over the pockets. Bake at 400 degrees for 8 to 10 minutes or until golden brown.

Makes 17

Cheddar Cheese Muffins

Great right out of the oven and even better toasted and buttered the next day.

2 cups sifted White Lily flour
4 teaspoons baking powder
1 tablespoon sugar
$^1/_2$ teaspoon salt
1 egg

1 cup milk
3 tablespoons butter, softened
Tabasco sauce to taste
6 ounces ($1^1/_2$ cups) shredded sharp
    Cheddar cheese

Sift the flour, baking powder, sugar and salt together. Combine the egg, milk, butter and Tabasco sauce in a mixing bowl and beat until smooth. Stir in the cheese. Add the dry ingredients and mix until moistened.

Spoon into greased muffin cups, filling $^2/_3$ full. Bake at 350 degrees for 30 to 35 minutes or until golden brown.

You may add spices and herbs to this basic recipe.

Makes 8

Banana Chocolate Chip Muffins

1 cup mashed banana
3 tablespoons half-and-half or milk
2 cups White Lily flour
1 teaspoon baking powder
$^1/_2$ teaspoon baking soda
1 cup sugar

1 egg
$^1/_2$ cup (1 stick) unsalted butter,
    softened
6 ounces (1 cup) semisweet chocolate
    chips
$^1/_2$ cup chopped pecans

Blend the banana with the half-and-half in a small bowl. Mix the flour, baking powder and baking soda together.

Combine the sugar, egg and butter in a large mixing bowl and beat until light. Add the dry ingredients alternately with the banana mixture, mixing by hand just until moistened after each addition. Fold in the chocolate chips and pecans.

Spoon into greased muffin cups, filling $^3/_4$ full. Bake at 350 degrees for 15 to 30 minutes or just until muffins test done. Serve immediately or remove to wire racks to cool.

Makes $1^1/_2$ dozen

Lemon Cheese Party Bites

8 ounces cream cheese
2 (8-count) cans refrigerator flaky buttermilk biscuits
sugar
3/4 cup sifted confectioners' sugar
1 1/2 tablespoons fresh lemon juice

Cut the cream cheese into 48 cubes. Separate each biscuit into 3 layers on a work surface. Place 1 cream cheese cube on each biscuit layer and wrap the biscuit to enclose the cream cheese; pinch the edges to seal. Roll in sugar and place on a lightly greased baking sheet. Bake at 400 degrees for 8 to 10 minutes or until golden brown.

Blend the confectioners' sugar and lemon juice in a small bowl. Drizzle over the baked party bites.

Makes 4 dozen

White Lily Biscuits

1/4 cup shortening
2 cups White Lily self-rising flour
2/3 to 3/4 cup milk or buttermilk
melted butter

Cut the shortening into the flour in a mixing bowl until the mixture resembles coarse crumbs. Add just enough milk to make a dough that leaves the side of the bowl, mixing with a fork.

Knead gently 2 or 3 times on a lightly floured surface. Roll 1/2 inch thick and cut with a biscuit cutter; do not twist the cutter to cut.

Arrange on a baking sheet lightly sprayed with nonstick cooking spray. Bake at 500 degrees for 8 to 10 minutes or until golden brown. Brush the tops with melted butter and serve warm.

Makes 1 dozen

Culinary

Low gluten content helps White Lily flour produce especially flaky pie crusts, magnificent pastry, and perfect light southern biscuits. For each cup of regular flour required in a recipe, use 1 cup plus 2 tablespoons of White Lily flour to make the weight the same. The recipes in this book were all written with White Lily flour in mind. If you don't have White Lily flour when making one of our recipes, remove 2 tablespoons flour for each cup called for and your recipes will turn out just fine. Happy baking!

Iced Cheese Sandwiches

These treats from Encore *were served at the first Show House Tea Room. They are great to have on hand for soups or to take to a gathering as an appetizer.*

1¹/2 cups (3 sticks) butter, softened
1 (15-ounce) jar Cheddar cheese
   spread
1¹/2 teaspoons Worcestershire sauce
1 teaspoon Tabasco sauce

1¹/2 teaspoons dillweed
1 teaspoon onion powder
1 teaspoon Beau Monde seasoning
2¹/2 loaves thinly sliced bread, crusts
   trimmed

Combine the butter and Cheddar cheese spread in a mixing bowl and beat until smooth. Add the Worcestershire sauce, Tabasco sauce, dillweed, onion powder and Beau Monde seasoning and mix well. Spread 3 slices of the bread with the cheese mixture and stack on a work surface. Cut into 4 squares. Spread the cheese mixture on the cut sides. Repeat the process with the remaining ingredients.

Arrange the sandwich stacks on a baking sheet and bake at 325 degrees for 15 minutes or until the edges are brown.

You may freeze the sandwiches on a baking sheet lined with waxed paper and remove to plastic bags until ready to bake. Thaw before baking.

Makes 5 dozen

Frozen Fruit Cups

Serve these for dessert too.

16 ounces sour cream
³/4 cup sugar
2 tablespoons lemon juice
salt to taste

4 bananas, mashed
1 (20-ounce) can crushed pineapple
¹/4 cup maraschino cherry halves

Combine the sour cream, sugar, lemon juice and salt in a mixing bowl and mix until smooth. Stir in the bananas, undrained pineapple and cherries. Spoon into oiled muffin cups or individual decorative molds. Freeze, covered with plastic wrap, until firm. Let stand at room temperature for 5 minutes or place briefly in warm water to loosen from the muffin cups. Invert onto serving plates.

Serves 8 to 10

Fireman's Chili

2 medium onions, chopped
3 tablespoons olive oil
3 garlic cloves, minced
1½ pounds lean ground beef
2 (16-ounce) cans crushed tomatoes
1 (15-ounce) can beef broth
3 tablespoons chili powder
1½ teaspoons ground cumin
½ teaspoon oregano
1 teaspoon salt
1 (15-ounce) can kidney beans, drained

Garnish
shredded Cheddar cheese
chopped onions
fresh cilantro

Sauté the onions in the heated olive oil in a large saucepan for 8 minutes or until tender. Add the garlic and sauté for 2 minutes. Add the ground beef and cook for 4 minutes or until brown, stirring until crumbly; remove with a slotted spoon and drain the beef mixture and the saucepan.

Return the ground beef mixture to the saucepan and stir in the tomatoes, beef broth, chili powder, cumin, oregano and salt. Bring to a boil and reduce the heat. Simmer for 2 hours or until the chili is thickened and the flavors blend.

Stir in the beans and adjust the seasonings. Cook until heated through. Ladle into soup bowls and garnish with Cheddar cheese, onions and cilantro.

Serves 4 to 6

A stone's throw from the Bicentennial Mall's interactive fountains is the Metro Farmer's Market. Fresh tomatoes, huge watermelons, and heaps of turnip greens are just a few of nature's delights waiting for customers. The permanent buildings house some of the best lunches available, with cuisine from Chinese to Middle Eastern to barbecue by Swett's.

Glazed Carrots

1/3 cup packed brown sugar
2 tablespoons butter
salt to taste
1 small package tiny carrots

Combine the brown sugar, butter and salt in a small saucepan and cook until the brown sugar dissolves, stirring to blend well. Add the carrots. Bring to a boil and reduce the heat. Simmer, covered, for 15 to 20 minutes or until tender and glazed, stirring occasionally.

Serves 4

Garlic Green Beans

1 tablespoon olive oil
1 tablespoon butter
1 pound fresh green beans, trimmed
2 garlic cloves, minced
1/4 cup white wine
1 chicken bouillon cube
pepper to taste
1/4 cup toasted sliced almonds (optional)

Heat the olive oil and butter in a 12-inch nonstick skillet over medium-high heat. Add the beans and garlic and stir to coat well. Reduce the heat to medium and cook for 4 to 5 minutes or until the beans turn bright green, stirring frequently.

Add the wine and bouillon cube. Bring to a boil and reduce the heat. Cook for 5 minutes longer or until tender-crisp, stirring occasionally. Season with pepper to taste and spoon into a serving bowl. Sprinkle with the almonds to serve.

Serves 4

President's Potato Salad

4 cups cooked chopped new potatoes with skins
   (2¹/2 to 3 pounds)
1 bunch scallions, chopped
3 tablespoons chopped parsley
3 hard-cooked eggs, chopped
1 teaspoon celery seeds
Tangy Dressing (below)

Combine the potatoes, scallions, parsley, eggs and celery seeds in a bowl and mix gently.

Add Tangy Dressing to the potato mixture and mix to coat well. Chill, covered, until serving time.

Serves 10

Tangy Dressing

³/4 cup mayonnaise
3 tablespoons Dijon mustard
3 tablespoons Durkees Deli Mustard Spread
¹/2 teaspoon salt
¹/2 teaspoon pepper

Combine the mayonnaise, Dijon mustard, Durkee sauce, salt and pepper in a small bowl and whisk to mix well.

Culinary

As with most mothers and daughters, recipes are handed down from generation to generation, and the mothers and daughters in the Junior League are no different. Instead of keeping recipes in the family, however, Junior League members began compiling and sharing them, and thus the tradition of the Junior League cookbook was born. President's Potato Salad was handed down from a past Junior League of Nashville president to her daughter. Enjoy!

Parmesan Mashed Potatoes

4 medium potatoes, peeled, chopped
1¹/2 cups milk
¹/4 cup (¹/2 stick) butter
¹/2 cup grated Parmesan cheese
salt and pepper to taste
dried parsley flakes to taste

Combine the potatoes with enough water to cover in a saucepan. Bring to a boil and cook for 30 minutes or until tender; drain. Reduce the heat to low and add the milk and butter. Mix with a spoon or use an electric mixer for a creamier texture.

Stir in the Parmesan cheese and season with salt and pepper. Keep warm over low heat until serving time; the potatoes will thicken. Spoon into a serving bowl and sprinkle with parsley flakes.

Serves 6

Baked Tomatoes

4 firm tomatoes
¹/4 cup grated Parmesan cheese
¹/4 cup mayonnaise
chopped green onions to taste
chopped parsley (optional)
paprika (optional)

Cut the tomatoes into halves horizontally and cut a thin slice off the bottoms to help them stand. Arrange on a baking sheet.

Combine the Parmesan cheese and mayonnaise in a mixing bowl and mix well. Stir in the green onions. Spread over the tomatoes and sprinkle with parsley and paprika. Bake at 325 degrees for 8 to 12 minutes or just until the cheese begins to brown.

Serves 8

Awesome Meat Loaf

3 slices white bread, crusts trimmed
1 large carrot, peeled and sliced
1 rib celery, chopped
1/2 medium onion, chopped
2 garlic cloves, chopped
1/2 cup loosely packed fresh parsley leaves
1 1/2 pounds ground round
2 large eggs, beaten
1/2 cup ketchup
2 teaspoons dry mustard
1 teaspoon Tabasco sauce
2 teaspoons salt
1 teaspoon pepper
2 tablespoons brown sugar
3 tablespoons ketchup
2 teaspoons dry mustard
1/4 teaspoon garlic powder

Process the bread to crumbs in a food processor and remove to a large mixing bowl. Add the carrot, celery, onion, garlic and parsley to the food processor and process until minced, scraping down the side of the processor. Add to the bread crumbs.

Add the ground round, eggs, 1/2 cup ketchup, 2 teaspoons dry mustard, Tabasco sauce, salt and pepper and mix just until evenly moistened. Shape into a loaf.

Place a wire baking rack in a baking pan and place a piece of baking parchment the size of the meat loaf on the baking rack. Place the meat loaf on the parchment.

Combine the brown sugar, 3 tablespoons ketchup, 2 teaspoons dry mustard and garlic powder in a small bowl and mix well. Brush over the meat loaf. Insert a meat thermometer into the thickest portion of the loaf.

Bake at 400 degrees for 50 to 60 minutes or to 160 degrees on the meat thermometer. Cool on the rack for 15 minutes.

Serves 8

Family Flank Steak

1 cup vegetable oil
1/2 cup soy sauce
1 tablespoon garlic powder
1 tablespoon ground ginger
6 tablespoons honey
2 tablespoons vinegar
1 bunch green onions, chopped
1 (2-pound) flank steak, double tenderized or scored

Combine the vegetable oil, soy sauce, garlic powder, ginger, honey and vinegar in a shallow dish and mix well. Stir in the green onions.

Add the steak to the marinade and marinate, covered, in the refrigerator for 24 hours, turning once. Drain the steak, allowing the excess to drip back into the dish.

Grill the steak over hot coals for 15 minutes or until done to taste. Place on a cutting board and slice diagonally. Serve immediately.

Serves 4 to 6

Birds of Paradise

3 or 4 skinless boneless chicken breasts
1 egg
1 teaspoon dill
1 teaspoon rosemary (optional)
6 ounces (1 1/4 cups) grated Parmesan cheese
1/4 cup (1/2 stick) butter

Cut the chicken into 1-inch pieces. Combine the egg, dill and rosemary in a bowl. Add the chicken and mix well. Coat with the Parmesan cheese.

Melt the butter in a nonstick skillet over medium heat. Add the chicken and cook until brown on all sides. Reduce the heat to low and cook for 20 to 30 minutes or until very tender, turning occasionally.

Serves 4

Perfect Pot Roast

1 (4-pound) boneless chuck roast
1/2 teaspoon salt
1/2 teaspoon pepper
2 large garlic cloves, finely chopped
1/4 cup White Lily flour
1 medium onion, chopped
1/3 cup olive oil
1 cup red wine
1 (8-ounce) can tomato sauce
1 teaspoon Worcestershire sauce
1 teaspoon prepared mustard
1 teaspoon prepared horseradish
1 teaspoon brown sugar
1 bay leaf
1 teaspoon dried oregano
1 teaspoon honey
1/2 teaspoon baking cocoa

Rub the roast with the salt and pepper. Cut several small slits in the roast and insert the chopped garlic. Coat with the flour. Sauté the onion in the olive oil in a heavy saucepan just until tender. Add the roast and brown lightly on all sides. Remove from the heat and add the wine.

Combine the tomato sauce, Worcestershire sauce, mustard, horseradish, brown sugar, bay leaf and oregano in a saucepan and mix well. Simmer until the brown sugar is completely dissolved. Pour over the roast and add the honey and baking cocoa. Simmer for 1 to 2 hours or until very tender and done to taste.

Remove the roast to a serving platter and serve with the cooking juices, discarding the bay leaf.

Serves 8

Easy Orange Rosemary Chicken

1 pound skinless boneless chicken breasts
1/4 cup White Lily flour
1/4 teaspoon paprika
1/4 teaspoon salt
cracked pepper to taste
1/4 cup (1/2 stick) butter
1/2 cup orange juice
1/4 teaspoon dried rosemary
salt to taste

Cut the chicken into 1-inch pieces. Combine the flour, paprika, 1/4 teaspoon salt and pepper in a sealable plastic bag and add the chicken; shake to coat well.

Heat the butter in a large skillet over medium-high heat until sizzling. Shake the excess flour from the chicken and add the chicken to the skillet. Cook for 3 to 5 minutes or until cooked through, stirring frequently. Remove to a plate and keep warm.

Add the orange juice to the skillet, stirring to deglaze the bottom. Add the rosemary and season with salt and pepper to taste. Cook over medium heat until slightly thickened, stirring constantly. Return the chicken to the skillet and cook just until heated through, stirring to coat well.

Serves 2

Lemon Oregano Chicken

3/4 cup olive oil
juice and grated zest of 2 lemons
1 teaspoon minced garlic
1 to 2 tablespoons chopped fresh oregano
1 teaspoon salt
1/4 teaspoon pepper
4 to 6 skinless boneless chicken breasts

Combine the first 7 ingredients in a medium bowl and mix well. Add the chicken and mix well. Marinate, covered, in the refrigerator for 2 to 12 hours, turning occasionally; drain.

Place the chicken on the rack of a broiler pan and broil for 5 to 7 minutes on each side or until cooked through. Serve hot or cold. You may grill this.

Serves 4 to 6

Antebellum Chicken

legs, breasts, thighs and wings of 1 chicken
2 eggs
2 cups milk
3 cups White Lily flour
2 tablespoons salt
3 cups shortening

Remove the skin from the chicken legs, breasts and thighs. Mix the eggs and milk in a medium shallow bowl. Mix the flour and salt in a medium shallow bowl. Heat the shortening to 325 to 350 degrees in a large skillet.

Dip the chicken into the egg mixture and then into the flour mixture, coating well. Add to the skillet in batches and cover. Cook for 45 minutes, turning every 10 minutes. Turn and test for doneness with a fork; juices should run clear and the fork should pierce the chicken easily. Fry for 10 minutes longer if necessary. Drain on paper towels.

Serves 4 or 5

Culinary

Although my mother's mother was a great cook, this recipe was actually handed down from her father who in turn learned it from his mother, Grandma Miller Carr, who was born before the Civil War. This East Tennessee recipe has been a favorite in our family. I always looked forward to eating dinner after church on Sunday and this was one of my favorite dishes. When my husband and I were dating, I used to make this dish for him. Marriage and three children later, I continue to make fried chicken part of our family tradition.

Tennessee Fried Chicken

4 chicken breasts, boneless or with bone
1 cup buttermilk
1 1/2 cups self-rising White Lily flour
1 teaspoon garlic powder
1/2 teaspoon paprika

1/4 teaspoon poultry seasoning
1 teaspoon salt
cayenne pepper to taste
1 teaspoon black pepper
3 cups shortening or vegetable oil

Combine the chicken with the buttermilk in a sealable plastic bag or shallow dish. Marinate in the refrigerator for 8 hours or longer. Combine the flour, garlic powder, paprika, poultry seasoning, salt, cayenne pepper and black pepper in a sealable plastic bag or shallow dish. Drain the chicken and add to the flour mixture, turning or shaking to coat well.

Heat the shortening to 325 to 350 degrees in a heavy 10-inch cast-iron skillet. Add the chicken and cover. Fry for 20 minutes, turning once. Remove the cover and fry until crisp and brown on both sides, testing for doneness with a fork.

Serves 4

Lemon Chicken and Rice

2 pounds boneless chicken breasts
3 tablespoons White Lily flour
3/4 teaspoon oregano
1 teaspoon salt
1/2 teaspoon pepper
3 tablespoons (or more) olive oil
3 garlic cloves, minced
1 large onion, chopped

1/4 cup lemon juice
1 1/2 cups chicken broth
hot cooked rice

Garnish
thin lemon slices
capers

Cut the chicken into small pieces. Combine the flour, oregano, salt and pepper in a small bag. Add the chicken and shake to coat well.

Heat the olive oil in a skillet over low heat. Add the garlic and onion and sauté for 3 to 5 minutes or until tender but not brown. Remove with a slotted spoon. Increase the heat to medium, adding additional olive oil if necessary. Add the chicken and sauté until brown.

Return the garlic and onion to the skillet and stir in the lemon juice and chicken broth. Simmer, covered, for 10 to 15 minutes or until the chicken is tender. Spoon over the rice to serve and garnish with the lemon slices and capers.

Serves 6

Picante Chicken and Rice

Good for dinner in a hurry.

3/4 cup coarsely chopped onion
3 garlic cloves, minced
1 tablespoon vegetable oil
1¼ cups chicken broth
1 cup medium salsa or picante sauce
1 cup uncooked rice
6 skinless boneless chicken breasts
salt to taste
1 avocado, sliced
1 medium tomato, coarsely chopped
2 ounces (½ cup) shredded Cheddar cheese or Monterey
   Jack cheese

Sauté the onion and garlic in the vegetable oil in a 10-inch skillet for 2 minutes. Add the chicken broth and salsa and mix well. Bring to a boil and stir in the rice.

Sprinkle the chicken with salt and arrange over the rice. Simmer, tightly covered, for 20 minutes. Remove from the heat and let stand, covered, for 5 minutes or until the liquid is absorbed. Top the servings with the avocado, tomato and cheese.

Serves 6

Culinary

Tomatoes have a better flavor if stored at room temperature. To peel them easily, make a cross in the stem end with a sharp knife and immerse briefly in boiling water just until the skins can be peeled off easily. The same process can be used with peaches. To ripen tomatoes, pineapples, and avocados, place them in a brown paper bag and leave in a warm place until ripe.

Chicken Potpie

2 carrots
2 ribs celery
1 medium potato, peeled and chopped
1 medium onion, chopped
6 tablespoons (³/4 stick) butter
6 tablespoons White Lily flour
2¹/2 cups chicken broth
1¹/2 cups half-and-half
¹/2 teaspoon dried thyme
¹/8 teaspoon ground sage
1 teaspoon salt
¹/2 teaspoon pepper
2 refrigerator pie pastries
4 cups chopped cooked chicken
1 to 2 tablespoons shredded Cheddar cheese

Cut the carrots and celery into ¹/4-inch slices. Combine with the potato and onion in a small amount of water in a saucepan. Cook, covered, for 5 minutes or until tender-crisp; drain.

Melt the butter in a saucepan and stir in the flour. Cook until golden brown, stirring constantly. Add the chicken broth and half-and-half gradually. Stir in the thyme, sage, salt and pepper. Cook for 5 minutes or until thickened and smooth, stirring constantly.

Line a 2-quart baking dish with 1 of the pie pastries. Sprinkle the chicken into the prepared dish and spread the vegetables over the chicken. Pour the sauce over the top and mix gently. Sprinkle with the cheese.

Top with the remaining pie pastry; seal and flute the edges and cut vents in the top. Bake at 425 degrees for 25 to 30 minutes or until the crust is golden brown.

Serves 8

Chicken Noodle Paprika

2 cups uncooked egg noodles
3/4 cup finely chopped onion
3 tablespoons butter
1/4 cup White Lily flour
2 teaspoons paprika
3/4 teaspoon salt
1/4 teaspoon pepper
2 cups chicken broth
3 cups chopped cooked chicken
1 cup sour cream

Garnish
chopped parsley

Cook the noodles using the package directions; drain well and keep warm.

Sauté the onion in the butter in a medium saucepan until tender. Mix the flour, paprika, salt and pepper in a small bowl. Add to the saucepan and mix well. Cook until bubbly. Add the chicken broth gradually and cook until thickened, stirring constantly.

Add the chicken and sour cream and mix gently. Cook just until heated through. Add the noodles and toss to coat well. Garnish with parsley.

Serves 6

Notable

With the graciousness of a true southern belle, Michael Lee West wrote the foreword for this cookbook in her usual lively and entertaining fashion. Born and rasied in Louisiana, she now lives with her family in a renovated funeral home just east of Nashville, and owns a childhood bed of Margaret Mitchell. These are just a few of the life experiences she draws on to write tales that entertain. With the wit and wisdom passed down from generations of great southern ladies and cooks, Michael Lee captivates us all with her stories of southern families and lets the world know why the South loves to cook. Thank you Michael Lee for the gift of your words.

Creamy Chicken Enchiladas

Always a hit when taken to a friend or neighbor's house.

1 medium onion, chopped
1 tablespoon butter
1 (4-ounce) can chopped green chiles
3½ cups chopped cooked chicken
8 ounces cream cheese, softened
8 (8-inch) flour tortillas
16 ounces (4 cups) shredded Monterey Jack cheese
2 cups heavy cream
1 (7-ounce) can salsa verde

Sauté the onion in the butter in a large skillet over medium heat for 5 minutes. Add the green chiles and sauté for 1 minute. Stir in the chicken and cream cheese. Cook until the cream cheese melts, stirring constantly.

Arrange the tortillas on a work surface and spoon 2 to 3 tablespoons of the chicken mixture down the center of each tortilla. Roll the tortillas to enclose the filling and arrange seam side down in a lightly greased 9×13-inch baking dish. Sprinkle with the Monterey Jack cheese and drizzle with the cream.

Bake at 350 degrees for 30 to 45 minutes or until bubbly and light brown. Serve with the salsa.

Serves 4

Old-Fashioned Peach Cobbler

1/2 cup (1 stick) butter
4 cups sliced peeled peaches
1/2 cup sugar
3/4 cup White Lily flour
2 teaspoons baking powder
1/4 teaspoon salt
1 cup sugar
3/4 cup milk

Melt the butter in a 9×13-inch baking dish in a 350-degree oven. Combine the peaches and 1/2 cup sugar in a bowl and toss to mix well.

Combine the flour, baking powder, salt and 1 cup sugar in a mixing bowl. Add the milk and mix until smooth. Spoon evenly into the prepared baking dish, but do not stir. Spoon the peaches evenly over the batter, but do not stir.

Bake at 350 degrees until the topping is light brown; the peaches will sink to the bottom. Serve warm or at room temperature with ice cream or whipped cream.

Serves 8

ulinary

For Sweet Heavenly Handfuls, melt 6 tablespoons unsalted butter with one 13-ounce jar chocolate-hazelnut spread and 6 ounces semisweet chocolate chips in a saucepan over medium-low heat, stirring occasionally. Pour over a cup of your favorite nuts and a 12-ounce package corn and rice Crispix in a bowl and mix gently to coat well. Sprinkle with 2 1/2 cups confectioners' sugar and 3/4 cup baking cocoa and toss to coat evenly. Store in an airtight container.

Fresh Strawberry Sorbet

2/3 cup sugar
2/3 cup water
2 pints fresh strawberries
1/4 cup lemon juice

Bring the sugar and water to a boil in a medium saucepan, stirring to dissolve the sugar. Reduce the heat and simmer for 3 to 5 minutes. Cool to room temperature and chill, covered, in the refrigerator.

Process the strawberries in a food processor fitted with the metal blade until puréed; measure 3 cups. Stir in the sugar syrup and lemon juice. Spoon into an ice cream freezer container and freeze according to the manufacturer's directions.

You may store the sugar syrup in the refrigerator indefinitely.

Serves 6

Flowerpot Pudding

Sprinkle the "dirt" layer with gummy worms for a colorful touch.

1/4 cup (1/2 stick) margarine, softened
8 ounces cream cheese, softened
1 cup sugar
3 1/2 cups milk
12 ounces whipped topping
2 (4-ounce) packages vanilla instant pudding mix
1 (20-ounce) package chocolate sandwich cookies

Cream the margarine, cream cheese and sugar in a mixing bowl until light and fluffy. Add the milk, whipped topping and pudding mix and beat at low speed until smooth.

Process the cookies in a food processor until finely ground. Alternate layers of the pudding mixture and cookie crumbs in a new 8-inch plastic flowerpot, ending with a layer of the cookie crumbs.

Store in the refrigerator until time to serve. Just before serving, insert silk flowers into the flowerpot and serve with a small garden trowel.

Serves 6

Fudge Cake

2 cups sugar
¹/₂ cup baking cocoa
salt to taste
1 cup (2 sticks) butter
4 eggs
1 teaspoon vanilla extract
1 cup (scant) White Lily flour
1 cup chopped pecans (optional)

Mix the sugar, baking cocoa and salt together. Melt the butter in a small saucepan and add to the cocoa mixture, mixing well. Beat in the eggs and vanilla. Stir in the flour and fold in the pecans.

Spoon into a 9×13-inch baking dish lightly sprayed with nonstick cooking spray. Bake at 325 degrees for 30 minutes. Cool completely in the dish on a wire rack before serving.

Serves 15

Culinary

Filled with vintage neon and chrome, Vandyland—formerly known as Candyland—and Elliston Place Soda Shop vie for the attention of lovers of great hamburgers. A great Nashville debate regularly ensues over which establishment has the best ice cream counter. You be the judge!

Oatmeal Cake

A favorite comfort food.

1¹/2 cups boiling water
1 cup quick-cooking oats
1¹/2 cups White Lily flour
1 teaspoon baking powder
1 teaspoon baking soda
1 teaspoon cinnamon
¹/2 cup (1 stick) butter or margarine, softened
1 cup sugar
1 cup packed brown sugar
2 eggs
Coconut Pecan Frosting (below)

Pour the boiling water over the oats in a bowl and mix until moistened. Let stand until cool. Sift the flour, baking powder, baking soda and cinnamon together.

Cream the butter, sugar and brown sugar in a mixing bowl until light and fluffy. Beat in the eggs. Add the oats and mix well. Add the dry ingredients and mix until smooth. Spoon into a greased and floured 9×13-inch cake pan and bake at 350 degrees for 45 minutes.

Spread Coconut Pecan Frosting over the warm cake and broil just until golden brown. Cool on a wire rack.

Serves 15

Coconut Pecan Frosting

1 cup packed brown sugar
¹/4 cup (¹/2 stick) butter or margarine, softened
¹/2 cup evaporated milk
1 teaspoon vanilla extract
1 cup flaked coconut
¹/2 cup chopped pecans

Combine the brown sugar, butter, evaporated milk and vanilla in a mixing bowl and mix well. Stir in the coconut and pecans.

Makes enough to frost one 9×13-inch cake

Apple Pie

Granny Smith apples are the best for this pie.

4 cups thinly sliced peeled apples
Oatmeal Pecan Crust (below)
3/4 cup sugar
1 tablespoon cornstarch
1/4 teaspoon salt
1/2 cup water
1/2 teaspoon vanilla extract
Oatmeal Pecan Topping (below)

Arrange the apple slices in the Oatmeal Pecan Crust. Combine the sugar, cornstarch and salt in a saucepan. Stir in the water and bring to a boil over medium heat. Stir in the vanilla. Spoon evenly over the apples.

Crumble the reserved Oatmeal Pecan Topping over the apples. Bake at 375 degrees for 40 minutes, covering with foil during the last 15 minutes of baking time.

Serves 8

Oatmeal Pecan Crust and Topping

2 cups White Lily flour
1 cup packed brown sugar
1/2 cup rolled oats
1/3 cup chopped pecans
1/2 teaspoon salt
3/4 cup (1 1/2 sticks) butter, melted

Mix the flour, brown sugar, oats, pecans and salt in a large bowl. Add the butter and mix well. Reserve 1 packed cup of the mixture for the topping. Press the remaining mixture over the bottom and side of a 9-inch deep-dish pie plate.

Serves 8

Christmas Angel Cookies

Layer the cookie mix ingredients in the order listed in a quart jar and fill to the top with the chocolate chips. Attach the instructions for completing the cookies. Let the kids help make and deliver the mix to neighbors during the holidays.

Oatmeal Cookie Mix
1/2 cup sugar
3/4 cup White Lily self-rising flour
1 1/2 cups rolled oats
1/2 cup chopped pecans
1/2 cup coconut
1/2 cup packed brown sugar
white chocolate chips to taste
milk chocolate chips to taste

Cookies
1 egg
1/2 cup (1 stick) butter, softened
1 teaspoon vanilla extract

To prepare the cookie mix, combine the sugar, flour, oats, pecans, coconut, brown sugar and chocolate chips in a bowl and mix well.

To make the cookies, combine the cookie mix with the egg, butter and vanilla in a bowl and mix well. Drop by spoonfuls onto cookie sheets and bake at 375 degrees for 15 minutes or until light brown. Cool on the cookie sheets for 5 minutes and remove to a wire rack to cool completely.

Makes 4 dozen

Peanut Butter Gems

1 1/2 cups graham cracker crumbs
1 cup chunky peanut butter
3 cups confectioners' sugar
1 cup (2 sticks) butter or margarine,
  melted

12 ounces (2 cups) semisweet chocolate
  chips

Combine the graham cracker crumbs, peanut butter, confectioners' sugar and butter in a large bowl and mix well. Press into a greased 9×13-inch dish.

Melt the chocolate chips in a small saucepan. Spread evenly over the peanut butter layer. Chill, covered, in the refrigerator. Cut into small squares.

Makes 2 dozen

Gingerbread Cookie Mix

Combine the cookie mix ingredients in plastic bags and attach unusual cookie cutters with ribbon. Attach handwritten directions for completing the cookies for a special gift.

Gingerbread Cookie Mix

2¹/₂ cups White Lily flour
¹/₂ cup sugar
¹/₂ teaspoon baking soda
³/₄ teaspoon ginger
¹/₄ teaspoon nutmeg
¹/₄ teaspoon cinnamon
³/₄ teaspoon salt

Cookies

¹/₂ cup molasses
¹/₂ cup (1 stick) butter, softened
¹/₄ cup hot water

To prepare the cookie mix, combine the flour, sugar, baking soda, ginger, nutmeg, cinnamon and salt in a large bowl.

To make the cookies, combine the cookie mix with the molasses, butter and hot water in a bowl and mix to form a smooth dough. Chill, covered, in the refrigerator for 2 hours.

Divide into 4 portions and roll ¹/₄ at a time to ¹/₄-inch thickness on a lightly floured surface. Cut as desired and arrange on ungreased cookie sheets.

Bake at 375 degrees for 8 to 9 minutes or until golden brown. Cool on the cookie sheets for 2 minutes and remove to a wire rack to cool completely.

Makes 4 dozen

Kids love to make homemade Playdough. Mix 1 cup White Lily flour with ¹/4 cup salt, 1 tablespoon cream of tartar and 1 small envelope of unsweetened powdered drink mix in a saucepan. Stir in 1 cup water and 1 tablespoon vegetable oil. Cook over medium heat, stirring constantly until it reaches the consistency of playdough. Knead on a floured surface for 1 minute. Store in resealable plastic bags or plastic containers. This is a great way to introduce kids to the kitchen!

MiMi's Sugar Cookies

Grandmother MiMi always made these crispy and light sugar cookies for Christmas.

1 cup (2 sticks) butter, softened
1 cup sugar
1 cup confectioners' sugar
2 eggs
2/3 cup vegetable oil
4 1/2 cups White Lily flour

1 teaspoon cream of tartar
1 teaspoon baking soda
1 teaspoon salt
1 teaspoon vanilla extract
sugar

Cream the butter, 1 cup sugar and confectioners' sugar in a mixing bowl until light and fluffy. Beat in the eggs and vegetable oil. Add the flour, cream of tartar, baking soda, salt and vanilla and mix well.

Shape into balls and place on cookie sheets. Press with the bottom of a glass dipped in additional sugar to flatten. Bake at 350 degrees for 15 minutes. Cool on the cookie sheets for several minutes and remove to wire racks to cool.

Makes 6 to 7 dozen

Potato Chip Cookies

2 cups (4 sticks) butter, softened
1 cup sugar
3 1/4 cups White Lily flour

1 teaspoon vanilla extract
1 1/2 cups coarsely crushed potato chips
confectioners' sugar

Cream the butter and sugar in a mixing bowl until light and fluffy. Add the flour and vanilla gradually, mixing well. Fold in the crushed potato chips.

Drop by rounded teaspoonfuls onto ungreased cookie sheets. Press gently with a fork dipped in water to flatten. Bake at 300 degrees for 15 to 20 minutes or until light brown. Cool on the cookie sheets for several minutes and remove to a wire rack to cool completely. Sprinkle with confectioners' sugar.

Makes 4 to 5 dozen

Yum-Yum Bars

A popular recipe from Encore.

1¹/₂ cups White Lily cake flour
1 teaspoon baking powder
¹/₂ teaspoon salt
¹/₂ cup (1 stick) butter, softened
1 cup sugar
1 egg
1 egg yolk
1 teaspoon vanilla extract
1 egg white
1 cup loosely measured light brown sugar
1 cup chopped pecans

Mix the cake flour, baking powder and salt together. Cream the butter and sugar in a mixing bowl until light and fluffy. Beat in the egg, egg yolk and vanilla. Add the dry ingredients gradually, mixing well. Spread in a greased 9×13-inch baking pan.

Beat the egg white in a mixing bowl until very stiff peaks form. Fold in the brown sugar and pecans. Spread over the first layer in the baking pan. Bake at 300 degrees for 25 to 30 minutes or until golden brown. Cool in the pan on a wire rack and cut into bars.

Makes 2 dozen

otable

Christie Hauck, the mastermind and master cookie maker behind Christie Cookies, was trying to recreate childhood cookie memories when he hit cookie gold in 1984. Hours of baking, testing, and tasting resulted in the ultimate chocolate chip cookie that Christie Cookies sells today. The Doubletree® Hotels thought Christie Cookies so good they tapped them to manufacture their signature chocolate chip cookie. Mr. Hauck's childhood dreams drove him to seek the finest ingredients to create the ultimate cookie. We think he succeeded and so will you!

Cookbook Committee

$\mathcal{W}$e would like to thank all of the Junior League members who have given their time, energy and wonderful ideas to the development and success of this cookbook. The creation of this cookbook was a process that spanned several placements and committees, and many members worked on the initial committee for more than one placement year. The committees that followed have assured the success of this endeavor by promoting our great cookbook throughout the local area as well as nationally.

Cookbook Co-Chairs

Virginia Lazenby, 2005–2006
Mary Catherine McAnulty, 2005–2006

Mary Morgan Bryan, 2004–2005
Mary Kim Shipp, 2004–2005

Jennifer Orth, 2003–2004
Avery Wilson, 2003–2004

Patricia Hall, 2001–2003
Jody Mattison, 2001–2003
Amy Mauldin, 2001–2002

2004–2005 Cookbook Committee (Second Printing)

Holli Anglin *Traditional Sales Chair*
Rebecca Ayer *Marketing Coordinator*
Stacy Beaty *Marketing Committee*
Silvia Castaneda *Marketing Committee*
Jennifer Collins *Traditional Sales Committee*
Cathleen Coyne *Traditional Sales Committee*
Anna Drinkard *Marketing Committee*
Cordenus Eddings *Special Sales Chair*
Shawn Haile *Communications Chair*
Tonya Hamilton *Traditional Sales Committee*
Nicole Hamway *Account Manager*
Tammy Hillebrand *Account Manager*

Jennifer Hinds *Special Sales Committee*
Susan Irby *Treasurer*
Mary Catherine McAnulty *Sales Coordinator*
Megan Neumann *Traditional Sales Committee*
Heather Perry *Special Sales Committee*
Susie Rieniets *Interleague Sales Chair*
Helen Scoville *Special Sales Committee*
Sara Beth Sheehan *Administrative Coordinator*
Jordan Thompson *Promotional Materials Chair*
Anna Wilson *Traditional Sales Committee*

A Special Thanks to...

Marcie Angle
Kent Ewing Ballow
Shelby Boyd
David Crace
Donna Dalton
Karen Fleming

Jenny Freeland
Barbara (Babs) Freeman
Fran Hardcastle
Beth Harrington
Patti Hart Smallwood
Camp Howard

Debbie Howard
Peggy L. Jennings
Marsha Mullin
Barbara Nance
Scott O'Neal
Linde Pflaum

Nancy Quillman
Mary Rigby
Christopher Schappert
Kay Scruggs
Tricia Whitehead
Montyne Winokur

The great staff at the Junior League of Nashville headquarters.
All of the spouses and families that gave of their time.

Underwriters for the First Printing

Publix Super Markets Charities
White Lily® Flour
The Tennessean
Davis-Kidd Booksellers
Jack Daniel Distillery

National Bank of Commerce
Dr. Jordan Asher and Jody Mattison
The Danner Foundation
Mr. and Mrs. Jay Hardcastle
Mr. and Mrs. Mike Mauldin

Mr. David McMahan
Patricia and Andrew D. Hall
Jenney and Tim Petrikin
Robin and David Puryear

Photo Shoot Acknowledgments

Photographer   Mike Rutherford
Food Stylist   Mary Ann Fowlkes

American Artisan
Belmont University, Office
   of Alumni Relations

Boater's World
Great Stuff!
Hatch Show Print
My Second Home

Obelisk
You're Invited!
Maurice M. Scruggs

Previous Junior League of Nashville Cookbooks

Nashville Seasons First Printing 1964
Nashville Seasons Encore First Edition; First Printing 1977
Encore! Nashville Second Edition; First Printing 1982

Board of Directors

2005-2006

Mary Lee Bartlett	President
Shana Alford	President-Elect
Kelly McMullen	Corresponding Secretary
Angela Moretti-Goddard	Vice President of Community
Mary Rigby	Vice President of Development
Mary Kate Mouser	Vice President of Education and Training
Anne Jenkins	Vice President of Finance and Operations
Donna Walsh	Vice President of Communications and Marketing
Wendy Foster	Vice President of Membership
Lisanne Hitt	Home Board Chair
Mary Kim Shipp	Parliamentarian
Catherine Beemer	Recording Secretary
Robin Puryear	Strategic Planning Chair
Melinda Cullen	Treasurer
Heather Kemp	Member-at-Large
Stacey Sullivan-Karrels	Member-at-Large
Ann Bumstead	Sustainer Representative

2004-2005

Patti Hart	President
Mary Lee Bartlett	President-Elect
Lisa Cole	Corresponding Secretary
Mary Kate Mouser	Vice President of Community
Linda Biek	Vice President of Development
Kathy Davis	Vice President of Education and Training
Anne Jenkins	Vice President of Finance and Operations
Karen Malone	Vice President of Marketing
Grace Paden	Vice President of Membership
Lisanne Hitt	Home Board Chair
Alana O'Brien	Parliamentarian
Erin Morrison	Recording Secretary
Kim Carpenter Drake	Strategic Planning Chair
Mary Jo Shankle	Treasurer
Julia Cashion	Member-at-Large
Dara Dickson	Member-at-Large
Julie Walker	Sustainer Representative

Recipe Contributors and Testers

Jodi Alderson
Martha Allard
Muff Alsup
Amanda Altizer
Margaret Anderson
John Angle
Marcie Angle
Kendall Archdeacon
Sheila Armstrong
Ashley Arnold
Paula Aspacher
Yvonne Ayers
Andrea Baker
Kaelin Bale
Josephine Ballentine
Kent Ewing Ballow
Cathy Baughn
Kate Boland
Kimala Bond
Karen Bone
Kathy Bonnet
Debbi Booton
Janice Bossing
Katherine Bostick
Danielle Boyce
Nan Bowers
Rosalie Boyd
Mary Barrett Brewer
Anna Bright
Kim Bright
Shauna Brooks
Amy Brothers
Dori Brown
Barbara Bundy

Jennifer Burns
Stacy Stokely Byerly
Alisa Campbell
Mary Campbell
Susan Carey
Julie Carpenter
Tricia Carswell
Lynn Casey
Marjorie Barr Castleman
Jacqueline Cavnar
Atlanta Gail Cervetti
Susan Chapman
Jessica Clark
Elizabeth Clarke
Julie Claverie
Eleanor Cobb
Susie Coles
Hanna Compton
Holly Conners
Beatrice Cope
Stacey Corley
Sandy Cornelius
Becky Cowart
Laura Creekmore
Laura Crenshaw
Sondra Cruickshanks
Katie Crumbo
Laura Currie
Donna C. Dalton
Elena Daniell
Anne Darken
Cleo Dasey
Mary JoAnn Dasey
Kathy Davis

Mary Lynn Davis
Rebecca Davis
Sarah Davis
Carter Dawson
Chris Dawson
Debbie Day
Janna Dedman
Mary Dempster
Rosemary Dinkins
Suzanne Dobbins
Hilary Doherty
Alisa Donato
Melanie Douer
Kim Carpenter Drake
Laura Dreher
Martha Duff
Laurel Leigh Duncan
Amy Dunlap
Mary H. Earthman
Tasha Elder
Mary Enkema
Susan Erb
Ann Ewing
Jody Ewing
Mary Alice Felker
Robyn Few
Elaine Finucane
Janna Fite
Beth Fitzgerald
Karen Fleming
Midge Folger
Jody Folk
Mary Ann Fowlkes
Maggie Frank

Recipe Contributors and Testers

Tracy Frazier
Jenny Freeland
Abby Frossard
Mary Stamps Gambill
Catharine Gardner
Susie Garner
Anne Garrett
Janice Garside
Ellen Gibbons
Wendy Gibson
Cindee Schreiber Gold
Mary H. Grant
Janelle Massey Grass
Meaghen Greene
Patricia Gregory
Allison Greiner
Lynn Grubbs
Anne Guerra
Bonney Guy
Leigh Haley
Patricia Hall
Carolyn Hannon
Stephanie Hardcastle
Beth Harrington
Estie Harris
Patti Hart Smallwood
Jean Jackson Hastings
Cate Hatcher
Leah T. Hawkins
Jane Haynes
Lucy Haynes
Candy Higgins
Judy Hill
Kittie M. Hill

Norman Hill
Tommy Hill
Reba Hilton
Sally Holland
Camp Howard
Debbie Howard
Catherine Parks Hubbard
Kirstin Humann
Jan Hunt
Holly Husband
Amy Jackson
Betty James
Willie Mae James
Anne Jenkins
Carolyn Johns
Lynn Johnson
Vicky Johnson
Lynda F. Jones
Heather Kemp
Heidi Kemp
Susan Ross Kennedy
Verel Kesler
Paula Kinard
Jane Knight
Betsy Koch
Mariam Miller Kohl
Jane Kramer
Laura Ladd
Lucy Kyger Langreck
Sandy Laszewski
Nancy Leach
Myra Leathers
Judith Lehman
Lorry Liotta-Kleinfeld

Laura LoJacono
Paula Lovelace
Nita Maddux
Laura Magevney
Dr. Jeff Manhin
Alice Marascalco
Chris Marcoy
Jody Mattison
Amy Mauldin
Ethan Mauldin
Mike Mauldin
Peggy Ann Mauldin
Mary Catherine McAnulty
Elizabeth Coble McDonald
Michel McDonald
Vickie McDonald
Blair McEvoy
Shannon McGahren
Angela Crawford McLaughlin
Lea Margaret McLaurin
Kelly McMullen
Sonja McMullen
Jennifer Mittry McRae
Diana Meade
Kristin Meadows
Connie Meranda
Kelsey Mitchell
Beth Moore
Pat Morel
Mariann Morris
Erin Morrison
Melanie Munnell
Carla Myers
Donna Kissiah Nelson

Recipe Contributors and Testers

Eric Sample Nelson
Peggy Newsham
Lucy Nichols
Mary Lawson O'Brien
Katherine Kelly O'Connor
Vivian O'Malley
Jennifer Orth
Martha Overholt
Grace Paden
Nancy Parker
Trayte Peters
Jenney Petrikin
Layne Heacock Pickett
Liz Piercy
Trish Poe
Virginia Anderson Porter
Sue Powell
Julie Price
Kathleen Pugh
Diane Purdy
Robin Puryear
Clare Quadland
Benning Ratliff
Sharon Reddick
Betsy Reineke
Heather Reisinger
Marcia Richardson
Mary Lee Richardson
Scott Richardson
Catherine S. Richie
Gay Roberts
Holly Roche
Delinda Rollins
Erin Roman

Sarah Heuer Ross
Mike Rutherford
Sharon Sandahl
Betty L. Sanders
Sargents Inc.
Robin Satyshur
Kathy Savage
Donna Schilling
Mary Schoettle
Mary M. Schoettle
Melissa Schramkowski
Carol Scott
Phillys M. Scruggs
Susan Scruggs
Cheryl Seaborg
Mary Jo Shankle
Deena Shapiro
Jane Sharp
Kristin Shoe
Silver-Palate Catering
Jodi Sims
Sally Smallwood
Amy Campbell Smith
Anne-Taylor Smith
Janna Smith
Kathryn Smith
Valerie Smith
Kathy Southall
Elizabeth Spurgeon
Cindy Stanley
Jennifer Stark
Angie Stiff
Amy Strohmeier
Joanne Sullivan

Stacy Sullivan-Karrels
Patty Swartz
Kelly Tabb
Amy Thomas
Ellen Tighe
Nancy Tirrill
Lynne Tolley
Julie Townsend
Courtney Travis
Lynne Trost
Ansley Tullos
Christi Turner
Dayna Turney
Valerie Van Eaton
Julia Vaughn
Patti Viars
Peggy Waldrop
René Ward
Anne Westfall
Judy H. Whittle
Lella Bromberg Wilbanks
Lisa Williams
Avery Wilson
Jennifer Winokur
Judy Wolfsberger
Lynn Woodall
Tara Woodlee
Trish Woolwine
Margaret Boyd Zibart
Cathy Zutell

Resources

Adventure Science Center
800 Fort Negley Boulevard
Nashville, TN 37203
(615) 862-5160
www.adventuresci.com

Arthur Dyer Observatory
1000 Oman Drive, Brentwood, TN 37027
(615) 373-4897
www.dyer.vanderbilt.edu

Belle Meade Plantation
5025 Harding Road, Nashville, TN 37205
(615) 356-0501 (800) 270-3991
www.bellemeadeplantation.com

Belmont Mansion
1900 Belmont Blvd.
Nashville, TN 37212-3757
(615) 460-5459
www.belmontmansion.com

Bicentennial Mall State Park
600 James Robertson Parkway
Nashville, TN 37243
(615) 741-5280
www.state.tn.us/environment/parks/parks/
Bicentennial/

Carnton Plantation
1345 Carnton Lane, Franklin, TN 37064
(615) 794-0903
www.carnton.org

Cheekwood Botanical Garden & Museum of Art
1200 Forrest Park Drive
Nashville, TN 37205
(615) 356-8000
www.cheekwood.org

Country Music Hall of Fame
222 Fifth Avenue South
Nashville, TN 37203
(615) 416-2001
www.halloffame.org

Davis-Kidd Booksellers
2121 Green Hills Village Drive, Nashville, TN 37215
(615) 385-2645
www.daviskidd.com

Downtown Franklin Association
P.O. Box 807, Franklin, TN 37065-0807
(615) 591-8500
www.historicfranklin.com

Downtown Presbyterian Church
154 Fifth Avenue, North, Nashville, TN 37219
(615) 254-7584
www.dpchurch.com

Fisk University
1000 Seventeenth Ave. North Nashville, TN 37208
(615) 329-8500
www.fisk.edu

Fort Nashboro
170 1st Ave. North at Riverfront Park
Nashville, TN 37201
(615) 862-8400
www.historicnashville.org/history/pioneer.shtml

Frist Center for the Visual Arts
919 Broadway, Nashville, TN 37203
(615) 244-3340
www.fristcenter.org

Gaylord Opryland Resort and Convention Center
2800 Opryland Drive, Nashville, TN 37214-1297
(615) 889-1000
www.gaylordhotels.com/gaylordopryland.com

Grand Ole Opry
2802 Opryland Drive, Nashville, TN 37214
(615) 871-OPRY
www.opry.com

Hatch Show Print
316 Broadway, Nashville, TN 37201
(615) 256-2805
www.countrymusichalloffame.com/about/hatch/

Resources

HCA Inc.
1 Park Plaza, Nashville, TN 37203
(615) 344-9551
www.hcahealthcare.com

Hecht's Department Store
3813 Hillsboro Pike, Nashville, TN 37215
(615) 383-3300
www.hechts.com

Hermitage Hotel
231 Sixth Avenue North, Nashville, TN 37219
(615) 244-3121 or (888) 888-9414
www.thehermitagehotel.com

Iroquois Steeplechase
P.O. Box 331547, Nashville, TN 37203
(615) 322-4814
www.iroquoissteeplechase.org

Jack Daniel Distillery
P.O. Box 199, Hwy. 55, Lynchburg, TN 37352
(888) 221-JACK
www.jackdaniels.com

Kandle Kitchen
432 Main Street, Franklin, TN 37064
(615) 261-7550
www.kandlekitchen.com

Meharry Medical College
1005 Dr. D.B. Todd, Jr., Blvd., Nashville, TN 37208
(615) 327-6000
www.mmc.edu

Nashville Zoo at Grassmere
3777 Nolensville Road, Nashville, TN 37211
(615) 833-1534
www.nashvillezoo.org

Phillip P. Shipp IV, DDS
3833 Cleghorn Avenue, Suite 200
Nashville, TN 37215
(615) 292-4100
www.phillipshipp.dds.com

President Polk Home
301 West 7th St., Columbia, TN 38401
(931) 388-2354
www.jameskpolk.com

Radnor Lake
1160 Otter Creek Road, Nashville, TN 37220-1700
(615) 373-3467
www.state.tn.us/environment/parks/parks/
RadnorLake/

Rattle and Snap Plantation
1522 N. Main Columbia, TN 38401
(800) 258-3875
www.rattleandsnap.com

Red Grooms' Tennessee Fox Trot Carousel
Riverfront Park, 1st & Broadway
Nashville, TN 37201
(615) 254-7020

Ryman Auditorium
116 Fifth Avenue North, Nashville, TN 37219
(615) 889-3060
www.ryman.com

Tennessee Performing Arts Center (TPAC)
505 Deaderick Street, Nashville, TN 37243
(615) 782-4000
www.tpac.org

Tennessee Walking Horse National Celebration
1110 Evans Street, Shelbyville, TN 37162
(931) 684-5915
www.twhnc.com

The Athenaeum Rectory
808 Athenaeum Street,
Columbia, TN 38401
(931) 381-4822
www.athenaeumrectory.com

The Danner Foundation
2 International Drive, Suite 510,
Nashville, TN 37217

Resources

The Factory
230 Franklin Road
Franklin, TN 37064
(615) 791-1777
www.factoryatfranklin.com

The Hermitage
4580 Rachel's Lane
Hermitage, TN 37076-1344
(615) 889-2941
www.thehermitage.com

The Parthenon
Centennial Park
Nashville, TN 37203
(615) 862-8431
www.nashville.org/parthenon

The Tennessean
1100 Broadway
Nashville TN 37203
(615) 242-NEWS
www.tennessean.com

The Tennessee Antebellum Trail
1345 Carnton Lane
Franklin, TN 37064
(800) 381-1865
www.antebellumtrail.com

The White Lily Food Company
218 Depot Street, Knoxville, TN 37917
(800) 264-5459
www.whitelily.com

Travellers Rest
636 Farrell Parkway
Nashville, TN 37220
(615) 832-8197
www.travellersrestplantation.org/

Union Station Hotel
1001 Broadway, Nashville, TN 37203
(615) 726-1001 or (800) 678-8946 (reservations)
www.wyndham.com/hotels/BNAUS/main.wnt

Van Vechten Art Gallery
1000 Seventeenth Ave. North
Nashville, TN 37208
(615) 329-8500
www.fisk.edu/index.asp

Vanderbilt University
2201 West End Avenue
Nashville, TN 37235
(615) 322-7311
www.vanderbilt.edu

Warner Parks Nature Center
7333 Highway 100
Nashville, TN 37221
(615) 352-6299
www.nashville.gov/parks/wpnc.htm

For additional information about Nashville and the surrounding area:

State of Tennessee:
www.state.tn.us

Metro Nashville Davidson County Government:
www.nashville.org

Metropolitan Nashville Arts Commission:
www.artsnashville.org

Nashville Convention and Visitors Bureau:
www.nashvillecvb.com

Nashville on Citysearch:
nashville.citysearch.com

Blue Shoe Nashville Travel Guide:
http:www.blueshoenashville.com

Insider's Guide to Nashville:
www.insiders.com/nashville/

Life in Nashville:
www.nashvillelife.com

Recipe Index

Non-Recipe Index

Notably NASHVILLE

a medley of tastes and traditions

**To order,
send or fax to:**

Junior League of Nashville
2405 Crestmoor Road
Nashville, Tennessee 37215

Telephone
615.269.9393

Fax
615.292.7563

Website
www.jlnashville.org

JUNIOR LEAGUE OF
NASHVILLE
Women building a better community

The proceeds from the sale of the cookbook support the vital mission of the Junior League of Nashville and continue to improve our community through the effective action and leadership of our trained volunteers.

Photocopies accepted.

Please send me:

_____ copies of *Notably Nashville* @ $28.95 each $_____

Shipping and Handling (see below) $_____

Tennessee residents add 9.25% sales tax $_____

Total $_____

Shipping and Handling:
    $6.95 for first book
    $1.00 for each additional book

Name   Telephone

Address

City   State   Zip Code

Payment Method:
    ☐ VISA   ☐ MasterCard   ☐ American Express
    ☐ Check payable to Junior League of Nashville, Inc.

Account Number   Expiration Date   Security Code

Cardholder Name

Signature

THE TENNESSEAN
Every day matters.   www.tennessean.com